HOW THINGS FALL APART

WHAT HAPPENED TO THE CUBAN REVOLUTION

ELIZABETH DORE

HOW THINGS FALL APART

WHAT HAPPENED TO THE CUBAN REVOLUTION

HEAD
ZEUS

An Apollo Book

First published in the UK in 2022 by Head of Zeus Ltd,
part of Bloomsbury Publishing Plc

Image credits: p. 1 DeAgostini/Getty Images; RAFAEL PEREZ/AFP/Getty Images; Sven
Creutzmann/Mambo Photography/Getty Images. p. 2 Olga Saavedra. p. 3 James Quine/
Alamy; Imageplotter Travel/Alamy. p. 4–5 Diego Grandi/Shutterstock. p. 6 Olga Saavedra;
Elizabeth Dore; Martyn Vickery/Alamy. p. 7 Olga Saavedra; Yamil Lage/AFP/Getty
Images. p. 8 marcin jucha/Alamy; Olga Saavedra.

9 7 5 3 1 2 4 6 8

A catalogue record for this book is available from the British Library.

ISBN (HB): 9781803283791
ISBN (E): 9781803283777

Printed and bound in Great Britain by
CPI Group (UK) Ltd, Croydon CR0 4YY

MIX
Paper from
responsible sources
FSC® C171272
www.fsc.org

Head of Zeus Ltd
First Floor East
5–8 Hardwick Street
London EC1R 4RG

WWW.HEADOFZEUS.COM

For Johnny

'*Life is not what you lived, but how you remember it.*'

Gabriel García Márquez

Contents

Prologue

Cuba is not the country it used to be. If you were a Cuban born on the island in the vicinity of 1975, you grew up with the promise of equality. You remember watching your classmates eating identical sandwiches and feeling: 'We are all part of the whole.' You were on the verge of adulthood when the country of your childhood vanished, following the fall of the Soviet bloc. You and your neighbours went hungry. Water and electricity were off more than on. Factories shut and fields of sugarcane lay idle. Fidel Castro announced that the Soviet Union had collapsed, but he did not explain what had happened. The US Congress tightened the economic blockade. 'We will wreak havoc on the island,' said the congressman who sponsored the bill, 'Fidel's days are numbered.' Cubans – perhaps you were among them – joked that Fidel's remaining days in power added up to a very big number.

Instead of laying the foundation for a self-sustaining socialist economy, the leadership that came to power after Fidel introduced market measures. They opened the island to tourism, legalised the US dollar and encouraged people to launch little businesses. The changes temporarily propped up the economy but ruined the country. The fortunate few who could rely on remittances turned to private enterprise and black marketeering to survive. Cubans called them *los nuevos ricos*, the new rich. Children asked their parents why some classmates brought ham sandwiches for lunch while they brought bread and dripping. 'Their families have dollars; we are just poor workers.'

Fidel vowed to rein in *los nuevos ricos* and rekindle Cubans' collective spirit. But the new leadership wanted to soften the rules governing private enterprise – even if it intensified inequality. Raúl Castro, Fidel's successor, declared, 'If we do not change we will be swept away.'

Purging Fidel's closest allies, Raúl announced that his government would 'update the economic model'. It was a euphemism for laying off public sector workers and expanding the private sector. 'Do not rely on the state to solve your problems; rely on yourself,' was the government slogan. It turned the founding principles of the Revolution on their head.

Raúl promised that the market opening would lift everyone's standard of living. 'No one will be left behind.' Many people were sceptical of the changes and opposed them. They feared losing their jobs, however poorly paid. They lacked the means or the inclination to start a small business. There was something else: many Cubans still believed in the promise of equality.

Los nuevos ricos and prominent economists opposed the new policies but for different reasons. They believed the economic opening was too halting and they called on the government to reduce regulations that held back the operation of market forces and slowed the rise of inequality.

The government's pro-market policies culminated in a historic declaration. Raúl Castro announced that egalitarianism, widely considered the Revolution's greatest achievement, was in fact one of its greatest errors. He said that guaranteeing all Cubans had a job and food discouraged individual initiative and promoted laziness. 'The notion that Cuba is the only country in the world where you can live without working must be erased forever.'

The government's austerity programme provoked enough opposition for it to be scaled back, but public sector layoffs combined with private sector growth altered the character of society. In Fidel's final years the state employed approximately eighty-five per cent of the working population. When Raúl Castro stepped down fifteen years later, forty per cent of the labour force was employed in the private and cooperative sectors working as part time, casual workers. A minority were self-employed microentrepreneurs. The shift from public to private employment, from secure to casual labour, from collective to individualised work reflected the advance of market forces. It also contributed to an increase in racism as Cubans of African descent lost out to white Cubans in the emerging market economy.

When Raúl Castro passed the presidency to his chosen successor in 2018, some island Cubans had more economic freedoms than at any time since Fidel had come to power in 1959. They were free to run a small business, hire and fire workers, make money, go bankrupt, sell their house and buy another, run a restaurant, get hired and fired on a nod and a whistle, go back and forth between Havana and Miami, run contraband, sell sex, vacation in Paris, own a smartphone and live off remittances. Other Cubans encountered a different kind of freedom. They were free to be poor and hungry.

The government attempted to maintain single party politics, but conditions had changed. Fidel's power rested on charisma, the promise of equality, fear, and Cubans' sense that they were a part of something larger than themselves. Fidel's successors lacked the vision and the resources to rule in the old way. When it became clear that market forces would not improve the lives of more than a tiny minority of the population, the leadership relied on repression and emigration to maintain control.

This book tells the story of modern Cuba through the life stories of seven islanders of the post-Soviet generation. These men and women grew up in the 1980s, a decade of relative comfort and equality. They came of age with the economic collapse of the 1990s, when they started questioning the ideology that governed their everyday lives. As young adults they faced poverty and shortages. A few encountered opportunities to make money and join the ranks of *los nuevos ricos*.

For six decades the Cuban government and Cuban exiles have portrayed the history of modern Cuba. This book tells Cubans' stories of their first-hand experiences of the Revolution.

1

THE NARRATORS

Mario Sánchez Cortés is Director of Digital Technology at the Ministry of Industry. Born in 1975, he has lived his entire life in two rooms in a tenement in San Isidro, a poor, majority-Black barrio in Old Havana. Mario is an iconoclastic member of the Communist Party who felt free, in the interviews, to question the Party's aims and methods.

Alina Rodríguez Abreu is a filmmaker who shot to fame when her documentary about Havana's squatter settlements, *Buscandote Havana (Looking for you Havana)*, was censored but subsequently won a prize at the Havana International Film Festival. Born in 1984, she lived on a tidy street in San Miguel del Padrón, an outlying Havana suburb known for poverty and criminality.

Juan Guillard Matus, a school dropout, is a rural jack-of-all-trades and talented raconteur. Born in 1968, he lives alone in a small cabin in Santa Ana de la Laguna, a two-hour drive east of Havana. The crux of Juan's life story is how he, an Afro-Cuban, felt the wounds of racism when he was growing up.

Esteban Cabrera Montes was a black marketeer and political rebel. Born in 1974, he lived with his brother in a 1950s subdivision on the outskirts of Havana in the house they inherited when their mother died in the late 1980s. Twice Esteban tried to escape by crossing the Florida Straits on a raft. Leaving was an obsession and, finally, he succeeded.

Barbara Vegas was born in 1972 and lived most of her life in a house on the verge of collapse in a majority Black neighbourhood in Regla. After quitting or losing one job after another she was hired as a night guard at the nearby Casa de Cultura and subsequently rewarded for her hard work with a promotion. She was appointed the head of administration. When we first met Barbara, she was applying for membership in the Communist Party and despite the Party's preference that women not complain about their partner's failure to do housework or childcare Barbara did just that. Her husband's machismo, and the subsequent burden of having to do everything alone, is a central theme of her life story.

Alejandro Espada Betancourt was born in 1985 and grew up in a spacious ranch-style house in Boyeros, an outlying Havana district. His father lived part of the time with him and his mother, and part of the time with his wife and their two children in Vedado. It was a very Cuban arrangement. At the age of nine Alejandro was diagnosed with leukaemia. With severe shortages of medicine, his mother persuaded government officials to allow her to take him to Miami for treatment, where he fell in love with PlayStation. After returning to Cuba, and graduating from university first in his class in industrial engineering, Alejandro had a plum job at Cuba Ron, the state company overseeing the rum industry. On the side he ran a small business in the underground digital economy. In 2015, Alejandro moved to Miami to join his mother who had left some years earlier. But the primary motivation for the move was that he wanted to live better than his state job plus his illicit business would allow.

When I interviewed Alejandro in Miami in 2016 he was trying to put on a good front. Finding work, an affordable place to live, and a big second hand car were more difficult than he had imagined.

Pavel García Rojas is an opposition activist. Once a fervent Fidelista, his narrative is a conversion story in which his current political stand is a prism through which he remembers the past. I interviewed him many times between 2012 and 2018 in the apartment in El Cerro that he inherited from his father who left.

Born in 1976 and growing up in Miramar, a once elegant Havana neighbourhood, Pavel fondly remembered the egalitarianism of his youth. Following the fall of the Soviet bloc he had an emotional breakdown and questioned his faith in Fidel, in socialism, and in the USSR. After studying history in the University of Havana's distance learning programme, Pavel enrolled at the privately funded Escuela International de Cine y Television (International Film and Television School), hoping to become a film director. Subsequently he worked as an administrator at the Film School.

At the end of 2014, Pavel's life changed dramatically. He was arrested en route to a demonstration, a political installation organised by the Cuban artist Tania Bruguera, and spent the next few days in jail. Pavel was fired by the Film School and ever since has been in and out of jail for a night or two for participating in anti-government events. Pavel writes regularly for online opposition publications to support his family.

Pseudonyms

I have changed the narrators' names for security and legal reasons. At the beginning and the end of each interview we asked the narrator to grant us permission to publish their life story, and we told them that we were changing their names. Although many narrators subsequently said they would be happy for me to use their real names, I decided not to.

Most of my Cuban colleagues on the project, the interviewers, asked me not to use their real names, and I have abided by their requests.

2

BACKSTORY

This book had a fortuitous beginning. At a conference celebrating Latin American women in 2000 I found myself sitting next to a smartly dressed woman at breakfast. She turned to me and said, 'If you had funding for a large research project what would you do?' I immediately said, 'I would do an oral history study in Cuba. I want to know how ordinary people feel about living the Revolution.' 'What a coincidence,' she said, 'I am in charge of the Ford Foundation's funding for Cuba.'

I first visited Cuba in 1972, when I was a graduate student studying Latin American history at Columbia University in my home town, New York City, and ever since wanted to conduct life history interviews on the island.

Several years after she and I met, I went to Havana to seek research collaborators and government authorisation. As the US embargo prohibited US foundations from funding Cubans' salaries and expenses, the Swedish Agency for International Development fortunately had agreed to co-finance the study. I met with academics and writers in Havana and Santiago, and soon had a team of ten Cuban and three British research collaborators. What I didn't have, and wouldn't for another few years, was permission to do the study.

The Cuban researchers and I made the rounds of officials in Havana who might help us secure approval. A vice-minister who asked to remain anonymous said, 'Your project is beautiful. I'd like to help, but remember Oscar Lewis. In Cuba oral history is taboo.'

*

In 1968, Fidel Castro invited Oscar Lewis, a famous US anthropologist, to interview Cubans about their lives. 'It would be an important contribution to Cuban history to have an objective record of what people feel and think… This is a socialist country. We have nothing to hide; there are no complaints or grievances I haven't already heard,' Castro reportedly told Lewis.[1] Lewis accepted, and with Ruth Lewis, his wife, and a team of young Cuban sociologists, he began interviewing people in several Havana neighbourhoods. Eighteen months later, in 1970, top Party officials abruptly terminated the project, and Raúl Castro accused Lewis of working for the CIA, though almost no one outside Cuba believed it. The most likely reason the study was closed was that Cubans acted exactly the way Fidel had predicted. They complained. They talked about their grievances. They described the government's accomplishments and its faults.[2] The Lewises were told to leave soon after Fidel announced that the historic campaign to harvest a record-breaking ten million tons of sugar would fall short of its goal. Its failure was the government's first major setback, and led many Cubans to question the revolutionary project. In that atmosphere, Cuban politicians did not want foreigners – or Cubans for that matter – interviewing people at random. Fidel still wanted an oral history of life in the Revolution, and in 1975 asked his close friend Gabriel García Márquez to write one. After a year of research, García Márquez abandoned the project, apparently telling friends that what Cubans said did not fit the book he wanted to write.[3]

In 2004, after umpteen attempts to get the project approved, I was on the verge of calling it quits when teammate Julio César

González Pajes suggested we appeal to Mariela Castro, Raúl Castro's daughter and the country's leading champion of LGBT rights. 'She has a reputation for fighting lost causes,' he said. The next day we met in her office at the National Centre for Sex Education (CENESEX), and she said without a moment's hesitation, 'Your project is exciting. I can't promise I can get it approved, but I will try.'

While we were waiting, the team met to work out exactly what we would do if the project went ahead. We decided in which provinces we would work and how we would select narrators. We agreed to conduct largely unstructured interviews because we wanted narrators to talk about what was important to them, not what we thought was important, and to start off each interview with a deceptively simple request, 'Please tell us the story of your life.' We conducted pilot interviews and drew up a short questionnaire to gather information about their family, education and work.

In 2005, one year after we first approached Mariela Castro, the project was approved. It was inaugurated at a ceremony in the Aula Magna of the University of Havana, and highlights of the event were broadcast on TV.[4]

We quickly discovered that many of the plans we drew up sitting around a table were not doable, and we ended up interviewing pretty much wherever and whoever we could. We improvised. At first I thought improvisation was a problem; soon I realised it was also a strength. We learned from our mistakes and adjusted the way we did things as we went along. About half of the team located interviewees through informal networks of acquaintances, relatives and co-workers, and half through official channels. The results of this two-track selection process surprised us. Although people said that Cuban society was deeply divided between supporters and opponents of the government, we learned that the divide was greatly exaggerated. Facing common hardships, the majority of the people we interviewed expressed similar hopes and grievances.

Another unexpected discovery was that so many people were willing to tell their life stories pretty much the way they remembered them. We had anticipated that interviewees would self-censor, and many did at the beginning. But telling the story of your life is often cathartic and many narrators said words to the effect, *I never said this to anyone before, but it feels good to say it*. We promised the narrators we would disguise their identity; we also reminded them that in Cuba anonymity only goes so far. Neighbours might inform. State officials might discover who they are.

Their openness generated problems. After listening to the black marketeer Esteban's interviews, Mariela Castro suspended the project. The ghost of Oscar Lewis kept me awake that night, and a week later I left Cuba not knowing when I might be back. Six months on I received a message from Mariela saying it was possible we could negotiate an amicable accord. When we met in Havana, she said the study could continue, but under less formal arrangements. I and half of the team accepted her conditions and we resumed interviewing, though less frequently. I took advantage of the shuffle to expand the pool of interviewers by asking younger, less politically attached, researchers to work on the project. Although I did not know it at the time, most of the Cubans I first invited to join the team were members of the Communist Party.

From 2004 to 2018 we interviewed 124 Cubans, some of them numerous times, Cubans living in the provinces of Havana, Artemisa, Santiago, Matanzas, Holguin, Sancti Spíritus, Bayamo and Granma. Approximately half of the narrators were from the City of Havana and its outlying districts.

When we began the project in 2004, many narrators believed that conditions in the country would improve. I didn't know then that we would be recording interviews over a span of fifteen years, and that taken together they would be a chronicle of the transformation of the Cuban Revolution.

Eventually, the audio interviews and electronic transcripts will be publicly available.

3

FIDEL'S FALL, AN OMEN

On 20 October 2004, one month after I arrived in Cuba, Fidel Castro gave a speech in front of the massive mausoleum that houses the remains of Ernesto 'Che' Guevara in the city of Santa Clara. The event was staged to promote the Battle of Ideas, a campaign to save socialism. 'The Battle of Ideas will put a stop to money lining the pockets of the new rich. Many inequalities will disappear. That is what true and irreversible socialism demands. Everything is a Battle of Ideas.'[1] The Battle of Ideas was Fidel's response to the rise of the inequalities engendered by private business, tourism and legalisation of the US dollar.

For Fidel and his followers, the Battle of Ideas was a struggle for the future of Cuba, a struggle between capitalism and socialism. As they saw it, Communist Party heavyweights who favoured expanding market forces, even if it amplified inequalities, stood on one side, and cadre calling for reining in the market and preserving equality stood on the other. In this feverish atmosphere, Fidel tried to inspire Cubans, especially the youth, to reconnect with the Revolution's founding principles. But he was old, his powers diminished, and the campaign quickly became an umbrella for a huge range of activities, from anti-corruption sweeps to making sure every woman received La Reina (The Queen), an electric pressure cooker that supposedly saved electricity. Many Cubans,

Fidelistas included, soon grew weary of the catch-all initiative and its never-ending call to arms.

That evening in Santa Clara, Fidel ended his speech in the usual way. '*Viva la Patria. Viva la Revolución. Viva el socialism. Hasta la Victoria Siempre.* (Long live the homeland. Long live the Revolution. Long live socialism. Ever onward to victory.).' As he stepped down from the podium he fell, breaking an arm and leg.

The next morning Cubans read a 'Letter from Compañero Fidel to his Compatriots' in the official newspaper of the Central Committee of the Cuban Communist Party, *Granma*. The letter combined an intimate account of his injuries and treatment, the sort of details usually reserved for family, with instructions regarding national security. To assure his compatriots that he was in the safest of hands he wrote, 'Into the ambulance speeding towards Havana squeezed various *compañeros*, including Carlitos... I spoke with Felipe. I asked him to stay in touch, which, despite its difficulties, was possible thanks to the wonders of wireless communications.' Cubans did not need to be told which Carlitos or Felipe. Carlos Lage and Felipe Pérez Roque were Fidel's closest allies, frequently named as potential successors, along with his brother Raúl.

The letter continued, 'Upon arrival at the Palace of the Revolution [the seat of government] various *compañeros* carried my stretcher in on their shoulders.' Fidel evoked a quasi-biblical scene. 'We agreed to operate on the kneecap immediately... The entire operation took three hours and fifteen minutes. The orthopaedic surgeons like weavers each attending to his own specialty reunited the fragments, solidly binding one to the other with a fine stainless-steel thread. A work of goldsmiths. The patient [Fidel referred to himself in the third person] asked the doctors not to administer a sedative... I explained that given my circumstances it was imperative to forego a general anaesthetic in order for me to be able to attend to numerous important matters. I remained in contact with my Chief of Staff throughout the operation... and I continued to receive information and give instructions as to the handling of the situation caused by this unexpected accident.'

The letter, evoking physical courage and absolute authority, reinforced Fidel's charisma, and let his enemies know that he remained in total control.

The next day I watched a rerun of the fateful night in a house in Miramar. The owner, whose grandson was a prominent dissident, was weeping. 'I love him like a son, I love him like a son,' she murmured.

Cubans believed Fidel's fall was an omen, and indeed it was. It foreshadowed not only his abdication two years later, but his successors' retreat from egalitarianism. In 2006, beset by illness, Fidel provisionally ceded power to his brother Raúl, who in 2008 was officially installed as president. The next year Raúl accused Felipe Pérez Roque and Carlos Lage of crimes bordering on treason and purged them from the government and the Party. They lost everything.

PART 1

THE 1980s

The decade began with an explosion of discontent. In 1980, 125,000 Cubans fled to Miami in the Mariel boatlift. Leaving was the ultimate taboo. Many narrators recalled with shame participating in *actas de repudio*, violent demonstrations against *los gusanos*, the worms, who left in the boatlift. When the government allowed the Marielitos to return to visit their families – because it needed their dollars – Cubans joked bitterly, 'The worms have turned into butterflies.'

In the wake of the boatlift, to forestall further unrest, the state increased the quantity of food and clothing, as well as cigars and rum, every household received. The emphasis on consumption reflected an ideological shift away from moral incentives – honorific medals and applause for vanguard workers – to material incentives: a pay bonus, a fan, a vacation in East Germany, and in exceptional cases a car, to raise labour productivity. The state introduced 'free market stores' where Cubans who earned more could buy items that were not available on the ration, such as blue jeans, evaporated milk and chocolate. In the Special Period, Fidel frequently reminded the population of the comforts they enjoyed in the 1980s, and many Cubans came to think of the decade as a golden age.

Although egalitarianism was eroding in the 1980s, Cubans still enjoyed an exceptional degree of economic equality. The ratio between the highest and the lowest paid was 4:1.[1] In addition to their earnings, Cubans had free healthcare and education, and heavily subsidised food, clothing, transport, housing and tickets to the ballet and baseball games. Narrators frequently talked about the atmosphere of equality in the 1980s, and recalled their shock when towards the end of the decade the government opened stores selling food, clothing and consumer durables that many Cubans could not afford.

As the 1980s wore on Cuba's economy pulled in different directions. Cuba was an ally of the USSR in the Cold War, but relations between the two governments frayed after 1985, when Mikhail Gorbachev liberalised the economy of the Soviet Union and advocated a measure of democratisation. Fidel denounced Gorbachev, and said he would never follow in his footsteps. The hard reality was that Cuba could not survive without Soviet assistance.

Tensions building throughout the 1980s played themselves out in the chaotic Rectification Campaign initiated by Fidel in 1986. He announced its goal was to rectify the errors undermining socialism, but many of the new policies had the opposite effect. They increased income disparities, and shored up privileges enjoyed by the bureaucratic elite. It is evident, in hindsight, that the Rectification Campaign was an attempt to resolve the country's intractable economic problems and preserve egalitarianism. Its failure paved the way for the Battle of Ideas.

A decade that began with an eruption of discontent in Cuba ended with a popular explosion that changed the world – the fall of the Berlin Wall. At the time few Cubans knew what was happening in Europe; the official media carried almost no news. The Cuban government drew a veil over the uprisings that toppled its communist allies for as long as it possibly could.

4

MARIO SÁNCHEZ CORTÉZ

Old Havana

Mario Sánchez Cortéz was a thirty-one-year-old computer technician when my colleague Lilia Campos first interviewed him in 2006, Fidel's last year in power.[1] Mario had recently joined the Communist Party and he was working at Cuba's first public internet centre. Much of the job was either technical – at the best of times the connection was very, very slow as the computers had to connect to the world wide web via satellite to get around the US blockade – or educational, both of which came easily to Mario, a tremendous admirer of the internet and its liberating possibilities. Part of Mario's job was to stop users going to websites prohibited by the government. He said he would have hated catching anyone and having to inform on them, so it was fortunate it never came to that; he always happened to be looking the other way. This anecdote is emblematic of his personality.

Medium tall, Black, with closely cropped hair, Mario is a sober dresser. Unlike many men of his generation he never wears jewellery or brand clothing. To me, at least, his distinguishing feature is his radiant smile. His face and eyes exude friendliness and good will. He speaks in a soft melodic voice that lets you know he's enjoying your company, and he puts people at ease.

Mario was born in 1975 in San Isidro, a poor barrio in Old Havana around the corner from the docks, where most families are of African descent. This was the height of the Soviet Period, so-called because Moscow's influence was at its strongest. The port was busy, and men in the neighbourhood worked as stevedores loading and unloading ships from the Soviet bloc. It's different now – the docks are a tourist attraction and lined with overpriced private restaurants and tacky souvenir shops. But few people living in San Isidro work in tourism; racism keeps them out. Walking around the neighbourhood, Mario pointed to a sign on the door of a swanky restaurant: 'Waitress needed. Preferably white, twenty to twenty-five years old, ideally blonde and blue eyed.'

In November 2020, San Isidro acquired a new kind of fame. Police raided a house where young Black artists were living, smashed their artworks and put several of them in prison. The artists and their art were calling for democracy and respect for human rights, and their arrest sparked the Movimiento San Isidro (MSI), and the first public protests against the government in twenty-odd years. Before San Isidro evoked an image of Black poverty; now it is a symbol of resistance.

Mario still lives in the same *ciudadela* where he grew up, a tenement built in 1900 to house the poor, with his parents and two siblings in two dark, damp rooms on the ground floor. The only window overlooks an interior corridor. Until he was in his teens the family shared a kitchen and a rudimentary bathroom with their neighbours. Now he lives in the same two rooms with his sister and her two children; they are his nuclear family.

Mario is a well-known figure in the barrio, celebrated for his concern for others and his university degree. Wherever we went it seemed that everyone on the street stopped him for advice. Youngsters wanted to know how to get the playground unlocked, and when he would join them in a basketball game. Oldsters asked where they could get their heart medicine as the pharmacy was out of stock. He spoke with everyone, put his arm around their shoulders, didn't hurry anyone along.

I always felt Mario was entirely open, even though we were recording the interviews. This was partly a question of trust, but also of principle. Humane and hard-working, he values perseverance and self-improvement, and is determined to focus on life's achievements rather than its infinite frustrations. Mario joined the Communist Party in a spirit of optimism: he supported its ideals but felt they weren't always reflected in reality. He wanted to change the Party, open it up, make it more like he thought it should be. His positivity and social conscience give him a great deal of natural authority and charm.

'I spent my childhood visiting prisons.'

When Mario was two weeks old his father went to jail for manslaughter. 'My father had issues with the man who ran the *bodega* [the state outlet that distributes the food ration]. They had an argument. The man was like a cockerel in a henhouse. He tried to dominate my father, but my father defended himself. The dispute got bigger and bigger until it reached the point where if my father hadn't killed the man, he would have killed my father. My father was jailed for eleven years. I spent my childhood visiting prisons.'

Mario's father was born in Granma Province in the eastern end of the island. Mario said his grandfather, a prosperous farmer, supported Fidel Castro and soon after the triumph of the Revolution he voluntarily turned over his land to the state and moved his family to Havana to work for the government. 'My father hoped to go to university, but when he failed the exams he became a high school chemistry teacher. In prison they taught him construction. He was somewhat unstable before he went to prison; by the time he was released he had become a violent man.'

Mario's mother, María, was a laboratory technician. She wanted to improve herself and studied biochemistry five nights a week at La Facultad Obrera y Campesina (the Workers' and Peasants' University), while her husband was in prison. For five years, she took her three children to the Facultad, where she put them to bed at the back of the classroom. When she was one course away from finishing, the Facultad changed the graduation requirements and she would have had to continue for another year. Instead she decided to quit. 'It was like a fireball dropped out of the sky and struck her down. Her years of sacrifice were for nothing. My mother was never the same. I vowed I would never let that happen to me; I would be a somebody when I grew up.'

Despite these difficulties Mario said his childhood was the happiest time of his life. It was, I think, because remembering equality and sharing brought him pleasure. 'Every child in the neighbourhood got a gift on Three Kings Day. We shared the presents; they were very simple, but we were content.' I asked if he played with dolls; he shook his head and broke into a you-must-be-crazy laugh.

'You looked to one side, then the other. Everyone was equal. You felt you were a part of the whole.'

La merienda, the school snack, was Mario's most cherished childhood memory. To the post-Soviet generation, *la merienda* symbolised the prosperity and equality of the 1980s – and its loss.

'In primary school we all got *la merienda*, a drink and biscuits and all that stuff. Everyone was content, partly because we all had the same. You looked to one side, then the other. Everyone was equal. You felt you were a part of the whole. *La merienda* was so plentiful we would grab a pastry or a biscuit just to throw it around. If I had known about the shortages we have now, I wouldn't have done that. At snack time each of us got our biscuit, hot chocolate, drink, crackers, our pastry filled with guayaba paste. I remember it all. The pastries were yummy. Everyone, every single one of us got our own *merienda*.' Looking back to the 1980s, Mario remembered the *merienda* not only as a sumptuous feast, but emblematic of shared abundance.

'In the 1990s, with the fall of the socialist camp, with the blockade and all that, they [the state] eliminated the *merienda*. They no longer give school snacks or lunches. Now children take to school whatever they can afford and a child's *merienda* reflects the money his parents earn. For example, my nephew takes who knows what to school, sometimes bread with meat paste, sometimes bread with dripping and a drink, a Toqui [cheap soda pop], or even one of those concoctions that shopkeepers make with powder. Children whose fathers work in a company or have a certain status, maybe they are *cuentapropistas* [self-employed], or taxi drivers, or run an illegal business which provides a good income, well that child brings every single day a ham and cheese sandwich and a can of genuine soda. This has an effect. The other children see it and their parents don't know how to begin to explain why there are such big differences.

'In the case of my nephew, he understands because we discuss it. Of course, he would like to bring a can of real soda and a ham sandwich, and he asks, "If others can, why can't I? Why do I have to eat bread with dripping?" What we do is explain that all families are not equal. We explain that he is from a family of ordinary workers and we don't have relatives abroad or anyone who sends us money and that's his lot in life. We try to explain. If he understands, good; if not, *bueno*, what can you do? We hope, we really hope, he understands. The fact is if he does or he doesn't he just has to get on with life.'

At that time, when many Cubans were facing food shortages, inequality felt raw and uncomfortable to Mario.

'In my time everybody was equal.'

'The difference between my epoch and now is your perspective, how you see things... In my time everybody was equal. Every child went to primary school carrying one pencil and one eraser, wearing the same *zapatos colegiales* [school shoes distributed on the ration]. Now some kids go to school in shoes their parents bought in US dollars, wearing clothes their parents bought, carrying notebooks their parents bought. This is creating differences, creating jealousy. I imagine that the other children also want to have the good stuff. No, I won't call it the good stuff because I don't know whether it is good or bad. It is different. I'm no child psychologist but I know from experience that in my day a child who went to school wearing a pair of Nikes felt like an outsider. A child who wasn't wearing the same as the rest of us felt left out. Now it's the opposite. In my day people felt differently than they do nowadays. Their point of view was different. Their consciousness was different. Dressing the same as everyone else was a source of satisfaction, of equality. Now it's the opposite. Equality is very, very important; that's what I want to say.'

'Unbelievable, me, the son of a nobody, going to school in Vedado.'

Mario recalls that by the age of eight he had decided to make something of himself. When neighbours remarked on his dancing, he resolved to become a famous *salsero*, salsa dancer, when he grew up. When a teacher praised his drawing, he signed up for after-school art classes at the local Casa de Cultura, the cultural centre in his neighbourhood, which was, appropriately, in the house where José Martí was born.[2] Artistic talent coupled with perseverance altered the course of Mario's life. Instead of going to the local middle school adjacent to the docks, and becoming a stevedore, Mario applied to a specialist art school in Vedado, from which most of the students went on to the celebrated Escuela Nacional de Bellas Artes, San Alejandro. Mario started art school in 1990, the year the Cuban economy fell apart. The school introduced Mario to the city beyond his barrio, and each day as he boarded the bus to Vedado he felt a rush.

'I am going to school in Vedado, Vedado, Vedado. Unbelievable, me, the son of a nobody, going to school in Vedado... I left home at six in the morning and arrived back at six at night... I learned many things that have served me well throughout my life: drawing, design, painting, engraving, history of art and architecture. But most importantly I was away from the barrio. I grew apart from my friends in the neighbourhood. Not because we had conflicts; I was always in Vedado and my new friends lived in different neighbourhoods.' The way Mario talked of leaving his barrio every morning and returning at night made it sound like a fairy-tale entitled 'The Prince of Vedado and the Pauper of the Docks'.

But the magic unravelled. In the first year Mario was conscientious and got good grades. Then his father came home. 'I had always dreamed of having a male figure in the house. At first, after he got out of prison, I was happy but we didn't know what was in store for us. Soon the problems started... I was eleven and this stranger stepped into my life saying that because he is my father he will impose his values, and if we don't obey he will force us the hard way. There were beatings and other things. He violently abused my mamá and my sister.' Mario talked about domestic violence at a time when the Cuban government refused to acknowledge its existence.

The next year Mario's grades fell. His father thought art school was a waste of time and forced his son to help him install a toilet and a concrete floor in the apartment. If Mario tried to explain he had homework his father beat him. Ashamed to tell his teachers why he hadn't done his homework he began to skip school, and spent his days hanging out on the Malecón. Mario remembers feeling that he was an outsider and didn't belonging at his school.

In his final year, when most of his classmates got into San Alejandro, Mario failed the exams. 'I was sad, very sad. I returned home crying.'

'Their clothes, and I am not talking just about clothes. You could see the status they wore.'

'While I'm not trying to blame others, I think that there was something big, something powerful, going on. I am the son of ordinary workers and, in the end, I did not have the same possibilities as other students. Some were sons and daughters of painters and positions like that. Their families had a different status. It was easy for them to get into San Alejandro. I was terribly, terribly disappointed that I did not achieve my goal.

'I began to see the marked differences in society. When there was a parents' meeting, cars arrived at school; the street was full of them. I, of course, had come by bus. I saw the other parents. Their clothes, and I'm not talking just about clothes, you could see the status they wore. Luckily, at my public exams the director said only students could enter the hall. Parents had to wait outside. Outside were all the parents, the so-and-sos. I was inside with their sons and daughters, and that was something. It made my mamá happy.' Fifteen years later Mario was still trying to understand his failure, still questioning how equalitarian Cuba really was in the late 1980s.

'Vedado, Vedado. At the beginning I was dazzled. Later I got to know the neighbourhood and discovered that Vedado is a lot like Old Havana – but with rouge. When people think of Vedado they think of [the famous intersection] 23rd and L; they think of Coppelia [the iconic ice cream parlour in the film *Strawberry and Chocolate*]; they think of the Habana Libre [before 1959 the Havana Hilton]. Yes, in Vedado there are many beautiful things, beautiful houses, beautiful buildings, beautiful people. But there is also ugliness and squalor. When I skipped classes I wandered into places you would never imagine were in Vedado. I saw humble people, some very humble; I'd even say marginal. When I saw that I said to myself, Vedado isn't what it used to be. It's fallen. Even so, life there was different. The hustle and bustle, the action was different. I remember back then if your mother gave you two or three pesos you could go to Coppelia, or to a cafeteria. Vedado had lots of life. Most of the action is still in Vedado.'

Lilia encouraged Mario to say more about his failure at art school. She and Mario were old friends; they lived in the same neighbourhood; they had been dancing partners. She asked questions I shied from.

Do you think there might have been a little, like, I don't know what to call it, racism, a little discrimination? You say that the fathers of the other compañeros were painters. Could you say more about this?

Lilia's question prompted Mario to consider whether race and racism had had anything to do with his failure to get into San Alejandro.

'When you fail at something you always try to justify it to others. You might say, it's because they are Black, or it's racism, other stuff like that. At the time I couldn't fathom it at all, not at all. I didn't have the consciousness. I couldn't interpret the subliminal messages or whatever they're called that people transmit. Do you understand what I am saying?... At that time there were only a few of us. The school had only a few Blacks. In my class of thirty-some students, there was me and one other Black. Two Blacks and neither one of us passed the exam. Well, let's discard the idea that it was because of that.' Mario doesn't say the word racism. 'But yes, yes, I believe there was a kind of predetermination in the selection in favour of those who had some influence at San Alejandro from the perspective of, who knows, they were artists, or they had a certain standing in society which could have influenced the process. Yes, those people got in without any problem. Then, I think, I don't know, but at the minimum [he hesitated] what happened wasn't fair. At that time San Alejandro was very elitist. I don't know about now because I am quite out of touch. Elitist places are places for the few. The people who go there are almost always from the elite, or in this case, they were the children of the elite.

'My family was not of the elite; I am not a child of the elite. I am the son of María, a worker, and of Juan, just another worker. That is the reason I did not have the, how should I put it, the opportunity to attend San Alejandro... There were mechanisms through which, I can assure you, *el hijo de mamá y el hijo de papá* [a Cuban expression meaning the son of affluent or powerful parents] wielded influence. It's true we all took the same exams, but there were only so many places at San Alejandro and I did not get in. Something else is important: there were only a few Blacks at San Alejandro, very few.'

Seeing the parents of his classmates opened his eyes. When Mario failed to gain admission to San Alejandro he realised that egalitarianism had another side. He felt he had been excluded from the elite school because his family was poor and yes, maybe because he is Black. The taboos surrounding race, the ideology that racism in Cuba ended with the end of capitalism, made it hard for Mario to say the word racism. Gradually over the next twelve years he talked more about the racism that is a part of his everyday life.

Mario's three years at middle school coincided with a sharp downturn in the Cuban economy, prefiguring the Special

Period, the name Fidel gave to the years of extreme austerity that followed the fall of the Soviet bloc. To build up foreign reserves the government introduced programs designed to earn hard currency. People with higher salaries and Cubans from the defunct bourgeoisie traded valuables they had hidden away for what passed for luxuries: blue jeans, trainers and art supplies. Differences in income and political status translated into material inequality. Mario remembered that his classmates purchased expensive paints and brushes while he had to make do with the materials they gave out in school and he wondered whether this disadvantage on top of all the others had contributed to his failure.

With San Alejandro beyond his reach Mario enrolled in a school in the countryside, the sort most students attended to prepare for university entrance exams. There the Special Period brought unexpected hardships.

5

ALINA RODRÍGUEZ ABREU

San Miguel del Padrón, Havana

Alina Rodríguez was an underground celebrity. *Buscándote Havana (Looking for You, Havana)*, her documentary about Havana's squatter settlements, started as a homework assignment and turned into a cause célèbre.

I arranged to interview Alina at her home in San Miguel del Padrón, an outer Havana district with a reputation for trouble. To avoid the two-hour bus ride, I asked my neighbour Alex to drive me in his rusty blue Lada. 'Fidel gave me this car almost twenty-five years ago when I nearly forfeited my life for the Revolution,' he said as I got in. Alex was wounded in Angola, in Cuba's African wars against apartheid. Alex appeared unstable. He drove with one hand on the horn, leaning out the window, shouting at passers-by. He told me he still was suffering from the trauma of fighting. Despite Alex's erratic behaviour he was president of the local CDR (Committee for the Defence of the Revolution), and he organised parties to celebrate state holidays and block meetings where neighbours could have their say about controversial policies. CDR heads were, in Fidel's words, 'the eyes and ears of the Revolution', whose job was to inform on anyone who exhibited counterrevolutionary tendencies. Doing illegal chauffeuring, Alex was in no position to grass on his neighbours.

Entering San Miguel we passed boarded-up factories and Soviet-style apartment blocks that loomed above dilapidated wooden bungalows, the remains of an old sugar mill, a mishmash of down-at-heel buildings. After looping our way through dusty roundabouts, we suddenly found ourselves in a street of tidy, pastel coloured stucco houses that looked like a tornado had picked them up in Kansas and plopped them here in outer Havana. I spotted a young, slightly built woman with translucent white skin, blue eyes, and a bubble of curly blonde hair calling excitedly from a rooftop patio. 'Liz, thanks so much for coming. There is a settlement at the end of the street, but you can't see it very well because it's hidden by brush. You really had to come out here. I wanted you to see where I live so that you could understand why I made the documentary.'[1]

Opening a metal-grate door Alina invited me in. I followed her upstairs to a small sunny apartment, crowded with cheery furniture, that she shared with her mother. Pictures of alpine shepherds hung on the walls, and an old man was sleeping in a rocking chair in the corner. Clearly irritated by his presence, Alina explained that it was her grandfather and she cared for him several mornings a week while her aunt, who lived downstairs, was at work.

'I wanted you to see my neighbourhood with your own eyes. La Corea, La Cuevita, Diezmero are barrios known for delinquency. Here most people live on the margins. Where I was born shaped what I did, am still trying to do. You can't separate this neighbourhood from the film I made. If I'd been born in Vedado I wouldn't have known there were illegal shantytowns in Havana, or if I happened to find out I wouldn't have cared. I first saw how squatters live right here. Every day I watched people walking back and forth in front of my house dragging bits of rubbish, rusted metal, broken pipes, everything you can think of. I saw kids my own age hawking old clothes, spare parts, vegetables, anything, and I knew they lived in the settlement at the end of my street. I have been surrounded by this kind of thing my entire life and I've had to live with it. Living in San Miguel definitely left its mark. I planned to make the documentary right here but the officials stopped me.' Alina's mobile phone rang just then; it was illegal and a sign of privilege.

Alina was born in 1984 in the enclave of San Miguel called Barrio Obrero, Workers' Neighbourhood, built in the 1940s by a US sugar company to house its American employees. Alina's home is a few minutes' walk from the Central Highway that runs the length of the island from Guantánamo to Havana, the road taken by migrants from 'Oriente', the east of the country, seeking a better life. Ever since the Soviet bloc crashed and maybe longer, Cubans have been leaving Oriente without permission, forfeiting their right to receive whatever the state delivers – food rations, healthcare, schooling, formal employment, sewage, electricity, housing – to make a life for themselves in Havana. They get off the bus, put down their belongings and put up a shack. The illegal settlements are known as 'llega y pon' (llega/arrive, pon/put), because the migrants arrive, put down whatever they are carrying and sink roots. Cubans call the migrants Palestinos, Palestinians, because they are people without rights, dispossessed.

As a child Alina avoided the children who lived in what she called 'the complicated barrios'. 'My lifestyle had absolutely nothing in common with theirs,' she said, which jarred with my sense of Cuba in the egalitarian 1980s. Attending primary school in a rough neighbourhood Alina discovered she had a talent for leadership. 'I was always the littlest girl in the class; they called me la chiquitica Alinita, but despite being tiny I was always the jefa del aula, head student. I'm sweet and kind and I got along with everyone. I'm not a born leader, the kind who calls attention to herself. I'm not egocentric, no, I'm not that way, but the teachers always chose me to be the head. I think it was because I liked helping my *compañeros*.'

Alina stood out not only for her blonde hair and pale skin, but for her helicopter parents. 'In my household I was the queen.' Alina's mother was in her middle thirties, her father in his forties, when she was born, and her only sibling, a half-brother on her mother's side, was a teenager. 'I have to admit I was definitely spoiled. I was born when the economy was the best we've ever had, and my mother and father tried to give me everything I wanted.'

Alina's parents came from farming families in the central provinces. 'Who owns the land now?' I asked. 'Fidel,' shouted her grandfather, who I had thought was sleeping. I asked him about the family's landholding, which Alina clearly felt was a diversion from the story of her documentary. This was supposed to be her chance to talk. She had been interviewed briefly on state TV but the presenter cut her off as soon as she mentioned the documentary. However, her grandfather was eager to talk and he explained that the family still owned and farmed approximately sixty acres, and sent food to their relatives in Havana, which got them through the Special Period.

Like many Cubans of their generation, Alina's parents went to university in Havana and never left. Her mother and aunt became epidemiologists; her father an industrial engineer. They joined the Party and were grateful to the Revolution for their professional advancement. Alina did not say that her father was living in Miami where he had a small business. Later on, I put two and two together and concluded that Alina's mobile phone and the new bathroom and kitchen fixtures must have been bought with remittances.

'My mother was divine, so was my father.' They gave little Alinita all the Revolution had to offer. At weekends they took her to Havana for all the lessons her heart desired. From age six she studied piano at the conservatory in Vedado, but when the school cut back its intake during the Special Period she had to give it up. She took ballet classes and when the buses stopped because of petroleum shortages, her father took her on his clunky Chinese bicycle the twenty-mile round trip to Vedado. She quit ballet and took Spanish dancing and drama classes. 'I was lazy. I never wanted to practise. I wasn't musical. I wasn't good at acting. I wasn't a good writer. I never ever thought of becoming a filmmaker. I never owned a camera or even held one in my hands, but I loved the world of the arts.'

6

JUAN GUILLARD MATUS

Santa Ana de la Laguna, Artemisa Province

Juan Guillard Matus was thirty-seven years old when my colleagues Marisol and Victoria first interviewed him in 2005, shortly before Fidel stepped down.[1] He lived alone in a dilapidated cabin, not much larger than a beach hut, in Santa Ana de la Laguna, a rural town thirty miles east of Havana, and scraped by working as a handyman and illegally rearing small animals in his front yard. 'My story is about what it's like to be a poor person in Cuba,' he began. Juan might well have said 'poor Black person', as many of his memories centred on how it felt to grow up Black in a predominately white town. But he didn't; talking about race was taboo in Cuba in 2005. Juan broke the taboo, but only to a degree. Instead of calling racism by its name he referred to 'that thing' or 'that idiosyncrasy' and explained that in Santa Ana he always felt different. Like all Cubans, Juan is fluent in the language of code.

Juan is the embodiment of *un personaje*, a character, as one of his neighbours put it. Graceful, muscular and with a shining mop of curly black hair, he clearly takes pleasure in his looks. Restless and always on the verge of laughing, he is affectionate and larger than life in ways that sometimes seemed designed to mask insecurity. In many interviews over thirteen years, Juan talked in a popular, garrulous, style known as *dando tremenda muela*, chewing the fat. He spoke rapidly, even by Cuban standards, using earthy, intentionally scandalous words. A natural performer, Juan clearly enjoyed shocking us, his mesmerised audience, with offbeat stories about racism, religion, politics, romance and life in Miami (though he'd never been) that he wove together into a narrative that was plainly at odds with the official history of the Cuban Revolution. Juan reminded me of the New York comedian Lenny Bruce, who combined satire, sex, politics, religion and vulgarity into a seductive but dangerous mix. I got the sense that Juan couldn't pass up the chance to shock the two stereotypically academic women from Cuba's illustrious Academy of Sciences, and me, the inquisitive foreigner, who miraculously landed on his front porch. I also suspected Juan's flamboyance was his way of coping.

Santa Ana, known before the Revolution as Havana's dairy, is a dusty one-horse town known nowadays for its large number of *balseros* – rafters.

Marisol said the entire neighbourhood seemed asleep when they went looking for Juan on a sultry Saturday in May. They found him dozing on his tumbledown porch while Elton John's *Sleeping with the Past* blared from his boom box. A fitting introduction to his life story, I thought as I listened to the recording.

Piglets and chickens squawked when Marisol opened the gate of Juan's mini-barnyard. Awakened by the clamour, he waved them in. 'Rosa told me to expect you. I thought she'd come to ask me to shore up the wall in front of her house. You can't imagine my amazement when she said she wanted me to do an important interview.' Rosa, our guide to the town, was that rare combination, a veteran Party member and an iconoclast.

Juan was dressed for company in an ironed T-shirt, olive green trousers and polished military boots; his outfit probably was army surplus. He jumped up to offer Victoria and Marisol water and a long apology for having neither ice nor juice. 'Things are not like they used to be. You know how it is. I used to be able to get just about every kind of fruit: guayaba, melon, fruta bomba, you name it.'

Juan began his life story with an upbeat account of his years doing obligatory military service. 'I enjoyed the military. Although many boys try to dodge the draft, not me. In the service they teach you all kinds of things. I was selected to participate in Bastión 1986 [a battalion that carried out special military exercises], and I received a medal for distinguished service.' And he dashed into the house to look for the medal but came out empty handed.

Perhaps Juan had decided beforehand to begin with his army stories. They were safe, and showed him in a good light. He also might have imagined – correctly – that a paean to the army would sit well with his interviewers.

Juan's life story quickly took a sombre turn. 'Ever since I was young, I've had a hard life. Nevertheless, I feel pretty good. I've learned how to survive life's difficulties, learned not to give in. It's true that sometimes I wish the earth would swallow me up. But what counts is not the number of times you fall down, but the times you pick yourself up... You've got to be an optimist. I'm a born optimist and I'll stay this way until the day I die. If you're feeling strong you can succeed. I've had hard times, but I never look back. That's because I am an optimist. If I set out to accomplish something I will. I'm an Aquarius, which explains my strength and my intelligence. Aquarius controls the world. That's why, despite all the things that have happened to me, despite all the troubles this country has suffered through, international difficulties and all that, I feel fairly strong. I am not a defeatist.' Over the years I learned that the importance of staying positive is one of Juan's core beliefs.

Many of the people we interviewed, of all ages and walks of life, attributed their fortune and misfortune to their signs. At first

Cubans' belief in astrology surprised me. I had expected people raised under communism to be scientifically minded. Some were, most were not. As support for the state declined many people had embraced spirituality and superstition.

While Juan was expounding on his philosophy of life, Marisol and Victoria surreptitiously peered around to locate the source of the odour permeating the porch. Juan apologised, and explained that the smell came from the pigsty on which they had arranged their papers. They mistook it for a table. This was the first of many cultural clashes. To ensure that nothing more went wrong, Marisol asked him to turn down the music. 'Of course, of course I will. I'll turn it off completely.' Juan wanted the interview to go well. But despite his enthusiasm, and my colleagues' efforts, the trio got off to a rocky start.

What is your telephone number?
'Well my work number was 89-8990, but I don't work there anymore.'

What's your neighbour's number?
'Umm, I don't know.'

Questions about phone numbers reflected my colleagues' social status and Havana-centred mindset. Beyond a small circle of functionaries, very few people in Santa Ana had telephones.

Where do you work?
'I used to work at the large [state] store but recently I changed jobs.' Juan sounded uneasy.

Were you an empleado, *white collar worker?*
'No, *jefe*, chief, of the warehouse.' Juan sounded apologetic for having a manual job, and said he had been the jefe, though he hadn't been.

Are you married?

'No, separated,' which was not true either.

Do you have children?

'No, but this year I want to make plans. I am no longer young, and now that I have a little more experience I feel ready.'

Do you live alone?

'Sometimes the women come here, sometimes I go there.' The misunderstanding was comical – and probably intentional on Juan's part.

No, I mean, do you live with your mother and father?

'No, my mother died.'

Marisol and Victoria hit one blank wall after another. You can hear their frustration. Juan was one of the first interviewees on the study and we as a team were trying to figure out what to say and not to say, and how to put the narrators at ease. At that moment, perhaps thinking it would dissolve the tension, Victoria introduced Marisol in a joking way. 'Marisol lives in Miramar, the neighbourhood of the upper crust.' Juan shot back in a voice thick with sarcasm, 'Yes, for people of rank.' You could almost hear the distance between them growing.

'We are researchers at a centre, part of the Academy of Sciences. This document describes our project, explains anonymity and...' Juan interrupted to ask for their phone numbers, 'In case of emergency.' The subtext was, you asked for my number, I'll ask for yours; you may be important, but so am I. Marisol followed with, 'Have you read *El Cimarrón* [Miguel Barnet's *Biography of a Runaway Slave*]? Our project is a little like that.' It would have been extraordinary if Juan, a rural jack-of-all-trades, had read *El Cimarrón*. To preserve his dignity, he murmured, 'No, but I think I may have heard of it.'

Despite the prickly start Juan was eager to forge ahead: 'I want to share the best and the worst moments of my life.' It is a tribute to Juan's exuberance, his desire to tell his life story to 'the whole wide world' as he puts it grandly, and to my colleagues' commitment to oral history, that the trio gradually forged a relationship of trust that extended to me.

Religion: coming out of the closet

Juan was born in Central Havana in 1968, 'The Year of the Heroic Guerrilla,' named to honour Che Guevara who had recently been killed in Bolivia. Juan said that his great-grandparents probably came from Martinique and Jamaica, though he bemoaned not having paid more attention to the stories his grandmothers told.

'My mother's people were from the middle aristocracy. My grandfather was one of the founders of the Capitol. He made my mother study piano and violin at the conservatory. It was like something out of a *telenovela*, a soap opera. But then she joined the Literacy Crusade and became immersed in all those kinds of things. To this day my relatives are fairly well-off. All of them came to my mother's funeral, but I did not see them again for twenty years. Mercedes Matus is one of my cousins. I'm sure you've heard of her; she's in the upper ranks of the Party in Havana.'

Prior to the Revolution Juan's maternal grandparents were skilled artisans and teachers, part of Havana's Afro-Cuban elite that Juan calls the middle aristocracy. From what I pieced together, his grandfather had worked as a site engineer in the construction of the Capitol building in the 1920s and 30s.

'My grandmother had me baptised and took me to church; my mother didn't get involved. At that time people didn't; they weren't supposed to. It was my grandmother who began going to church again... My godparents are the kind of people who own a car and all that stuff. They've always had a certain status.' Juan frequently complained that after his mother died her relatives ignored him. Maybe they considered him a country bumpkin, maybe they found his politics and religion embarrassing; whatever the reason Juan felt doubly abandoned.

Juan's father came from a line of rural labourers in Matanzas Province. 'They all had *santos* and practiced Santería. It comes from our ancestors. My father practices, he has all the ceremonial stuff. I practice too, every now and then, but I am not like those fanatics who buy my chickens [for use in ritual Santería sacrifices] … Occasionally I also go to church, but I don't do confession or communion, just the normal stuff. I especially like the processions. The other day they were parading the statue of Jesus Christ. I don't know if it was for the day he was born or the day he died, but I got all dressed up and led the procession.' Juan's lack of familiarity with the major Christian holidays makes me think his religiosity leaned toward Santería.

Soon after coming to power the Communist Party declared that Cuba was an atheist country. The 1976 constitution recognised atheism as the official non-religion, and the state actively discouraged religion. Twenty-five years later, following the fall of the Soviet bloc, the leadership allowed for more religious expression, and in 1992 the constitution was amended to guarantee freedom of religion. But the stigma remained. In 2002, the Academy of Sciences, which was affiliated to the Party, published a report which concluded, 'Devotees of Santería are primitive and prone to anti-social behaviour.' Understandably, Juan was somewhat cagey about religion. 'I am not like those fanatics,' had become the standard trope that Cubans used to hide their religious affiliation.

Fidel Castillo, a middle-aged Afro-Cuban Communist Party militant, explained in an interview in 2008 how attitudes toward religion were changing.[2] 'There was a time when being religious was not such a good idea. If you were thought to be religious, you were suspect. There were certain jobs you couldn't hold, careers you couldn't pursue. You were not allowed to be in the Party or in high government posts. If a neighbour reported having seen you carrying a palm leaf into your house it was assumed you were using it in Santería rituals and you were expelled from the Party. Religion no longer is outlawed. So long as you are not in the Party or in the Union of Communist Youth there's less of a taboo. Now there is a margin of flexibility, if not tolerance.'

As we gained Juan's confidence, he talked more about religion. 'My godmother said I was born under the protection of the Virgin of Regla, which makes me the son of Yemayá [the Santería sea goddess]... But I am not fanatical. I do things when body and soul call. My friends say, "I don't think you really believe." "Maybe so," I reply. I just do the normal stuff.' At that moment Juan jumped up and dashed into the house; he emerged with a handful of blurry photographs. 'That's Santa Ana, our town's patron saint. We paraded her statue on her saint's day, the 26th of July. Can you pick me out? I am the negrito, Black guy, in front, carrying the statue. Everyone comes to watch.'

Juan recalls that as a child he was hurt when classmates shouted negrito to taunt him, but he describes himself as 'the negrito in front'. It's contradictory, yes, but it also shows that Juan implicitly understands that the meaning of words depends on who is speaking and their intent.

It seems extraordinary that on the 26 July, the Revolution's holiest of holy days, when hundreds of thousands marched in the Plaza de la Revolución to commemorate the attack on the Moncada Barracks led by Fidel Castro, Juan and a contingent of townspeople paraded their patron saint around the town's dusty streets.[3] Juan's narrative reveals a hidden side of Cuban life.

Ten years later, in an atmosphere of greater religious tolerance, Juan told us that religion gave his life meaning. The walls of his house were papered, inside and out, with pictures of Pope Francis's recent visit to Cuba, and with biblical quotes he had carefully copied on lined paper. Gourds, glasses of water and an array of ritual objects used in Santería ceremonies were displayed around the room. Juan was publicly and proudly religious.

The move from Central Havana to Santa Ana

Over her father's objections, in 1961 Juan's mother joined the Literacy Crusade and went to the countryside to teach people to read and write. After the campaign ended, she worked at the headquarters of the Ministry of Education in Havana. In 1968, soon after Juan's birth, she was transferred to *el Valle de la Leche* (the Valley of Milk), a rural hamlet on the outskirts of Santa Ana, to teach school.

Nineteen sixty-eight was a turning point. Under the slogan 'The Revolutionary Offensive', the state expropriated the small private enterprises that had remained in private hands – corner shops, bars, barbers, dressmakers – and introduced measures designed to encourage Cubans to live like Che. All adults were issued a Libreta de Trabajo, an employment report card, which recorded their jobs, dismissals, voluntary labour, political attitude and behaviour. I asked Juan if national events or Party politics had played a role in his mother's transfer from Havana to the backwaters of Santa Ana. He did not know.

Juan's father accompanied his wife and newborn to Valle de la Leche, but did not stay long. The outback was not to his liking and he returned to Havana where, according to Juan, he landed a choice job in the Ministry of Tourism. 'My father was a famous chef. He was always on the move, preparing meals for famous international dignitaries at the Hotel Sevilla in Havana, in Holguín, Pinar del Río, the central provinces... I have eight or nine siblings on my father's side. To be honest,

45

I've lost count.' Juan enjoyed bragging about his father's virility and womanising.

Barely three years old when his parents separated, Juan lived throughout his childhood with his mother in a *bohío*, a rustic hut. He enjoyed roaming the countryside and recalled fishing in a dam stocked with 'Fidel's fish'. 'Now only a few of Fidel's fish are left. I caught most of them.' He meant this as a joke, but only partly. To Juan's way of thinking almost everything in Cuba belonged to Fidel, even the fish. Juan's joke was a skewed version of the quasi-official paternalist ideology.

Racism

Have you ever felt discrimination?

'Yes, yes, of course I have.' Juan sounded surprised; he wasn't expecting this question from a white researcher at the Academy of Sciences. After Fidel Castro announced in 1962 that racism had withered away, talk about race and racism was taboo. 'I felt it in school; you saw it a lot. The kids would call out, "*Oye*, listen, *negrito*." ... At Tarará, [youth camp] I felt it too. My classmates enjoyed making fun of me, pestering me, keeping me up all night touching my hair... It continues nowadays. Romana, one of my girlfriends, used to come here a lot, and her father constantly complained, "When Romana goes into town she goes to that negrito's house, that negrito's." Romana's mother would reply, "Look, just forget the colour of his skin. Stop that discrimination."'

Contrary to Juan, some Afro-Cuban narrators denied having ever experienced racism, or if they admitted to it, they explained it away. 'The guys didn't mean it.' 'My friends simply didn't understand what they were saying.' 'When people shout at me in the street I pretend not to hear.' 'They don't know any better.' 'They mean it affectionately, negrito is a term of endearment.' Juan did not excuse racism; he did not try to prettify his experiences. He talked about 'that idiosyncrasy' more than almost anyone else we interviewed. Thomas Holt, a US historian of race, wrote, 'It is the everydayness... the daily acts of name calling and petty exclusions through which racism is reproduced and continually remade.'[4]

So, you're saying there was discrimination in Santa Ana?
'Yes, yes, it always existed in this town.'

Is that so?
'Yes, always. There's less now, but in this town development came late. In Havana you'd rarely hear, "Listen, the guy is Black." Rarely. In Havana there's a lot of mixing. I've seen it myself, even in the Anti-Imperialist Tribunal, negritos with dreadlocks, can you believe – they give me the... err... those *chorongo* braids look like they haven't been brushed for a year – with a little white girl with a great body, hugging and kissing. I said to my friends, "Hey guys, look at that Black man!" I told my mates here in town, "There in the barrio everything is adjusting." But before, yes, it existed. A Black boy with a white girl, shhh [long whistle], that was a scandal. Later on, well everyone started to hook up. But to this day that idiosyncrasy persists here and there, in corners. That idiosyncrasy is still around. But everything is changing, people adapt. That's the way the world is. Everyone is adapting, everyone is adjusting, it's becoming normal. But yes, I felt discrimination... Yes, I felt it.'

Juan talked about the racism he experienced; he wanted us to understand his pain. But corn braids and dreadlocks, they disgusted him. The government had stifled manifestations of Afro-Cuban identity for so long that even race-conscious Juan was shocked by Afro hairstyles. Possibly his only connection with a culture of Black Pride came from seeing Angela Davis on TV way back when, and African-American tourists. Juan's dislike of corn braids also may have reflected a fixation with personal cleanliness. For a very long time, Afro-Caribbeans have adopted a strategy of hyper-cleanliness and cultural assimilation in an attempt to blunt white people's racism.

Recognising the symbolic power of hair, a group of leading Afro-Cuban artists, writers and activists founded El Club del Espendrú (the 'Fro Club – *espendrú* means Afro, as in hairdo) in Havana in 2017 to promote Afro-Cuban culture and Black pride.

What marks did discrimination leave? I mean how did it affect you?

Juan replied with a soliloquy.

'Do you really want me to tell you how it made me feel? I always felt more, I felt I am stronger than the atom. Besides, I have my sign. I am a legitimate Aquarius. I am the son of water, of Yemayá. I can put out fire and quench thirst. If they shove me aside and light a fire under me, psssst, I extinguish it. Sometimes I tell people, "No one can live without me." But I have a defect that is kinda bad. I am not resentful, but I am vindictive. If I give you flowers, why throw stones? Sooner or later you'll have to pay for this nastiness. I'm not saying you will die. No, no, I'm not saying that. No, no, that's not what I want. What I am saying is that you will have to pay for what you did. If I don't deserve it, why are you doing it? Tell me frankly because I don't like any of this. Besides, I have my luck. I have *ashé*, spiritual powers. I can see into the future, though I admit that sometimes I can't. I have the power of my *santos*, and I can see above and beyond. I can predict what will happen and what won't. Stuff happens and I say to myself, give it time. But how much time? It's already been going on two years. Give it time. Then, when the time is right, there it is. It happens.'

To communicate his pain and anger, and his powerlessness,

Juan elaborated an anti-racist fantasy. Racism leaves scars, he says, and he imagines what he would say, if he dared, to someone whose words hurt like arrows. Juan's fantasy reveals his frustration with the official policy of denial.

Juan's mother died in 1981 from pregnancy complications. 'My best times were my first fourteen years when I had my mom. I can't complain because I had everything. I had a beautiful childhood... My mother was the motor that propelled me through life. A mother is everything. You can get close to your father, your siblings, a guardian, but it's the mother who always wants the very best for her son. Mothers know how to bring out good and discourage evil. My mother would have made me take schoolwork seriously. If my mother had lived I could have become a somebody. I would have grown up to be an important person.' Juan said this frequently. It was one of the stories he lived by.

Juan's memories of childhood centre on his mother and food. 'Growing up we had everything... For my mother's outstanding work the Revolution gave her a fan and a food blender.' ('The Revolution gave' was a popular expression that embodied the state's paternalist ideology.) 'I still have them, and I have an American refrigerator, a Westinghouse. It's a family heirloom, and I am very attached to it. It belonged to my grandfather, my mother, and now to me. But the Comandante says he's going to take it away. That will hurt because the refrigerator occupies a soft spot in my heart. I could have bought an up-to-date tape recorder, but I didn't; I used the money to repair my refrigerator.' Juan did not blame bureaucrats for confiscating his beloved Westinghouse, or state institutions, he blamed Fidel. To his way of thinking the Comandante was in charge of everything, from the country's role in world politics to the fate of his refrigerator. Many Cubans viewed Fidel just the same way.

The beginning of the oral history study coincided with the start of Cuba's refrigerator conversion programme and refrigerators were on everyone's lips. Although the programme aimed to save electricity, many Cubans saw it differently. They complained that they had to part with a reliable old fridge, and buy a flimsy, Chinese model they didn't want, and they would end up paying for it through salary deductions over many years.

Remembering the 1980s

'I tell my friends, the younger ones, you don't have any idea what life used to be like. The shops had stacks of glass jars filled with chocolates, candy, egg creams, delicacies that you can't even imagine. These days we don't have anything like that. The kiosks were furnished with beautiful antiques that had belonged to the propertied classes. I remember a kiosk run by Benigno. He was an old man; he's long dead. We used to buy all kinds of delicacies from Benigno, strawberry soda, syrups, candies. When you went into the little Coppelia in town they would ask, "Do you want a sundae, or this or that, and with syrup on top?" They would hand you a little aluminium cup with piles of wonderful stuff.' Juan's memories of childhood centred on fairy-tale sweets that may have existed only in his fantasies. For Juan's generation, sugary sweets symbolised a paradise lost.

'I say to my young friends, "You can't even imagine; it was all before you were born." I am speaking about my childhood, up until when I was fourteen or fifteen. Life was improving until I was about twenty.' Juan was twenty in 1988. 'With a normal salary you could buy everything you needed, everything was within reach. We lived well, how to describe it, people could go to restaurants, to any restaurant. There was only one currency and salaries were enough to go to any restaurant.' Juan was nostalgic for a time when Cubans lived decently on a state salary.

Remembering as a form of resistance

When Juan was ten or eleven his mother was promoted and began teaching at the Facultad Obrera y Campesina, the Workers' and Peasants' University, in Guanabo, a forty-five-minute bus ride from Santa Ana. Juan said she was rarely at home. If she wasn't at the Facultad, she was at a meeting. *Cubanas integradas*, Cubans involved in the revolutionary process, went to lots of meetings: meetings of the CDR, meetings of the Federación de Mujeres Cubanas, the official women's organisation, Party meetings.

Donata, a relative who lived nearby, cared for Juan after school. 'I felt lonely and abandoned but I did not know how to express my simmering rage. One day I tried to set fire to our house. I was very restless, very unsettled, as a child. Even now as an old man [Juan was thirty-seven] I feel very restless and unsettled.'

Juan was plagued by memories of an *acta de repudio*, a state-organised protest to shame Donata who was leaving in the Mariel boatlift. 'The memory still haunts me. She lived here in this very house. It was 1980, and I was about ten years old. She planned to leave in the boatlift. Along with my neighbours, I shouted *gusano*, worm. We hurled eggs and all of that. Every time I remember, ay *caballeros*, gentlemen.' (Juan often addressed Marisol and Victoria as caballeros, maybe it was a sign of respect, maybe it was a joke.) After a long pause he continued, 'When they [Cubans who left in the boatlift] came back they were treated like kings. That's why I don't like politics.' My Cuban teammates told me 'I don't like politics' was a code for I don't like the government.

bell hooks, anti-racist writer and activist, said, 'People resist by telling their stories.' Decades after the Mariel boatlift the government discouraged talk about the *actas de repudio*. Yet many narrators described their participation; I feel it was an act of catharsis. Jorge, a middle-aged editor at a state publishing house, said, 'The *actas de repudio* were a turning point... They opened my eyes... Never again could I feel the same as before [about the Revolution]... I look back with horror on the time the government incited neighbours against neighbours.'[5] Carlos, a fifty-year-old from Santa Ana, said, 'Remembering makes me ashamed.'[6] Fernando, a young librarian in Holguin, described watching people throwing stones at a family who lived across the street when he was four. 'It was a day I will never forget.'[7] Juan's moan, '*Ay caballeros*,' and his uncharacteristic pause conveyed his pain.

'I had to throw myself into life's hustle and tussle.'

'It wasn't easy after I lost my mother. I had to face life alone. I had to get through adolescence all on my own.' Juan lived with his best friend's family for a year. 'I can't complain. Leo's family treated me like a son. But they were poor. Their house was too small for their five children plus me. I felt uncomfortable.' Juan moved into Donata's empty house and lived alone. 'I lost my balance. I felt crushed. I couldn't concentrate and I got left behind in school. A neighbour helped me. She told me I had to face life by myself. My stepfather wanted to help but he couldn't do much, he wasn't around. [He worked in Cuba's merchant marine.] Eventually I got myself under control. I buried my memories in my subconscious and I carried on.'

Juan wanted to talk about his feelings, his suffering, his trauma, his ongoing psychological problems, and his efforts to erase memories. He seemed relieved to be able to unburden himself to sympathetic strangers. Oral history often has a liberating effect.

Juan dropped out of school at age fourteen. 'I couldn't stay to finish school because I had economic problems and my stepfather did too. We weren't the kind who had a bit of a margin. Joaquín, my teacher, who lived in Quebrada Roja, Red Ravine, said I shouldn't quit. I explained my problem, I said I had to. There

I was, not yet fifteen years old, and having to support myself. I had to find pennies here and there to make my own way. I had to throw myself into life's hustle and tussle.' At the time, the early 1980s, very few Cubans supported themselves through illicit work. A decade later almost every adult living on the island was plugged into the underground economy one way or another.

'Many people told me, "Don't quit school, school gives you a future." They said this, and they said that. People who don't have problems find it easy to say things. But if you have problems it isn't easy; it's difficult. How was I going to live? My stepfather couldn't help. He was at sea most of the time. I had to find work to support myself.'

Marisol asked why relatives didn't take him in, why the government didn't provide support, why he fell through the cracks. Juan said he didn't know the answer. Perhaps he was embarrassed to say; perhaps he had something to hide. None of my colleagues had ever heard of a teenager having to drop out of school in the 1980s. But it's unlikely that Juan was unique, there must have been others, people whose stories haven't been told, Cubans who didn't or couldn't benefit from the Revolution's famous schooling.

How did you survive?

'I worked for myself... and my neighbours taught me to cook. At first, I frequently burned food, and I had to throw lots away. I hurled pots against the wall out of hunger and frustration, hollering *coño*, cunt. [One of Cuban men's favourite swear words.] Little by little I figured out how to survive. People dropped by, "Hey, if you'll build me a wall, I'll pay you forty pesos. I'll give you fifty pesos to paint my house. Could you move a pile of cement blocks from A to B?" I eked out a life.

'Many people have said, "*Coño*. Juan, you raised yourself." It's true. What's more, I never did the stuff many people do. I've

had all kinds of friends, of all colours, with every kind of flaw –
thieves, druggies, you name it, but I've never ever been in trouble
with the law or anything like that.' Juan likes to think of himself
as a lone cowboy. 'It's like I'm out of a Hollywood Western.'

At age sixteen Juan tried to enlist. He hoped the army would
give him the education, the structure and the support he needed.
'They weren't interested in me.' When he turned eighteen he
was drafted in the normal course of things. But by the time
he completed his two years of service the world he knew had
evaporated.

7

RACISM

The Revolution's fight against racism had a promising beginning. Soon after coming to power, Fidel launched a campaign against racial discrimination that eliminated segregation in schools, workplaces and clubs.[1] But the campaign ended abruptly three years later when Fidel announced to the world that when the Cuban government abolished capitalism, discrimination had come to an end. To understand his claim, we need to place it in its geopolitical context. In 1962, president John F. Kennedy and his Latin American advisors wanted Cuba expelled from the Organisation of American States (OAS), and they lined up the presidents of every member state to go along with Washington. Following Cuba's expulsion, Fidel gave a fiery speech in which he boasted that unlike in the country to the north, discrimination was not tolerated in Cuba. Fidel's riposte was part of a propaganda war designed to make Cubans proud of their beleaguered nation, and to shame leaders throughout the Americas who kowtowed to US pressure.

But Fidel came to believe the propaganda, and in the aftermath of his speech racism was hushed up and hidden away like a dirty family secret. The official narrative was that the problem of racism had been solved, and measures to combat it were not only unnecessary, but dangerous, as they would undermine national unity, and provide ammunition to the enemy.

For forty years the subject of race was taboo. Calling out racism could endanger not only your membership in the Communist Party, but your job. Alexis Esquivel, a Cuban artist, was quoted in *The Washington Post*, saying, 'You can joke about race all you want, but you can't talk about it seriously.'[2] Paradoxically, at the same time as it suppressed discussions of race, the Cuban government celebrated Angela Davis, the Black Panthers, and the US Black consciousness movement.

Disparities between white and Black Cubans declined dramatically, a result of the Revolution's race-blind, egalitarian agenda, and Afro-Cuban men and women built prestigious careers in fields that had previously been the domain of elite white men.[3] But refusal to talk about race – the traits Cuban society attributes to skin colour – and to address racism, operated insidiously to keep Black Cubans out of important sectors. Afro-Cubans, especially Afro-Cuban women, were greatly underrepresented in the political arena, and on TV – spheres of high visibility.[4] And Afro-Cubans were greatly overrepresented in sports, singing and dancing, which reinforced racist stereotypes.

As Raúl Castro's government relaxed restrictions on private enterprise, Afro-Cubans lost out relatively to white Cubans. The *clase emergente*, the emerging economic elite, is predominately white, largely because remittances sent by affluent white Cuban-Americans are behind many of the new businesses. Few Afro-Cubans have a well-to-do family network abroad to call on. The regeneration of historic privilege combined with everyday racism is recreating the pre-revolutionary racial divide.

Back in 2005, Esteban saw the upsurge in racism coming. 'Now you see people who have a little more money looking down their noses [at Blacks]. I'm talking about people who have cars, who live a little bit better than the rest of us. You can see and feel it happening. This is what Cuba is turning into, can you believe… It's outrageous. I know there are problems like this all over the world… But, please, it's not like we're living in Europe. We're in the Caribbean where everyone is a great mixture. We Cubans are all a great mixture.'

Breaking the silence

In 2016, Raúl Castro acknowledged the underrepresentation of Afro-Cubans, women and youth in the political sphere, and said the government would correct it. Frustrated by the slow, sometimes imperceptible, pace of change, Afro-Cuban intellectuals and activists took matters into their own hands. Groups such as El Club del Espendrú in Havana began holding discussions about Black pride.[5] Ten years earlier the government might have disbanded the club. In the economic crisis, state officials were inclined to tolerate some independent organisations, particularly if they generated hard currency, and did not threaten the Communist Party's hold on power.

8

ESTEBAN CABRERA MONTES

Fontanar, Havana, 2005–06

Esteban was a black marketeer. When I met him at dinner at my house in Havana he followed me into the kitchen. 'I want you to interview me. I have a story to tell,' he said. Esteban was thirty-one, graceful and lean, with watchful eyes and very short hair, practically shaven. Dressed in a plain white T-shirt and jeans he looked unadorned, spare, as if trying to be inconspicuous. Though he could easily have passed for white-skinned if he had wanted to, he explained in the interviews that he was a *moreno*, a light-skinned man of African descent. Esteban listened attentively to the dinner table conversation but said little. After he left Julia, my British colleague, said she would do the interviews. She and Esteban were the same age and already had established a rapport.[1]

The next morning she went to his house in a far-flung suburb near the Havana airport that he shared with his brother. Soon his motives became clearer. He was desperate to leave, had tried twice, and hoped we might be able to help him. Esteban's interviews were charm offensives designed to persuade Julia to give him an invitation to Britain. One minute he was the innocent victim of the police, the neighbourhood watch, the bosses of the factories where he intermittently worked, the next he was an opposition activist forced to put himself forward by the apathy of his fellow Cubans. He was analytical, funny, contradictory and relatively fearless. Like an outlaw in a Coen brothers movie, he had a magnetism, a way of revealing vulnerabilities and saying truths that got under your skin. He was deeply unpredictable. In a sense the only constant was his obsession with leaving the country.

Esteban lived well compared to the vast majority of Cubans. He had a mobile phone when they were illegal. He ate steak, imported cheese and other illicit delicacies. Intelligent, witty, and shrewd, Esteban was the embodiment of an anti-hero, and his rejection of officialdom revealed a great deal about Cuban society that was left out of the master narrative. His interviews almost cost us the whole project.

'He is an anti-social. You'd better destroy the recordings,' said Marisol, my colleague, when our team was listening to his first interview. I knew that Mariela Castro would soon hear about the scandalous interview, so I decided it would be best to give her the recording myself. Several days later she called a meeting to inform the team that the government was suspending the project. Fortunately, six months later we were allowed to continue.

A year or so after Julia's second interview with Esteban I phoned his house. A recording said the line had been disconnected. I suspected he had left, which he was always trying to do. His ex-girlfriend confirmed my suspicion.

'Politics tore my family apart.'

Esteban was born in 1974 in Havana to a politically divided family. His first memory was of lying in bed at night listening to his parents quarrel. 'Politics tore my family apart,' he said, and he recalled always feeling caught in the middle. His mother, Teresa Montes, was an ardent supporter of the Revolution. 'When she was a child she didn't have a hard time. Under the previous government her family had money. She grew up in a sprawling house in El Cerro, near the Plaza Cívica, now the Plaza de la Revolución. It was a very wealthy neighbourhood, like Vedado, and her father was a businessman.' Despite her privilege, and her father's implacable opposition to Fidel, she embraced the revolutionary cause. Teresa joined the Literacy Crusade and went to teach in the mountains.

'She was young and she was carried away by the fervour of youth, by Fidel's speeches, by the changes. At that time a lot of people believed in Fidel, as everyone knows, and a lot were tricked. Fidel gave an infinite number of speeches and the people believed him, especially the young. They were in the vanguard. I think the Literacy Crusade was very positive. Teaching people to read and write was a very good thing… Giving land to the peasants, that was very good too, and all those other things.' Esteban sounded apologetic, as if he were betraying his cause. 'My mother saw all those things and she thought they were good. The feelings, the fervour, she thought it was all good. What more can I say?'

Esteban suspected that his maternal grandfather worked with American gangsters before the Revolution. A case of history repeating itself, you might be thinking. His grandfather's activities were a family secret. 'No one ever talked about his business.' After Fidel came to power the state confiscated his property, including the sprawling house, and late one night he fled to Miami, leaving his wife and children behind. Esteban said the family never heard from him again but learned through the grapevine that he remarried and had more children. Esteban's mother used to say, 'Good riddance to that old traitor, that *gusano*, counterrevolutionary worm.' Esteban was more forgiving. He remembered that as a child he used to dream that his grandfather came back for him and together they flew to Miami where they lived happily ever after.

When the Literacy Crusade ended Teresa worked as a secretary at the Ministry of Education in Havana. She died of asthma when Esteban was twelve. (The parallels with Juan's life are uncanny.) Esteban recalled adoring his mother but objecting to her revolutionary zeal. 'She was too ardent, too gullible.' Every May Day, every 26th of July, she marched in the Plaza de la Revolución with little Esteban on her shoulders. 'Clap, wave your little flag, cheer for the Comandante,' she told him. 'She was headstrong. She stubbornly stuck to her ideas. No one could change her mind. She was ultra-revolutionary. She is dead, and I don't want to offend the memory of the dead, but she was more than a revolutionary; she was a communist. She was with the Revolution one hundred per cent, always always on the government side.'

Teresa met Esteban's father, Alejandro Cabrera, in the Literacy Crusade. Later, when both were working at the Ministry of Education, they began living together in a consensual union. Teresa had two sons from a previous relationship. Esteban said he never understood why his father joined the Literacy Crusade. 'Maybe he was swept along by the fervour in the air. More likely he joined out of opportunism. My father is ultra-radical.[2] He holds extremely, extremely radical ideas. He is not with the system, not in the least. I think this affected his mind. He has never, ever been with the government. He even listens to Radio Martí [a radio station financed by the United States government]. He reads banned books about resistance; he always has. He is very, very political. In another country he would be a politician, maybe even a senator. If not a senator, something.' Esteban's comment took me by surprise. I had been thinking that in another country, the Soviet Union or the German Democratic Republic (the former East Germany), his father would have been sent to the gulag.

'When I was growing up he didn't pay me any attention. When I was an adolescent he didn't bother about my education. My parents did not get along ideologically. They were always arguing.

My father couldn't stop. Everywhere he went he argued with everybody. It was his crusade. He ignored his personal life. He ignored me, his only child. Now my father is in his fifties and he has never managed to live a normal life, not with me, not with partners, not with himself.'

Alejandro left Teresa when Esteban was three. Before Teresa's death, father and son rarely saw one another. After she died Esteban lived with him for a short while. 'That was when my father brought his influence to bear.' Esteban said his father tells everyone he quit his job at the Ministry of Education, but he suspects that his father was sacked. 'For the past three decades he has been a Havana bus driver. You know, he drives the buses that never come.'

Esteban's paternal grandfather had been a foreman on a minor sugar estate who developed a side-line making sweets from the discarded cane. His business thrived in the 1950s, and he purchased a house in Vedado. When the state abolished all private enterprises in 1968, it shut down his confectionery business. Esteban said his grandfather never forgave Fidel. Esteban saw him as the perfect grandfather. Every Sunday they went on outings, and sometimes Esteban's father came along. Esteban said that the two men totally agreed about politics. 'Their mentality was what you might call Americanised, maybe it was because almost all of their family lived in the United States… Most of my family is American. I have lots of relatives over there who I don't even know.'

Esteban felt betrayed by the family he never met, or never heard from after they left.

'Family separation… the national tragedy.'

'Cuba is a nation traumatised by family separation. It is the national tragedy… Here we have a saying, the Cuban who emigrates bites the apple of oblivion. After the first morsel they forget everyone, even their family. Once they're in Miami they forget everyone they left behind. Not everybody acts like this, but the great majority do. Take me and my family; the last of my cousins left more than five years ago and I haven't heard from her since. No letter. Nothing. It's not my tragedy. It is the national tragedy. Cuba is a country in mourning, a nation traumatised by separation.

'Let me tell you why it is so difficult to keep families together. The leavers think those who remain have so many needs that we will forever be asking for something. Asking, asking, asking. I don't even like to think about it. I have my pride. I manage with what I have… I survive by my wits. If my family *al otro lado* [on the other side] wanted to give me something, sure, I'd accept it. But I won't go asking. No, nothing like that. If every Cuban thought the way I do, it would be perfect. But not everyone does. There are always tensions between the leavers and the remainers, always. It causes distancing, estrangement, rifts. What has happened?… Emigration has wreaked havoc within the Cuban family. All our families are in chaos. We used to have large families, now we have small ones. A nation of large families turned into a nation of small ones. Family breakdown is the Cuban tragedy.' Almost every Cuban we interviewed lamented the breakdown of families.[3]

When I heard Esteban say (on the recorder), 'Cuba is a country in mourning, a nation traumatised by separation,' I looked around the room. My teammates looked uncomfortable. At that moment, in that room, those words seemed more subversive than anything Esteban had said about the government, his criminal activities, his attempts to escape. Right before the meeting one of my colleagues confided that her nephew had just been arrested for attempting to flee, and she had visited him in jail the night before. Victoria's son had gone to a conference in the US and defected. She said she never would have guessed. Many members of Marisol's family left. Her grandmother and two beloved aunts left in 1960; she never saw them again. Her ex-husband took a temporary post abroad and didn't come back. Her daughter left, leaving behind her two small children for several years. Cubans across the ideological spectrum shared the pain of family separation.

'Our American connection.'

When did you first think about leaving?

'I fell in love with American music when I was an adolescent. That's what young people do, they latch on to something. My friends in secondary school were not with the system either. It was inevitable; they also followed American music and fashion. They were very influential. We watched American movies on TV. Yes, Cuban TV showed American movies; it's always been like that. This created a sense of, there's always been a strong sense of our American connection, always. Even people in the government feel it.' Louis A. Pérez Jr., a leading historian of Cuba, puts it this way, 'The Cuban encounter with the United States... influenced the context in which Cuban identity and nationality acquired recognisable forms.'[4]

'We listened to American music on the radio. I had a short wave that got all the FM stations. I mostly listened to the stations broadcast out of Key West, Florida. As soon as I got home from school I'd switch on the radio and rush through my homework, or, left it to do the next day in school, so I could listen to music. They played the best music very late at night, all the stations did... They played music from all over the world. All my contemporaries, everyone who was young, loved it. They were with me on this. Then music videos became all the rage. All this made people, made me, you get what I'm saying? I began to think [about leaving]. My friends did too. Many of them left when they were twenty-five or thirty because they saw this wasn't going anywhere.'

Was this way of thinking common?

'Of course it was. There came a time when I began to criticise, young people criticised the socialist countries. "Like it is all so, so ridiculous. Like it is all absolutely dreadfully designed. Like it's all shit."' Esteban laughed so hard he could barely speak. 'Get it? We criticised everything. We criticised other young people too.'

In the 1980s did your generation share a vision?

'No. Among young people there were always some who thought one way and some who thought another. Sometimes we got into arguments. Sometimes we provoked them. The arguments got pretty heated, but they didn't go anywhere because we had two different ways of thinking.'

What did they teach in school?

'I don't think school has changed much, well maybe a little bit. How should I put this? Sometimes I had problems. Once, in secondary school, I had a big problem with the teacher of the Political Foundations class. They don't teach that subject anymore. Just remembering it makes me laugh.' After uncontrollable laughter Esteban said, 'It's been a while since I thought of Political Foundations. You can imagine what it was: Marx, Engels, Lenin.

'When I was twelve, maybe thirteen or fourteen, I got into a discussion with the teacher because I told her some true stuff; I told her my point of view, the way I do. I don't remember exactly what we were talking about, but it was a polemical topic. I stood up and gave my point of view. She sent me to the director and I got into trouble, but not that much. It wasn't that serious. It wasn't over the top. The director called in my brother, by then I was living with my half-brother; he was caring for me. After that I paid less attention in that class. I ignored what the teacher said because I didn't want to get into trouble.

'When I had to move out of my father's house, my half-brother took me in. I was twelve, he was hardly out of adolescence himself. Although he was very young, he took care of me. He made sure I got an education of sorts. Well, he had to. He did fairly well, even though at the time [late 1980s] the situation in this country was somewhat difficult. Well, now that I am thinking about it, it really wasn't so difficult. In this country the situation has always been difficult.'

Because of the blockade?

'Yes, the blockade and US hegemony. All this stuff between the US and the Cuban governments has been very negative. As you might imagine I don't go along with it. The truth is I don't support the US government with all its stupid laws and other things. But let me be clear about one thing. Our government should have taken more advantage of the help we received from the socialist camp. If they hadn't been so preoccupied with politics, politics all the time, we could have developed the economy. Always pushing politics puts you on a par with the US. You're playing the same game.'

Craving trainers

Esteban recalled his craving for trainers, his desire to dress like American teenagers, his first feelings of disillusion. He described the day in 1986 when his mother took him to Central Havana to buy him trainers for his twelfth birthday. They got off the bus on Calle Galiano and walked to Fin del Siglo. Before the Revolution, Fin del Siglo had been a swish department store. Esteban remembered the moment he entered the cavernous space and saw piles of blue jeans and trainers, and lots of TVs, record players and kitchen appliances in the adjoining hall. Esteban had never seen anything like it – except in Hollywood movies.

He said he felt like he had just gone to heaven. 'The stores had everything. In the 1980s they had everything. There was nothing they didn't have. Thanks to help from the socialist countries we had everything. You could find whatever you wanted.' It all came from the USSR.

Esteban was trying on a pair of trainers when his mother whispered, 'I can't afford them.' He remembered thinking to himself, '"Is the system we have here really so great? If it were truly good my mother would be able to buy me the trainers I really, really want. But she can't..." The prices were sky high, super, super high. Everything was very, very expensive. A pair of trainers cost what one person earned in a month. That's what I mean by expensive. Now people talk about the 1980s as a time of plenty. They say in the 80s we had this, in the 80s we had that. Rubbish. Everything cost a lot of money and my mother couldn't afford to buy the trainers. Well, after that happened a couple of times I thought to myself, this system sucks. What we have here is not good, not good at all. Those feelings grew and grew.'

The late 1980s was a confusing time. Household consumption rose, the state implemented some egalitarian policies, alongside programmes that increased inequality, like the Gold and Silver Stores which Pavel, the dissident, describes. Esteban's narrative captures the tensions of the era when imported luxuries, such as blue jeans, trainers and washing machines were available for the first time since the triumph of the Revolution, but not all Cubans could afford them. His disillusion set in the moment it dawned on him that access to the luxuries was not equally shared, that his mother, a single head of household with three children who worked as a secretary, was not in a position to enjoy the prosperity.

'Fashion brands... have destroyed young people psychologically.'

Ironically, despite his current affluence, and the memory of his anguish over trainers, Esteban lamented the new consumerism.

'In the 1980s you could live OK; we didn't have shortages. You could buy enough food and that sort of thing. Food was not a problem. Life was not a struggle. It was not hard to get by. Clothing, well that was a little more difficult. But in this country all this stuff about fashion brands simply did not exist. We did not have any of the brands. You did not see any of that kind of clothing, the kind you see for sale these days. I don't know if it was because we didn't have any of that stuff – you couldn't buy Adidas or brand this or brand that– I just don't know, but it was not a part of our lives.

'Then came Perestroika [economic liberalisation in the USSR in the 1980s], and the influence of the capitalist world. Then all those things became important and we discovered all that stuff. It has destroyed young people psychologically. I tell you, it has destroyed us. It particularly destroyed the generation younger than me, kids just entering that delicate stage, adolescence. They wanted to have everything, to experience absolutely everything. Now we are in the middle of two political systems, two different systems: the capitalist system and socialism of the kind we have in Cuba. We are caught in the middle. Young people are paying for this. Yes, they're the ones paying for this. It is unbelievable.'

Esteban with his mobile phone and his unconsummated love affair with the US was an unlikely critic of consumerism. Yet he was nostalgic for the ethos he remembered from his adolescence and appalled by designer fads. To his way of thinking, consumerism was doing young people's heads in.

'We had to begin again at zero.'

'When the 1990s came around, this country was in crisis. We hadn't developed, not the slightest, zilch. We had to begin again at zero. We had to open ourselves up to foreign companies, European companies. Thanks to you Europeans we received a lot of assistance and we began to develop, but just a tiny little bit.' Esteban's gratitude to Europeans seemed designed to ingratiate himself with Julia.

'But this tiny bit was more development than we had had in all the years prior to 1990, during all the years of the Revolution. Isn't that amazing? The country is still bankrupt. We still don't have any development. We have no industry, no industry of any sort. Unbelievable. Now a lot of people are coming to see this. All that assistance from the socialist bloc came to nothing. It was all about politics, and politics doesn't feed anyone.'

In fact, the Soviets propped up the Cuban economy and provided food to Cuba for thirty years. Yet despite – or because of – Soviet assistance and the US blockade the Cuban government never developed a viable economic strategy.

Esteban's narrative of life in the 1980s clashes with the official story. He recounted events and attitudes other narrators might have remembered but refrained from describing. Esteban was a contradictory rebel who recalled his growing disenchantment with socialism yet lamented the loss of the egalitarianism and anti-consumerism of the 1980s.

9

BARBARA VEGAS

Regla

Ada and I ran to catch the ferry to Regla, a town on the other side of the Havana harbour, to interview Barbara. Regla occupies a special place in Cuban history. It is known as the cradle of Santería for the inhabitants' attachment to the Yoruba beliefs, brought by slaves to Cuba, which subsequently became mixed with folk Catholicism. Close to the spot where the ferry lands, there is a small sanctuary devoted to the Virgin of Regla, the Black Madonna, who is worshipped as a Catholic saint and a Yoruba deity. Regla's claim to fame also rests on its support for Fidel when he was fighting in the Sierra Maestra, the big mountains. Hence the town's nickname, la Sierra Chiquita, the little mountain.

Barbara was on edge when members of our team arrived at her house on a busy side street in the centre of Regla, the house where she had grown up and lived her entire life.[1] The building was supported by poles that blocked the sidewalk. Born in 1972 – she had recently celebrated her thirty-third birthday – Barbara was prematurely grey, with worry lines etched into her face. She spoke slowly and with an exaggerated politeness, avoiding eye contact with me. She was wearing a high-necked grey dress that jarred with the flamboyant clothing used by her contemporaries.

The only decorations in the dark room were a tattered poster of the Sacred Heart of Jesus, a vase of plastic flowers, and a table mat crocheted by her mother.

'The three adults in this household are committed to some degree, *de cierta forma*, to the Revolution. What I mean is we try to fulfil our obligations. We pay our dues to the CDR, the Committee for the Defence of the Revolution, and the Trade Union. I am up to date with my payments to the Federation [of Cuban Women, the official women's organisation]. We attend neighbourhood assemblies and participate in everything we are supposed to do, yes, everything. In that way we keep up to date with the changes taking place that benefit all Cubans.' It was the slogan of the day. 'To be honest, people around here do not support the Revolution. They want to make money, buy good food, a new TV, and paint the house,' she explained later.

Barbara was against the economic changes, the private restaurants, the B&Bs, the tiny businesses people set up in their front room. She said that Cubans who did not support the Revolution, who had left as *balseros*, rafters, and returned, lived far better than she could on her state salary, and she felt the government did little to stop them breaking the law. Barbara shared Mario's view that the economic changes were generating inequality and creating a new class, *los nuevos ricos*, the new rich.

We met Barbara through Party channels. My teammates knew her boss, the director of the Casa de Cultura in Regla, and asked him to give us names of people to interview. He recommended Barbara. The strong probability that everything she said would get back to him made it more surprising that she said that she supported the Revolution, but only to a degree. It was a strong statement that showed her frustration.

'My people are very humble but very respectable.' Occasionally narrators invented stories about growing up poor to fit the

71

template of a workers' state. Barbara didn't need to. She was raised in a poor, Black, working-class household in Regla. Before the Revolution her extended family rented a house from an urban landlord. 'It's hard to imagine twenty-one of them crammed into such close quarters.' When the landlord fled to Miami the new revolutionary government acquired the property title, but officials at the Housing Ministry refused to give it to Barbara's family. Their explanation was that the building was not structurally sound. Barbara described how her family had been battling the Ministry for forty-five years to obtain the title.

'As you can see, this house is on the verge of falling down. It's my biggest problem. We have been trying to resolve this situation for a very long time – first my grandmother, then my mother, and now me, but we didn't want to do something that would damage the family's reputation. The rest of the family moved out a long time ago. My ancestors didn't have money or power, and to repair a house you have to have one or the other. That's why for half a century our house has been decaying. We've gone to the Housing Ministry numerous times to ask why the building isn't covered by the Housing Laws. An official told my mother that they would give us the title, and we would be entitled to housing benefits, but only if the house were inhabitable. Imagine, it has to be inhabitable before they will give you construction materials to make it inhabitable. Let's just say it's... I don't know what to call it.' 'It's a contradiction,' said Ada.

Many classic Cuban films – *Death of a Bureaucrat, Alice in Wonderland, Guantanamera* – are parodies of the cumbersome state bureaucracy. Barbara's description of her family's battle with the Housing Ministry sounded like a film script.

Barbara grew up in the condemned house with her grandmother, mother and brother. Her father lived in Central Havana with his family. It was not an unusual arrangement. He died when Barbara was three years old.

'My parents were simple workers.' Her father worked as a carpenter in Ultra, a state-owned department store. Her mother was a machine operator at a large rice mill in Regla. When the mill closed the state reassigned her to a mill in Matanzas but she refused to go because her mother was dying of cancer. 'Although my mother never held a regular job again she always earned a little money doing this and that.' They relied on state provision: subsidised food, clothing, free healthcare and education. Housing was always in short supply and the housing laws created inequalities.

'The adults in my family were devoted to their jobs. My brother and I worked hard in school. We did everything we could for the collective good and we wouldn't dream of doing something that might reflect badly on us.'

Barbara's worry about her family's reputation may have had a racial element, a way of separating good Blacks from vulgar Blacks, deserving versus the undeserving.

'Four members of my family live here now: my brother, my husband, my little son, and me. We are simple workers. My husband is a gardener at the Victory at the Bay of Pigs Medical School. My brother is self-employed and works in the farmers' market. My son goes to nursery in the neighbourhood. When I was hired at the Casa de Cultura I was on the night guard. A year and a half ago, I was promoted and now I am the head of administration. In my household everyone earns a low salary, but little by little, thanks to the opportunities the Revolution gave us, we have been able to buy a few things, such as this fan which makes us a bit more comfortable. As you can see for yourselves, I don't have expensive furniture, and my house needs major repairs. It was condemned, but we have nowhere else to go. Thanks to the Revolution my mother was given the cement blocks in the corner, and I got roofing paper at the local slaughterhouse before the last hurricane.' Ada told me later that Barbara probably bought the construction materials on the black market.

Barbara's repeated expressions of gratitude to the Revolution chimed with the official narrative, but clashed with her statement that she supported the Revolution but only to a degree.

Switching to safer ground, she described the pleasures and the solidarity she remembered from the past and she lamented the loss. 'I had a very happy childhood. I took advantage of everything the Revolution gave us, like Tarará, and the outings for young Pioneers.' Tarará was a beach camp outside Havana where schoolchildren vacationed for several weeks each year. 'We were still in the socialist bloc, and enjoyed all the things that Cuban children don't have today because of the many problems this country is facing. But for now *Vamos Bien*.'

Fidel had just announced that the Special Period of hardship was over, and the slogan '*Vamos Bien*' (We're Doing Well), appeared on billboards throughout the country.

Barbara quickly corrected herself. She knew that Cubans were not doing well. 'What I meant to say is that despite the economic situation, we're doing OK, *Vamos Bien*. Education remains good, even if it isn't like it was in my day. As a young girl, I participated in everything, but especially in local activities. I was active in all the campaigns to tidy up our neighbourhood. I did all kinds of volunteer work and I had lots of fun. Yes, I had a very good childhood.'

Barbara considered voluntary labour and solidarity fun, and lamented their demise. She said that because Cubans were busy solving individual and family problems they kept to themselves and had lost their sense of solidarity.

10

FIDEL CASTRO

Everyday life came to a standstill. The day after I arrived in Cuba to begin the oral history study, Hurricane Ivan battered the Caribbean. Forecasters predicted it would make landfall in Pinar del Rio, Cuba's western tip, and hit Havana. Our research team postponed the meeting we had planned and spent the day boarding up windows at our office near the Plaza de la Revolución. Late in the afternoon, when my teammates went home, I walked to Old Havana. Everything was boarded up and the only person on the street was an elderly woman who took me by the hand and told me to go back to my hotel.

I went home. Home was the apartment I had rented in Vedado. I turned on the TV and there was Fidel on the beachhead in Pinar del Rio directing the anti-disaster operations. He looked like God in Michelangelo's *The Creation of Adam*. His beard and long grey hair were blowing in the wind; he appeared frail, older than his seventy-eight years, but resolute. Shouting over the sound of howling wind, he explained in minute detail, with the precision he was famous for, how they were evacuating the area.

Fidel had a genius for seizing opportunities. When most Cubans were inside taking refuge, he rushed into the eye of the storm. With the country watching, he announced that the wind was abruptly changing course and the hurricane would not hit Havana. The next morning everyone on the street was talking about Fidel's courage and joking about his standoff with God. My neighbour said, 'When God saw Fidel on the beach he quickly altered the hurricane's path.' I could see for myself why Cubans regarded Fidel with a mixture of 'intimacy and awe'.[1]

Fidel was frequently on TV talking about economic goals, production shortfalls, reciting long lists of statistics – always to two decimal places – and saying whatever popped into his head. Cubans only half-listened while they impatiently waited for the telenovela, the soap opera, that came on next. One evening while I was listening, Fidel, apropos of nothing, said he liked a thimble full of milk in his morning coffee and held up a preternaturally elongated pinkie to show the measure of his drop of milk. I thought nothing of it.

The next day all my neighbours were out in the street. 'How dare he. I would be happy enough with a bit of real coffee; I no longer dream of milk.'[2] 'No, it isn't right that he [she stroked her chin] gets to have milk,' said another.[3] Habaneros carried on for days about Fidel's thimble of milk. They enjoyed pretending that Fidel ate what they did. It made them feel more important, and him more ordinary.

Cubans' feelings toward Fidel depended largely on their age. Many older narrators talked about him as god-like. Alejandro's mother, Olga Betancourt, recalled, 'After [the triumph of the Revolution] Fidel replaced the God we had believed in... We thought of him as our God the saviour.'[4] Salomón, a trade union functionary and Party member, described Fidel as a God-like, Jesus-like figure. 'Fidel has extraordinary vision. He can predict the future. He foretold events even experts could not have imagined. He warned us. His kind of genius, for he is a genius, does not often come into the world. Fidel made many sacrifices. He sacrificed his life to give us life.'[5]

The state, when Fidel was *Comandante en Jefe* (Commander in Chief), encouraged Cubans not just to support him, but to love him.[6] Yeyé, an elderly Black woman who worked as an assistant cleaner in a government office in Regla, thanked Fidel over and over. 'I had a hard life, I suffered. Then came Fidel Castro who put everything right for everyone. After the triumph of the Revolution my life changed. I became a person. But I have to tell you, as a worker I had no opportunity to study. I am illiterate but not totally, totally, I can sign my name. Aside from that I give enormous thanks to Fidel Castro. For a poor person I have everything.'[7]

Interviewing in Cuba was a delicate business. A narrator's tone of voice, body language, and silences gave important clues to the meaning of their words.

Cubans of a certain age believed that when things went wrong – when food was short, or prices soared – it wasn't Fidel's fault; it was the fault of his underlings. This is called the Good Tsar Syndrome, as it is often associated with Russia's tsars in the era before the Bolshevik Revolution when peasants (supposedly) believed that the tsars were benevolent, or wanted to be, but their advisors lied about conditions in the countryside. Petra, a retired state official in Santa Ana, is a Fidelista through and through. She said, 'If only the Comandante knew of our suffering he would ensure that we all had enough food and he would lower prices, but his advisors do not tell him the truth.' This is a classic example of the Good Tsar Syndrome.[8]

Jorge, an editor at a state publishing house, described falling in love with Fidel when four doves landed on his shoulder during a victory rally in Havana, just days after the guerrilla army defeated the US backed dictator, Fulgencio Batista. The image of Fidel and the doves acquired an almost religious quality in the Revolution's iconography, and I wondered if Jorge had actually been at the rally, or whether the image was so much a part of the collective memory that Jorge remembered being there himself.

Whether or not he was present doesn't matter very much. Jorge remembered it as the moment he fell in love with the Revolution. Fidel's charisma, and the future he promised, persuaded young Jorge, a student at an elite private school, to throw in his lot with the new government.[9]

Narrators also described falling out of love with Fidel and the Revolution.

Carlos, a custodian at a state warehouse in Santa Ana, recounted his growing disaffection. 'I always thought I loved the Revolution, but that wasn't true. I was hypnotised by the collective hysteria... They make you believe certain things. I don't know if something like mass psychological manipulation exists, I don't know, but it should, because they make you believe that [nervous laughter] you love, they make you believe that you applaud, that you are jumping for joy, that you are happy. I just don't know. They repeat things so many times, they make you think that.[10]

A notable difference between the life stories of older men and women is that men told stories that highlighted Fidel's flaws, particularly his stubbornness. I feel this was a demonstration of machismo, both the narrators' and Fidel's. Socrates, a veteran of the Bay of Pigs invasion and the African wars, revered Fidel. Yet his stories emphasised the Comandante's pig-headedness. Describing a long-ago meeting between Fidel and locals in Santa Ana, he said, 'El Comandante had made up his mind before he got here... We told him moringa won't grow around here, but he wouldn't listen... We are farmers, we know the land, we know what will grow and what won't. But he was stubborn and he got his way.'[11]

Lorenzo, an agronomist who had worked on Fidel's infamous cattle project, also emphasised his stubbornness. 'Experts from all over the world told him it was impossible to breed a cow that would survive in our tropical climate and produce enormous quantities of milk, but he simply pretended not to hear them.' Lorenzo said working with Fidel was so frustrating that he resigned three times. 'But he was obstinate and refused to let me quit.'[12]

The post-Soviet generation described a different Fidel, an old man out of touch with their lives and aspirations, a historical anachronism, a charismatic megalomaniac. Mario said, echoing Raúl Castro's implicit criticism of his brother, 'Fidel was an exceptional thinker on the international stage, but his moment has passed... I think he was far, far too paternalist and now we are paying the price [*pagando los platos rotos*, paying for the broken plates].'... 'As Carlos Varela [a famous Cuban folk singer] says in his songs, a father needs to pass the reins to his son and allow him to make his own mistakes.'[13]

11

PAVEL GARCÍA ROJAS

El Cerro, Havana

'We took equality for granted.'

If asked to picture a young Cuban revolutionary, I would probably see someone exactly like Pavel García Rojas, a pro-democracy activist. Tall, gaunt, sometimes bearded, with a gentle but unrelievedly serious manner, Pavel has skin the colour of moonlight and long unruly black hair. I first met him in 2004, soon after I began interviewing Cubans. The son of a friend, I frequently saw him coming and going but we never spoke beyond a hi, how are you, as he always seemed preoccupied.

In 2012, when he was thirty-six, I began to interview him at my friend's suggestion. She hoped the process of telling his life story might make him reflect on – and alter – his politics. He was keen, but for other reasons. He wanted to expose what life in Cuba was really like, and besides he was interested in oral history, having conducted interviews himself. The entire series of interviews, recorded over the next six years, were punctuated by the rap of his fingers on the table, beating out the rhythm of his story. Pavel spoke quietly, but intensely. He rarely smiled. The impression he gave was of complete attention, measuring every word. Whether describing family, school, or films, his theme was always *Castrismo*, Pavel's word for Cuba's political system. His life story is a narrative of political awakening.[1]

'I have always been *muy politizado*,' he said early on, conjuring up the image of himself as a ten-year-old avidly reading *Granma*. The precocious youngster was a devout Fidelista almost from birth. His middle-class grandparents supported the Revolution from the beginning. His parents formed part of the Fidelista intelligentsia, the 'revolutionary aristocracy' as some Cubans call it. His epiphany at the age of thirty was therefore all the more momentous and the ardour with which he now opposes the Castros reflects in equal parts a conviction that they betrayed egalitarian ideals and his belief in an open, democratic society.

Pavel repeatedly drew my attention to the disparities between his relatively comfortable circumstances growing up and the lives of others. He did not want me to forget he had avoided the worst of the hardships suffered by most Cubans in the Special Period and he seemed to harbour something like class guilt. By the same token he felt it was incumbent upon him to conduct himself in a transparent way. 'I declare my opposition publicly. I like to be open. It gives me pleasure. I am not someone who mutters to his friends, "Everything is bad." I have taken a public stand.' That can be a dangerous thing to do in Cuba, not just for oneself but for one's family and friends, and I ended up changing Pavel's name, like everyone else's. It wasn't what he wanted – government opponents are accused of hiding behind anonymity as often as they are said to be in the pay of the US – but Pavel graciously accepted my decision, so long as I inform readers that he would have preferred to use his real name.

He grew up in a large, but not opulent, red brick house on a leafy boulevard that runs between Fifth Avenue and the sea in Miramar, once the neighbourhood of Cuba's plantocracy. His maternal grandparents, Arturo and Rebeka, rented the house in 1958. Originally from Santiago de las Vegas, a small town outside Havana, they moved when Arturo opened a public relations company in the capital shortly before the triumph of the Revolution.

The timing of the move was unfortunate for Arturo's PR career, but very fortunate regarding the red brick house. With the revolutionary government's urban reform of 1960, ownership of residential property passed to sitting tenants upon payment of small fee. At a stroke Arturo and Rebeka became owners of one of the most desirable houses in Cuba. Pavel's mother and her two sisters subsequently inherited the property, and unless something untoward happens – for example, if the house is returned to the descendants of its pre-revolutionary owners – it will remain in Pavel's extended family.

Arturo's PR business petered out after the revolutionary government came to power. Pavel says his grandfather bore no grudge and offered his services to the new leadership. With fluent English which he had acquired in US private schools, and a flair for publicity, Arturo worked first at ICAP, the Instituto Cubano de Amistad con los Pueblos, the Cuban Institute for People's Friendship. After several years he was sent to Indonesia as part of the diplomatic corps. Indonesia was an important post because left-wing President Sukarno enjoyed the support of the USSR. Arturo's diplomatic career was cut short. Pavel said it was because his grandfather did not hold a university degree. Pavel's mother said it was because her father was in the habit of speaking his mind. Pavel's grandmother said her husband did not like to be separated from the family. Whatever the cause, Arturo never again held a prominent post. He worked as a high school history teacher before taking early retirement.

Pavel's grandmother Rebeka came from a more modest background than her husband. Before the Revolution the females in her family worked as telephone operators at the Cuban Telephone Company, partly owned by the US-owned

International Telephone and Telegraph Company, ITT. When the Cuban government expropriated ITT in 1960, Rebeka's mother, aunts, and sisters moved to the US. Rebeka was the only one to remain in Cuba. She exchanged several letters with her family in the US, but the correspondence soon stopped. Castro's government discouraged people communicating with the *gusanos*, the worms, who had fled.

Like so many other white, middle-class families, Pavel's was divided by the Revolution. Four decades later, when Pavel travelled to the US to speak at international conferences, he visited cousins in Chicago and Miami he had never met. He also saw the cousins he had grown up with in Miramar, who had joined the more recent exodus to the US.

Rebeka remained a loyal Fidelista throughout her long life. She worked for the Cuban telephone company, ETECSA, until 1991, when she was sixty-five. She wanted to carry on but in the depth of the Special Period her family persuaded her to retire. With almost no buses on the streets, she would have had to ride her bicycle the five miles to her office in the gruelling heat.

Before the Revolution Pavel's paternal grandparents, Francisco and Magdalena, owned several bars. In the 1950s their businesses prospered, and they sent Pavel's father to the exclusive Havana Military Academy. Pavel says that despite their class aspirations Francisco and Magdalena supported the Partido Socialista Popular, Cuba's Moscow-affiliated communist party. In the middle 1950s, when Fulgencio Batista was President of Cuba, they rented a modest apartment in a three-family house in a middle-class neighbourhood in El Cerro, near the iconic memorial to José Martí in the Plaza Cívica, now the Plaza de la Revolución. Like Arturo and Rebeka, they were beneficiaries of the revolutionary government's urban reform. While they had long supported the struggle to overthrow the Batista dictatorship, Pavel says their Fidelismo was cemented the day they became homeowners. Pavel and I met to record the interviews in that same airy apartment in El Cerro.

In the 1968 Revolutionary Offensive, Francisco and Magdalena's bars were confiscated. Pavel said he never once heard them complain. Thanks to their home ownership they were Fidelistas through and through. His grandfather took a job in the Ministry of Foreign Commerce where he worked for the rest of his life. His grandmother was manager of a large spaghetti factory until she became head of the first Diplo-tienda [dollar shop for diplomats] on the island.

Pavel grew up in the large red brick house in Miramar along with his maternal grandparents, his parents, his sister, two sets of aunts and uncles and six cousins. The house was large, but not that large. The family slept dormitory style. Pavel says he enjoyed the communal atmosphere. Both of his parents had PhDs from the Academy of Sciences in Moscow. His father taught at the University of Havana where he attracted a large following. His mother was head of personnel at a government research centre.

Pavel remembered that when he was eight or nine he heard his father saying things he had never heard before. 'My household was very revolutionary, very Fidelista. I lived all that. My father sparked a political crisis in the household. He considered the Revolution a good thing, but he was more critical than anyone else in the family. Come to think of it by then my grandfather was also quite disaffected. My point is, I remember overhearing my parents arguing, it must have been in the early 1980s. I can cite my father's words, "Nothing is working... things are bad." Yes, I remember his words very clearly because in school there was no political debate, hardly at all.'

Pavel's primary school was an ornate pink palace on Fifth Avenue in Miramar, which, like many school buildings after 1959, had once been the home of sugar magnates who had fled to Miami. Pavel recalled staring at the frescoes on the ceilings when he got bored in class and playing in what remained of the sculpture gardens.

He lamented the day in the 1980s when the government relocated the school to an ordinary building and leased the pink palace to a foreign embassy. He said that every time he walks past his old school he is reminded of its fate. 'The changing face of Fifth Avenue mirrors the history of the Revolution. By the 1980s politicians had abandoned their ideals. They became pragmatists and figured why waste these extraordinary buildings on schools when our country needs beautiful embassies.'

Pavel believes that in 1959 Cuba had two revolutions: a popular rebellion and an authoritarian coup. 'The spirit of the 1960s was defined by the great masses of Cubans throwing themselves into revolutionary activities. Ordinary men and women left the comfort of their homes to go to the mountains to teach people to read and write. For me that spirit defines the 1960s. At the very same time the leaders revealed their repressive side, executing people by firing squads. The two revolutions happened simultaneously. It was a very contradictory moment. When most Cubans were giving their all to create a new society, Fidel Castro was having his opponents shot at La Cabaña.'

Pavel's narrative illustrates Cubans' struggles over memory. For government supporters, La Cabaña, the magnificent colonial fortress across the bay from Havana, is a symbol of the country's cultural achievements. The international book fair is held there every year. For opponents, La Cabaña symbolises repression. They refuse to forget that the fortress was a political prison and a site of executions.

To Pavel, the relocation of his primary school exemplifies politicians' betrayal of the people's revolution. 'By the 1980s Cubans had lost their hope and enthusiasm. The generation that had devoted their lives to justice and equality was replaced by opportunists whose careers flourished within the bureaucracy. For example, university professors said to themselves, why should I go and teach children in the mountains; it involves a lot of extra work. Cubans gradually lost their spirit of solidarity. By the mid-1980s people had figured out how the system works, and how to play it to their advantage. This created fertile conditions for opportunism... and laid the groundwork for what we have today. The disaster of our entire system has its roots in the 1980s.'

'We took equality for granted.'

What else do you remember about growing up in the 80s?

'I am, let's say, part of Cuba's intellectual middle class. In Cuba, to define oneself as middle class is, to my way of thinking, a fairly recent thing. I believe that class divisions, the idea that you belong to a certain class, effectively disappeared in Cuba, though in reality it continued to exist. For example, when I was ten or eleven years old, and I will never forget this, I told a classmate that my mom earned 400 pesos. He burst out laughing because he thought it was a lie... he was sure I was lying about my mother's salary. Four hundred pesos was something like double his mother's salary. In Cuba at that time 400 pesos seemed to be too much because there weren't the contrasts that are normal in any other country... That's the reason he could not believe it was true.

'What was striking is that in school you were with children of all social strata. He and I, despite our differences, were in the same classroom; me, the son of intellectuals, he the son of a woman without any education. Still the fact remained that in Cuba the area where you lived determined the social milieu you moved in. I was born in Miramar and everyone in Cuba knows that Miramar is a middle-class neighbourhood, at that time it was upper middle class. Nevertheless, that boy, he was the school thief, he stole books and other things, and he grew up to be a delinquent, but that's beside the point. The point is he lived very near me. That would not have happened before 1959, no doubt about it. I am telling you this to locate myself in terms of social class, which is a way of thinking that came into being only later, more recently. As a child I had no awareness of this at all. Nobody talked about it when I was a kid. We took equality for granted. Though in reality there were social differences, no one felt they belonged to this or that class.'

Even after Pavel turned into a fierce government opponent, he continued to value the equality and racial tolerance the Revolution once achieved. He contrasted the blatant racism he sees now with his childhood. 'When I was a child although there was hypocrisy in the adult world about racism and things like that, racism wasn't common. It was not common for Cubans to refer to the colour of people's skin. No, as far as I can remember it was not common at all. It would have been very difficult for someone to say, "He is Black"... or "That man did it because he is Black." No, I don't remember hearing that when I was about ten years old. It came with the crisis of the 1990s, absolutely, and now it is scandalous, absolutely scandalous. It is something that really distresses me every single day... Remember, I am talking about Miramar, where I lived, where I was born.'

Is Pavel's story about what people in his neighbourhood said or did not say twenty-five years earlier believable? After all, memory is fallible and people forget. Whether or not it is true, it is valuable in important ways. It reveals his feelings about his childhood, his perception of how attitudes to race have changed, and his political stance.

Memories of the past to fit the present

When I asked Pavel if he remembered formative moments in the 1980s – the occupation of the Peruvian Embassy and the

Mariel boatlift – he cautioned me about the tricks memory plays.[2] 'Mariel was one of the most important events in Cuba... But no, no, I have no memories of those events. Remember, I was only four years old. I was born in 1976, they happened in 1980. To answer your question, I could imagine that I remember Mariel and the events at the Peruvian Embassy, but in reality I don't know if my memories are accurate.'

Pavel recalled visiting the Museo de la Marcha del Pueblo Combatiente, the Museum of the March of the People's Resistance, that presents the official history of events surrounding the storming of the Peruvian Embassy which sparked the famous Mariel boatlift.[3] The exhibitions led the young Pavel to question what he had been taught to believe. He recalled feeling shocked when he realised that what happened at the Embassy was different from what the government said had happened. He said the museum triggered his political awakening.

'I remember going to the Museo de la Marcha del Pueblo Combatiente when I was young. I will never forget the bloody shirt on display under glass. Listen carefully because this is very significant to me. I figured out from looking at the shirt that the man guarding the Embassy had not been killed by a person storming the building. I figured out he had to have been killed by another guard in crossfire. The people in the bus that broke through the Embassy gates were not carrying arms, of course not. They would have been shot immediately. But no one ever, ever said that, nobody. I grew up thinking the guard was a hero because he had been shot by the people storming the Embassy. I grew up believing he was the courageous man of socialist realism, a powerful hero who threw himself in front of the guns. The victim... No one ever said, never, ever, I never heard anyone say it was an accident, that he died in a crossfire. For me this is very significant.'

Memories change as people reimagine the past to make sense of who they are and to understand their society. Listening to Pavel's story, I was left with the feeling that perhaps his memories of the museum had undergone a change to fit in with his narrative of political awakening.

The Gold and Silver Stores: a missing piece of history

Thinking back to the 1980s, Pavel recalled events that, he said, had played an important role in his own political development, but had been erased from the official story of the Revolution.

'I want to tell you about a part of history that should not be forgotten, the Tiendas de Oro y Plata, the Gold and Silver Stores. No one ever talks about them, but, as I've said, *yo soy muy politizado*, I am very politicised. I don't know when they began exactly, it must have been 1987 or 88, I don't know, but we are talking about twenty-five or thirty years after the 1959 Revolution. For thirty years people gave everything of themselves, and what happened? They [the state] took everything away. We have a state that never hesitates to take away, to take everything away.' Pavel was speaking from a position of privilege. As he himself said, the vast majority of Cuban families had nothing to take away that had a monetary value.

'Historically, Cuba is a country with major social differences. Before the Revolution there was great prosperity. In the 1950s, Cuba had a very prosperous upper middle class. After the Revolution there was a continuous process of impoverishment, a vile process of impoverishment. It occurred to Fidel Castro, it had to have been Fidel Castro's idea, or the idea of another Castro, that the upper middle class must have a lot of gold and silver hidden in their homes, along with valuable works of art and similar possessions. The question was how to take it from them? Well they could have employed the Soviet method that Aleksandr Solzhenitsyn describes in *The Gulag Archipelago*. Steal it outright and kill anyone who resists. But no, that's not what happened here. We don't have such a brutal Revolution. It occurred to them that if they gave Cubans access to consumer goods they could do a trade. They could exchange consumer goods for gold and silver, but with one simple detail, a very Fidelista detail. The Cuban state would buy their gold and silver way below the world market price, way, way below, and sell consumer goods at prices way above.

'To me, this act was so corrupt that, taken on its own, it delegitimises the entire revolutionary process. This act alone demonstrated enormous irresponsibility towards a people that had given everything. Trading necessities for the only possessions they had left: to me it is enough, there doesn't have to be more. To my way of thinking this stained Castrismo forever. What I demand of this system is accountability towards a people that have given of themselves so brilliantly, so completely, so fully. To me this act is sufficient, I need nothing more. I swear I need nothing more to sustain my convictions.'

Pavel was shaking with indignation. The contrast between the soft voice and the hard words underscored the importance he gave the story.

'Let me tell you what I did, at ten years old. I came here to my grandparents' apartment, this very apartment where we are sitting.' Pavel's apartment had a surreal feel, like a Fellini film set. It was furnished in a bizarre mix of dark, heavy, baroque furniture, his grandparents' legacy, and found objects he used as props in his films. In one corner stood a fire hydrant, from the ceiling hung a huge traffic sign. Above the dining room table, among fading family photographs, hung a beautiful and unusual photo of Che smiling a soft almost coquettish smile that had been given to his grandparents or to his father, he didn't know which. 'I knew that my grandparents in Miramar had no gold and silver, but the ones who lived here did. So, I came here and began searching through their closets for anything made of gold or silver. I was only ten years old remember. Ten years old and I was desperate to find gold and silver to exchange for a colour TV.

'My grandparents had a large box of beautiful silverware, with silver spoons, forks and knives. I remember even as a young boy thinking the set was exquisite. Of course, it was the first thing to go. They exchanged it for two televisions. One they gave to my mother [by that time Pavel's parents were divorced]. It was the first TV we ever had. One they gave my father. They themselves already had a TV. Although dollars were prohibited my father had managed to buy them a TV through special connections, friends and all that. Theirs was a Chiro, made in Korea. Ours was a Sanyo; I still have it; I'll show it to you. The one they gave my father was a Toshiba, but it wasn't made well and before long it broke. I remember going with my grandparents to the Tienda de Oro y Plata. It was the first time I was in a real store where they had lots of things, beautiful things.

'Only a very small group had gold and silver, and they were from families that had money before 1959 but had not managed to get all their valuables out [of the country]. Many succeeded in getting their valuables out. I am not talking here about people who had been lower or lower middle class before the Revolution. My grandparents, for example, the ones who lived here were middle class, solidly middle class.

'At the Tienda de Oro y Plata you could even buy a car. I know someone who did. He had enough gold and silver and jewellery to buy a car. Can you imagine, Liz, how much gold and silver you had to take to the Tienda to buy a car, and the price! I had a friend whose father bought a car at the Tienda de Oro y Plata. But, of course, I'm from Miramar. Wait a minute, I just remembered, yes, I'm pretty sure that my uncle Joaquín bought his car at the Tienda de Oro y Plata. But, and let me repeat, I'm from Miramar. If I had grown up in this apartment in El Cerro,

I probably would not have known anyone who could buy things at the Tienda de Oro y Plata.'[4]

Pavel's narrative contains multiple contradictions, but rather than invalidating his life history, it is more revealing. Frequently contradictions alert us to subjects a narrator finds particularly uncomfortable, and wants to hide, or highlight. How a narrator interprets an event helps us understand their feelings, their politics, and their circumstances. Frequently contradictions and factual mistakes are clues to a story's meaning. In this passage Pavel wants to demonstrate that pre-revolutionary class differences resurfaced in the 1980s.

'Now we are going to build socialism.'

When Pavel's grandparents were exchanging silver spoons for colour TVs, Fidel Castro initiated a campaign aimed to strengthen Cubans' commitment to socialism. It baffled just about everyone, not least because, although Fidel talked about the need to recover the ideals of Che, the state implemented measures that intensified material inequalities, such as the Tiendas de Oro y Plata.[5]

'In 1986 they [the state] inaugurated a campaign called the Rectification of Errors and Negative Tendencies. In reality, as a ten-year-old, it didn't mean a great deal to my life... Some prices went up as part of the Rectification of Errors. What I know about the campaign came from people who were adults at the time, from hearing them talk about Fidel's famous slogan, "Now we are going to build socialism." Remember, we are talking about twenty-seven years after the triumph of the Revolution, twenty-five years after Fidel declared that the Revolution was socialist. I heard many adults, including my father and his friends, and the people in my house, say, "If it's only now that we are going to build socialism, what have we been doing so far?"'

'To tell the truth, in those years my friends and I mostly watched out for new Ladas and Moskvitchs.' Pavel and his friends sat on the curb in Miramar hoping to spot cars that people had bought at the Gold and Silver Stores, or received in recognition of their loyalty and work. The Ladas and the Moskvitchs speeding down Fifth Avenue exemplified the creeping inequality that the Rectification campaign promised to overturn.

Why do some Cubans refer to the 1980s as a golden age?

'You have got to remember [after the 1959 Revolution] Cubans always lived modestly. We never had abundance. One thing or other would suddenly disappear, sweet potatoes, rice, whatever, and we got used to not having this or that. We took shortages in our stride and learned to make do. It wasn't a big problem.'

Pavel believed that Cubans recall the 1980s as years of abundance not because they had so much, but because in the years before and after they had so little.

'People remember the 1980s as the period of greatest abundance within the Revolution because you got condensed milk on the ration. Only once in her lifetime has my seven-year-old daughter had condensed milk; I bought it for her to taste. It is not readily available. In the 1980s the ration included beef. The generation now in their twenties does not know what beef tastes like. In the late 1980s, if you had the money you could buy certain luxuries outside the ration, on the *mercado libre*, the free market. We thought they were expensive but at prices that now would be next to nothing. Chocolate, for example, was available in the 1980s, but at a price most people could not easily afford.'

From the Special Period onwards eating beef had been prohibited. It was legally available only at tourist hotels and restaurants and the clandestine sale of beef carried a ten-year prison sentence. Prohibition only added to Cubans' longing and when I asked one narrator his dreams for the future he answered with one word: steak.

Stories Pavel forgot to tell

Pavel sent me several long emails recounting events he remembered after listening to the recordings.[6] 'There is an important topic I forgot to tell you about. You should know how Cubans lived *la cultura militar*, military culture. In the 1980s all children [in Havana] between the ages of ten and twelve were taken to the Pioneers' Palace in Lenin Park where we ate the best *merienda* of our lives. They took us there in special buses. I went when I was ten years old and I recall the place was very, very clean. I took classes in anti-aerial defence, we learned to use a typewriter, to load and unload a Makarov, a regulation Soviet pistol, and to operate a military radio. Our teachers were from the army. It showed that the military was our friend. There was another organisation called SEPMI, which had its own magazine. There we learned other skills and received training. I don't know what SEPMI stands for.'

I typed SEPMI into Google and zing, the *Cuba Annual Report 1989* appeared on my screen. The *Cuba Annual Report* was a CIA-type manual, published by the Radio Martí Program of the Voice of America in collaboration with the United States Information Service (USIS). It was, quite obviously, part of the US effort to undermine the Cuban government.[7] I learned that SEPMI stands for Sociedad de Educación Patriotico-Militar, Society for Patriotic Military Education, and that beginning in the early 1980s SEPMI trained youth in 'militarily oriented sports and outdoor activities'. It extended its coverage to ten-year-olds only in the late 1980s, when in addition to its regular programs, it 'delivered courses in the use of the AKM rifle [the Kalashnikov modernised automatic rifle], tractor driving, radio telegraphy, and cooking.' The cooking classes were probably for the girls.

The *Report* explains that the Cuban government named 1989 'The Year of Defence Preparation' because, quoting Fidel Castro, Cuba's leaders sensed the US might soon be making peace with the USSR, and the country would have to defend itself. This would explain young Pavel's military training. The *Report* concludes, 'The United States is once again raised as the most persistent danger the Revolution faces,' implying that the Cuban government's analysis of US politics was oh so tiresome and out-of-date.

In 1992, following the collapse of the USSR, the United States Congress passed the Cuban Democracy Act, referred to as the Torricelli Act, which tightened the blockade against Cuba by prohibiting foreign-based subsidiaries of US companies from trading with the country, and Cuban-Americans from sending family remittances. Put simply, the US government acted exactly the way Cuban leaders had predicted.

'Soviet superiority was a truth I lived by,' wrote Pavel in his email. 'It goes without saying I was proud of Soviet armaments most of all. I took pleasure in knowing the names of every weapon and everything about them. I firmly believed in the Soviet Union's superior military capacity. Cubans saw the army as their friend, and it has been difficult over the years to dismantle that image. I struggle to teach my children about the character of the military. It seems what children are taught in school remains pretty much the same as it was in the past, even though other things have changed radically.'

The Cuban Revolution was a messy, complicated process and Pavel's memories of the 1980s are contradictory, as they would be. The first instalment of his life story is a homage to egalitarianism, a narrative of creeping social divisions, and a denunciation of the betrayal of the people's democratic revolution.

PART 2

FIDEL AND
THE COLLAPSE
1990-2006

When communism in Europe collapsed, the head of every country in the Soviet bloc fell except Fidel. His survival was not solely a tribute to his extraordinary charisma; Cubans took pride in his implacable opposition to Washington, it gave their life meaning. But their lives changed dramatically at this point. The USSR had supplied food, petroleum and machinery in exchange for sugar. When that arrangement stopped Cubans lacked sufficient food and electricity. Factories closed. Buses sat idle. Rusting tractors littered the landscape. Fidel dubbed the crisis the Special Period of wartime hardships in a time of peace.

Cuba was the only Soviet bloc country still at war with Washington – a cold war.[1] To undermine the Cuban government, the US Congress tightened the blockade, strengthening, in the process, Cubans' nationalism, but also intensifying their hunger and desperation. Many Cubans tried to flee illegally by crossing the Florida Straits on flimsy rafts. The exodus was a reprise of the Mariel boatlift but driven less by politics than by deprivation. In the summer of 1994 discontent boiled over and hundreds of protesters gathered on the Malecón, Havana's seawall, chanting '*Libertad, Abajo Fidel*' ('Liberty, Down with Fidel!') When Fidel waded into the crowd the shouting stopped. 'We admired *el Caballo's* courage but feared his anger,' Miguel told my colleague Lilia Campos.[2] Cuban men frequently referred to Fidel as *el Caballo*, the horse, in homage to his famed womanising. Castro announced that anyone wanting to leave was free to go, the police would not stop them.[3] In the following months an estimated 30,000 Cubans attempted to cross the Florida Straits on anything that would float in an exodus known as the *balsero* (rafter) crisis.

The Mariel boatlift and the *balsero* crisis exposed Castro's difficulties. They also contributed to his success. On those rare occasions when dissatisfaction spilled into the streets the government released an escape valve and allowed opponents to leave. The strategy got rid of potential troublemakers and curbed unrest. Opponents figured, why risk imprisonment? If I keep my head down, sooner or later they will let me leave.

Pundits described Cuba as 'tropical socialism', partly because in contrast to the Soviets who sent opponents to the gulag, Fidel sent some of his enemies to prison but most to Miami with a goodbye and good riddance.

Cuba's leaders decided that to revive the economy they needed foreign exchange and they set about developing tourism. They encouraged Cubans abroad to send remittances, allowed US dollars to circulate, and legalised small businesses hoping to bring hard currency into the country. The narrators describe how the government's strategy altered their lives, altered every facet of existence.

With the economy in transition, the government attempted to practice politics as usual – the one-party system, managed elections and repression. But the mood had changed. Cubans were less obedient than before. Many narrators said, (I am paraphrasing), I feel at liberty to speak my mind because my salary is so low it wouldn't matter if I am fired, and besides most of my income comes from my work *por la izquierda*, under the table. Feelings like these were in the air.

The hardships and the everyday hustle to survive took a tremendous ideological toll. Warning of the dangers posed by private entrepreneurs and the emerging business culture, Fidel told students at the University of Havana, 'If the Revolution is destroyed it will not be by our enemies, but by ourselves. We can destroy the Revolution through our own errors, and it would be entirely our fault.'[4]

Cuba's economy grew modestly in Fidel's last years, largely because the Venezuelan government under President Hugo Chávez sent oil to Cuba in exchange for doctors. The upturn prompted Fidel to announce in 2005 that the Special Period was over. Billboards appeared throughout the island with the slogan, *Vamos Bien* (We're Doing Well), alongside a picture of a younger, smiling, Fidel. '*Vamos Bien*' was an exaggeration, but Cubans wanted to believe the worst was over. For some it was. For most it wasn't. The country's social structure had changed, and the very limited economic recovery was not equally shared. A small minority of Cubans lived in relative comfort; the vast majority endured hardships.

In failing health, in 2006 Fidel temporarily ceded power to his brother. Two years later the handover was made permanent. Many Cubans suspected that Fidel's retirement was not entirely voluntary, that he had been encouraged to resign by opponents eager to liberalise the economy.

12

MARIO SÁNCHEZ CORTÉZ

Old Havana

When Mario failed to get into the San Alejandro School of Art he enrolled in an *escuela en el campo*, a school in the countryside, to complete his secondary education and prepare for university entrance exams. Fidel had just told the country they had to prepare for a Special Period of hardship.[1]

Escuelas en el campo started in the heady 1960s to help break down the division between mental and manual work. Students combined classes with agricultural labour. Older Cubans we interviewed had fond memories of *las escuelas* back in the days. They recalled enjoying the collective ethos and most of all their liberation from parental authority. In the Special Period it was different. The *escuelas* developed a reputation for bullying, sexual abuse and appalling living conditions. Pavel managed to avoid going to a 'pre' (pre-university school in the countryside) because his father, a prominent intellectual, finagled a medical exemption. For Mario, working the system was not an option; his parents had no influential connections.

Mario remembered suffering during his first year from hunger, fear and depression. 'When I entered the building I felt I was in a prison. I felt I was being locked up against my will simply because I wanted to go to university. My friends felt that way too. For someone like me, born in the city, it was a shock to suddenly find myself in the countryside. The change was stark. There was nothing but red earth, red earth as far as I could see and it depressed me.

'I put up with it for one reason. It would have been worse at home with my father. Also, I had to go to a pre in the countryside if I wanted to go to university. After a while I got over my depression and I adapted; I had to. You had to fight, and I really mean fight, if you were going to survive. I had to defend myself all the time. My friends at home weren't like that; they weren't fighters. Sometimes I had to fight an entire gang of boys, an entire gang.

'In my first year I was in the same dormitory with students about to graduate. They were practically grown men and women. Like in a prison you had to impose your self-respect. To tell the truth having to fight shocked me. I fought with anything I could. I remember pulling out a machete. I fought with knives. It was terrible, terrible. In the dormitory the students were always fighting. If you didn't impose your self-respect, they would humiliate you. Finally, I managed to adapt. I invented ways. Mostly I ran away; I escaped into the outback.

'I was always hungry. They didn't feed us enough so I went scavenging for food. It was also a way to avoid the bullies. I dressed like a *campesino*, peasant, and before long I fell in with some *guajiros*, rustics, living by the grace of God. We stole anything: horses, bananas, yucca, oranges, anything. I took food home to my family. In Havana the situation was dire.'

Yanelis, Mario's neighbour in Old Havana, said she was lucky to be at an *escuela en el campo* in the worst years of the Special Period. 'There was no food at home; at *la escuela* at least I ate enough to survive.'[2]

Many of Mario's classmates dropped out of school. Some opted for technical training, others tried their luck in the black market. Mario was on the verge of quitting but resolved to stick it out. 'I would not be crushed. I would not allow the countryside to break me. I would not forsake my dream of graduating from university.'

Mario's memories of the school surprised me; I had heard nothing but praise for Cuba's education system. But schools were badly hit in the Special Period. Veteran teachers left the profession to drive taxis, clean hotel rooms or to go abroad. Their replacements were young and inexperienced. Soon after Raúl Castro became president he closed the *escuelas en el campo* partly because the government could not afford to keep them open, partly because of their reputation.

'My second year at the school was worse. I totally abandoned my studies... I wondered whether the reason I had messed up so badly was that I was some sort of brute. Maybe I was a brute but that didn't explain my problems. My brother was in prison. He was always the black sheep of the family. He started stealing from our neighbours and finally he got caught. When I was supposed to be preparing for my exams I had to visit him in prison. We [Mario's family] had to take him food and everything else. Because I didn't have time to study I requested a suspension from school... As if all this wasn't enough we had blackouts almost every single day. Most of the time we had no electricity or water. With so many problems it was impossible to contemplate life beyond tomorrow.

'I returned [to school] the following year. I was fairly conscientious and managed to graduate... I already had my status and I didn't have to defend myself. I spent my time drawing and doing stuff like that... and I passed my courses without any problems.' Although Mario graduated, he was refused a place at university because his grades were not high enough. 'I was very depressed and completely disillusioned.'

Almost everyone we interviewed of the post-Soviet generation talked about their depression and disillusion. They felt their future had been taken away; yet people reacted differently depending on their circumstances and their attitude.

'Just as I was finishing pre, I received a letter from the army. It was an appointment for a medical examination for obligatory military service. In May 1994 I graduated; in August I was drafted.' Mario laughed and added in a voice heavy with sarcasm, 'My country called and I had to fulfil my duty to *la patria*, the homeland.'

Mario and Juan completed obligatory military service. Pavel and Alejandro managed to avoid the draft. Esteban said nothing about army service, which makes me think he avoided the draft. From the lives of these five men we might suspect that the poor were more likely to be drafted than the more comfortably off, and we know that Afro-Cubans were overrepresented among the poor and underrepresented among the more affluent groups.

My brother the *balsero*

Mario reported for military duty in August 1994, the month of the Maleconazo, the legendary street protest when a crowd mostly of men gathered on the Malecón shouting anti-Castro slogans. Raydel, fifteen years old at the time, recalled that when the protesters saw El Caballo wade into their midst they fell silent.[3] Raydel said they listened to Fidel out of admiration for his fearlessness, also to avoid reprisals, and to their astonishment he announced they were free to leave. Fidel's speech sparked a mass exodus of men, women and families who attempted to cross the Florida Straits on *balsas*, improvised rafts. Mario's brother left in the *balsero* crisis, as did Juan's best friend and his entire family. The *balsero* crisis altered the political landscape on both sides of the Florida Straits.

'My brother was a carpenter. He made *balsas* and sold them to people leaving. He had been in prison and he always had problems with the law. That summer he was in some kind of

MARIO SÁNCHEZ CORTÉZ

difficulty and there was a warrant out for his arrest. One day a balsa was leaving but some of the passengers decided not to go. A man said to him, go ahead, take my place. My brother got in and just like that he left. He always liked fishing. Fishing and the sea are part of us. When I was three he took me fishing on the Malecón. I learned to swim on the Malecón.'

A year later Mario's family received an official letter saying that his brother had been rescued at sea by the US Coast Guard and was at the US Naval Base at Guantánamo awaiting processing. A year later they received an envelope postmarked Pittsburgh, Pennsylvania, with $300 in cash. At the time $300 was a fortune, Mario said. Twice they talked to him from a neighbour's phone; Mario's family never had a phone. After that nothing.

When was the last time you received news from your brother?
'We received no news from him; we received news about him. A woman in San Miguel del Padrón told my aunt that my brother and her son were together in a US prison. I would have asked which prison, in which state. But my aunt didn't ask, so we don't have any more information. I would have figured out a way of communicating with him, there are means. But not knowing which state, no, your country is too big for that.' Mario thinks of me as first and foremost a North American.[4]

Turning the army to my advantage

As fate would have it, when Mario was reporting for military duty, his brother was leaving on a raft. Mario was assigned to Unidad Militar 3146, a tank, artillery, anti-aircraft and chemical warfare unit. He said conditions on the military base made his suffering at pre seem like child's play.

'My introduction to military life was marching, shooting, crawling in mud, learning to camouflage myself. Because I had

107

graduated from twelfth grade, after basic training I was sent on a course to learn to drive tanks. When I returned to my unit I was the tiniest bit better off than the others because sometimes I was exempt from guard duty, though that wasn't much of a consolation. Even though I worked in communications I suffered the same as everyone else. I was sent to the *calabozo*, the stockade, two or three times; it is a normal part of military life. I managed to complete my second year in the army enduring all of the ordinary miseries of army life: the food, the boredom, the lack of privacy, the pain, the *calabozo*.

'The army affects some people more, others less. Many of my *compañeros* ended up in the high security prison on the base. That's where they send you if you try to escape. I managed to get through the army without too many problems because I said to myself, if I must be in the army for two years I have no choice but to survive. After all, it's only two years out of my entire life. I never threw acid in my eyes. I never wounded myself, or broke my own arm, as did many of my fellow recruits. A lot of them injected petroleum into their feet and sadly some died... As for me, I promised myself that I would get out of the army in the same condition as I went in, or stronger. I had to figure out how to turn the army to my advantage. I began to reflect on my mother's life with three children. She failed to achieve what she wanted. She tried to improve herself and I used to think that if she had managed to graduate all of us would have had a better life. Then I thought why shouldn't I succeed and graduate from university. I don't have to support anyone else, no one at all.

'At the end of the year I was informed, along with everyone who had completed twelfth grade, that if I wanted to continue studying I could enrol in Orden 18, the army's pre-university programme. Five hundred of us started the one-year intensive programme. If you did not pass all of your courses you were booted out. Everyone in Orden 18 was invited to join the Young Communists and almost everyone did. Quite simply it was expected. I studied very hard. I took the entrance exams for university and thanks to my artistic ability I got in to the Instituto Superior de Diseño Industrial.

'I don't know if this applies to every single student in Orden 18, but many faced economic limitations. Like me, they had limited clothing, limited food, limited everything, as you would after two years in the service, two years of not working, two years of not earning. They paid us thirty pesos a month, equivalent to one dollar. Like every Cuban of my generation I wanted things, it was that time in my life. But I had to forget that. I devoted myself to studying. In 1997 I started university.'

Tell me a little more about the period when you were in Orden 18, a little more about your economic limitations.

'What is there to say? I've been poor since the day I was born. For better or for worse I've never been middle class, always poor... Then all of a sudden, in a flash, the situation got much, much worse. It was the 1990s, the Special Period. By 1997, the year I entered university, we had gotten through the worst but we were still in a Special Period. Let me tell you something, I believe we Cubans have always been in a special period. Sometimes it's tougher, sometimes a little easier.'

Mario could not afford to buy shoes

'When I was in Orden 18 I was no longer a child. I was an adult and wore adult shoes, size 45. Shoes my size were no longer available on the ration. Previously, with your *libreta de abastecimiento*, ration book, you got clothes and housewares at reasonable prices, prices everyone could afford. By 1996, when I was in Orden 18, you had to buy shoes in *divisas*, hard currency. My family had no *divisas* so there was no way. My mamá could not afford to buy me shoes no matter how much she saved.

She could not spare that little bit of money. One day I went to a store and saw that shoes my size cost twenty-three dollars. (Twenty-three dollars was equivalent to approximately a month and a half of an average state salary.) Twenty-three dollars even though they were terrible, *malísimos*. When I discovered that I wanted to give up. But I began selling pastries in Orden 18.'

Mario started laughing and I asked why. 'Picturing myself at military school selling pastries on the sly... I went home right after school and studied until late at night. First thing in the morning I went out in search of bread, then I came home and prepared my pastries. At recess I sold the pastries and with that money I could more or less buy the bits I needed. I could get by. I bought the shoes. Of course, they weren't the best or the prettiest shoes in the world but they covered my feet and I could walk in them.'

Mario's story exemplifies the divide between those who had hard currency and those who did not. Unless you had relatives in Miami who sent dollars, or you received dollar tips from a job in the tourist sector, you had to invent some kind of illegal venture, just as Mario did, to buy shoes. This anecdote illustrates Mario's perseverance.

'I wanted a life.'

'Orden 18 was far from home. I got up at six in the morning and took a *camello* [a reviled double-humped trailer bus nicknamed the camel that came to symbolise the miseries of the Special Period]. I got off at a dirt road and had to walk uphill for about three miles. We had morning classes, they gave you lunch, then more classes in the afternoon, then the three mile walk to catch the bus home.

'In the beginning I lived at school but that didn't last long. When I boarded at pre, I had to eat the kind of food fed to inmates. After that I was in the military, and I wasn't about to starve like that again.' Mario chuckled, recalling the lousy food. 'I stopped staying overnight and began to commute back and forth. Sometimes we were lucky and caught a ride on the teachers' bus, but rarely. The driver was a son of a bitch. Usually late in the afternoon I had to walk the three miles downhill, catch a bus home, only to get up at six the next morning. Fortunately, many of the teachers helped us hitch rides on their bus because they wanted us to have more time to do homework.

'The economic situation was bad. I wanted to study. I wanted to succeed, but there was also this other thing. I wanted a life, you know what I mean. I was doing well in school. I was passing my courses, I was improving myself, but when the weekend came you wanted, how to explain it, you wanted to get hold of ten pesitos and have a good time.' Mario meant ten *pesos nacionales*, equivalent to forty cents in US dollars. 'But you couldn't have a good time unless there was a little fiesta in the barrio or something like that. You couldn't because everything was in *divisas*, in dollars. It was incredible. To have a good time, and I am not talking alcoholic drinks, what I had in mind was nothing more than a simple soda and a piece of pastry of whatever kind, a *pan dulce*, bread with anything at all plopped on top. But everything was in dollars. The same with *paladares,* private restaurants. You couldn't afford to go anywhere. It was all so expensive, you just couldn't.'

In the middle noughties, 2004 to 2008, every single young Cuban we interviewed said they were angry because they were not allowed to go to the 'for tourists only' beaches and clubs. Several narrators called the policy apartheid. Fidel explained on television that the prohibition was to prevent Cubans becoming contaminated by capitalist decadence, but that did nothing to assuage their fury. When Raúl Castro became president he quietly shelved the law.

Relaxation of the ban made little difference to Mario. He explained that a two-dollar entrance fee plus a couple of dollars to pay for a drink kept him out of discos as effectively as any government decree. Mario said he knew that in Miami the amount of money in your pocket separated the rich from the poor, but that was Miami. In Havana it wasn't supposed to be that way. The power of money opposed everything the Revolution stood for. Mario's thinking may well have been influenced by the Battle of Ideas.

'In the service I decided I wanted to be a somebody.'

Do you think military service helped you in any way, maybe in making a man of you? Lilia asked.

'Look, no one wants to do military service because throughout those two years you keep saying to yourself, this is a great big waste of my time. But the army taught me to be self-reliant, to solve my own problems, to get along with people who don't think the way I do. And it's true, to a certain extent it taught me to be a man, to take responsibility for my own actions, be tactful, ultra-careful because you are walking around with real guns and live ammunition. It also taught me to accept – in the army at least – the relationship between the *jefe*, the leader, and his subordinates. There are people who like the military, and I am not criticising them. But the most important lesson the army taught me is that I never ever want to have anything to do with it again.' Mario laughed at his joke about the army. 'At the same time it gave me something. It strengthened me. During long nights on guard duty I had lots of time to think. I estimate that in my two years in the service I spent one year on guard duty. I thought a lot. I contemplated the meaning of life. I analysed myself. I thought about what I wanted to accomplish. I had completed twelfth grade; how much further did I want to go?

'When I was in the service I decided I wanted to be a somebody, *ser alguien*. I began to dream. At pre, I dreamed of going to university but I lacked the self-discipline. The hardships I endured in the army strengthened me. They forged my willpower, my spirit. They reinforced my determination to achieve. When I was in the service I mapped out my future. I would graduate from university. Luckily, I persevered and I accomplished my goal. I'll show you my diploma.' Mario rummaged through a plastic-covered mountain of books and papers beside his bed until he found it.

Fewer Cubans graduate from university than I realised. According to government statistics, in 2017 approximately ten per cent of Cubans were university graduates. Mario said that in his neighbourhood it was hard to find someone who had gone to university. 'My friends in the barrio scoffed at my ambition. This diploma is my revenge… True it's not worth much right now, in the sense that as a professional I do not have a salary that allows me to live the way I'd like. But I made my dream come true. I learned that I can achieve my goals. Although many people don't think a university degree is worth much, to me it is very valuable. It gives me tremendous satisfaction. That's the way I feel.

'To work hard and to succeed, it stays with you your entire life. That's what being in the service gave me. You might find it hard to believe but the service gave me fortitude. It forces you to do things you think you can't do. For example, when there's an order, "Run six kilometres in x amount of time," and you say to yourself, I don't think I have the physical strength. You overcome that feeling, you do it, and you realise you have accomplished something. You say to yourself, if I can do those things when I have to, I can do them voluntarily. I can accomplish the goals I set myself. Why shouldn't I?… I believe that everyone who goes through the military comes out with a different mentality. They are more adult. They leave their youth behind. In the military you take your first steps to adulthood.' While regretting the time he spent in the military, Mario appreciated what the army taught him about perseverance, and about himself.

Cubans by and large hold the army in high regard. They see it a privileged caste, under the protection of Raúl Castro, that offers jobs for life, good salaries, housing, hospitals, clubs, educational opportunities and social mobility. A number of the young men we interviewed in rural towns said they hoped to have an army career.

'To remain at university I had to have courage.'

Mario was thrilled when he started university, it was the fulfilment of all his years of sacrifice. But after a few months he had to drop out. 'My deepest desire was to stay until I graduated, but I couldn't. University is a higher level, it requires a different way of life and my parents could not support me. My family did not have enough money even to buy food and clothing, in addition they wanted to improve our housing conditions.'

University was free, but by the time Mario enrolled students no longer received a living stipend. Mario quipped that most of his classmates didn't need one; they got money from mamá and papá. He recalled that when he entered university the gap between richer and poorer Cubans was widening, and his family counted themselves among the poor. His father believed university was a luxury they could not afford, and the little money they had was better spent cementing the walls and installing a sink, than paying for his son to do nothing but study.

One of the paradoxes of contemporary Cuba is that in the Soviet period some students were barred from university because of their politics. In Mario's generation they were effectively barred because of their poverty.

Profoundly dejected and fearing that all his sacrifices had come to nought, Mario spent weeks looking for a job. A decade before, when the state guaranteed employment, he would have found work quickly. But in 1997 legitimate jobs were hard to come by and paid a pittance. Mario did not want to work illegally, like most of his friends. Eventually he took a job as custodian at a warehouse that belonged to CIMEX, the Cuban Import-Export Corporation. Mario feared, at the end of his first year at CIMEX, that if he did not re-enrol at university he would end up a dropout, like his mother. He decided to attend classes during the day and work nights at the CIMEX plant in Guanabacoa, on the far side of the Havana harbour.

'I worked at that job during my five years at university. After my night shift I went home to shower before heading to class. I knew that working until dawn, often going to lectures after a sleepless night, was a problem. It affected my schoolwork… Frequently I handed in assignments late, or not at all. But I persevered in my struggle. I longed to stop working and dedicate myself full-time to university. *Tuve que hacerme de tripas corazón*, a Cuban expression meaning, I had to have courage. If I didn't work how was I going to support myself? Neither my mother nor my father could help me. As time went on I passed my courses, every single one of them, and I managed to graduate.'

Mario's story of poor students working their way through university, while rich students glided through supported by their parents, is at odds with Cuba's reputation for universal, free education. Mario's coming of age coincided with the withering away of the old system, and birth of the new.

Racism: 'My facial characteristics do not fit the part.'

Mario commuted by bicycle from his temporary home in San Miguel del Padrón, where his mother took refuge from her husband's violent abuse, to his night job in Guanabacoa, to university in Central Havana. The triangular route covered some thirty-five miles. 'One night, just before dawn, I fell asleep riding my bicycle and crashed into a dumpster. The bike was finished. I hurled it into the bin and from then on I hitched rides. But rarely with cars.'

Why not with cars?

Mario's smile disappeared and he asked if I was prepared for some uncomfortable truths. 'Let's see, how should I begin? I was a student, hardworking, *un muchachito integrado*, a young man who participated in the Revolution. But my facial characteristics do not fit the part, if you get what I mean. On the street I am taken for, how should I put it, a *negrón*, a big Black man. On the street folks I don't know shout *negrón* as I walk by. I think, given my appearance, people can't imagine I am a university student. That's why I didn't waste my time trying to hitch rides with cars. Now do you understand? It was very unlikely people who had cars would stop and give me a break. But with truck drivers, I am a... they'd call out, "*Hermano*, brother, come on let's go, jump in the back." Sometimes I'd ride in a truckful of construction materials, sometimes full of grease. I'd carry soap and wash when I got to school. I remember, once I jumped into a truck full of oil. My hands were completely coated when I got to university.'

Tell me, what does a university student look like?

'I think it dates from a long way back. The Revolution has been going for fifty-plus years, but there are many ways of thinking from before that haven't changed. The most difficult thing to change is people's minds. The way I see it, it's not discrimination in the sense that all Cubans have the same opportunities... But people still have prejudices. I don't have the statistics, but Black people make up most of the prison population. Why? Because they grow up in marginal barrios. Their families may be problematic. They may have suffered from a lack of parental attention when they were young.'

There are no official statistics on Cuba's prison population by race. But in 2005 Esteban Morales Domínguez, one of Cuba's leading specialists on race, said that approximately eighty-five per cent of the Cubans in prison were 'dark skinned'.[5]

Do you think there could be a problem with the police?

'Yes, definitely. The police stopped me mountains of times. I'll tell you why. At that time university students specialising in art and design wore their hair in weird ways. They looked like they'd never picked up a comb. They wore old clothes. I had my hair in braids, dreadlocks, shortish ones, sort of like corn braids but different. I looked the prototype of a *jinetero*, a sex worker, the type tourists go for. I'll show you my old university ID.' Mario found a faded photograph of his younger self. 'As an art student I was plugged into a different scene. I was a student but to some I looked like a *jinetero* and everywhere I went police would ask for my identity card. Not only would I show it, I would say, look here's my identity card, my university card, my Young Communists card. "OK, OK," they'd say, "move along." I'd take one step and another would ask for my identification.' Recalling these incidents made Mario give a nervous laugh. 'After I cut my hair and changed my haircut they stopped me less. When I started wearing glasses they stopped me even less. With glasses and closely cropped hair I didn't fit the image of a *jinetero*... I don't see this as discrimination so much as a lack of vision, let's call it obtuse vision, short-sightedness. The police on the beat are from the lowest ranks. They don't have sufficient culture or education to make judgements.'

Many police on the streets of Havana are Afro-Cubans from Oriente, the eastern provinces. The racial profiling Mario describes is not white police stopping Black people, often it is Black police stopping Black Cubans – and Black tourists.

When I interviewed Mario in 2016, a month after President Obama visited Cuba, he began by talking about Black exclusion and his own experiences. Perhaps seeing President Obama among Cuba's almost exclusively white leadership prompted him to think again about racial discrimination.

'In art school there were two Blacks in my class of thirty students. At San Alejandro, the college I never attended, there were very few Blacks, very few. In my pre in the countryside there was a rich mix of students. The proportion of Blacks, whites, and *mestizos* [mixed race students] was about equal. The same goes for military service and Orden 18. When I got to university of the 380 students in my year at the Advanced Institute of Industrial Design only ten of us were Black. That is something like .001 per cent.' (Actually it is 2.6 per cent, but Mario remembered feeling he was the only Afro-Cuban.) 'The faculties with a higher proportion of Blacks are sports, where there are many Blacks, and, well, I can't name any others, maybe medicine.'

Despite Afro-Cubans representing approximately thirty-six to sixty-five per cent of the Cuban population,[6] Mario's experience was that at the elite institutions he attended – a specialist middle school and university – there were few students of African descent. But in the army and in his ordinary pre there was a 'rich mix'. The low proportion of Afro-Cubans at elite schools is not surprising; Cuban analysts of race have been pointing this out for years. I was interested to hear Mario say that a highish proportion of medical students are Afro-Cuban, a judgement an Afro-Cuban medical student confirmed.

When Lilia asked Mario in 2006 whether racism might have played a part in his rejection from San Alejandro he seemed uneasy, before admitting it might have. Ten years later he was more comfortable talking about racism. His new attitude may have reflected changes in the public discourse, as well as a certain openness that comes from narrating your life story. In 2003, in a rambling and contradictory speech Fidel said the Revolution had not been entirely successful in eliminating differences between Black and the white Cubans. Fidel's dictum combined with pressure from Afro-Cuban intellectuals gradually opened up conversations about racism, but not at the highest political levels. Several manuscripts languishing at the back of publishers' drawers saw the light of day,[7] and the government became more tolerant of Afro-Cuban cultural, literary and feminist groups.

Mario's explanation of the causes of racism is compatible with the official narrative. He said, in effect, that after racial segregation had been outlawed in 1959, institutional discrimination ceased to exist. Continuing racism in the form of harassment, profiling, name calling and Afro-Cubans' relative invisibility at the upper echelons of officialdom reflected historical prejudices and a culture of poverty that would eventually die out. In the official framework racism is a holdover from the past, not a phenomenon continually recreated by economic and social conditions.[8]

An egalitarian fantasy: 'It was something like socialism is supposed to be.'

Mario recalled the consequences of economic inequality at university. 'In my university days some students could afford to buy soap, detergent, clothing, and go out to clubs. Others, including me, didn't have those possibilities. Some students had parents who not only were able to *resolver*, provide, their day-to-day needs, but parents who gave them more, sometimes much much more. Some students even had a car and a computer at home. Their living conditions were completely different from mine. At a time when government offices did not have colour printers they submitted assignments printed in colour at home.

'Universities had become very elitist by then [the late 1990s]. People went to university because they enjoyed certain social conditions and had parents who supported them economically. Others did not have those advantages. Many of the students who started university with me dropped out. Now they are working at who knows what. They are employed, like I was, as an assistant custodian or something like that. They work to survive, to earn a couple of pesos. Some students who graduated in my class are, like me, working in the state sector. In addition to our government jobs we have to work the street doing whatever, selling paintings in the tourist market, making crafts, anything to earn a few dollars without which we could not survive. We just about get by, *inventando*, making do, from one day to the next.' Mario's use of the verb *inventar* implies they worked in the shadow of the law.

When Mario was at university his idea of paradise was going with friends to the Coppelia ice cream parlour in Vedado. He remembered one outing to Coppelia as 'something like socialism is supposed to be. From each according to their means, to each equally.'

'My crowd at university, we called ourselves *los alternativos*. We were interested in studying and we came from different social backgrounds. Some were the sons and daughters of papá y mamá. Papá y mamá resolved their economic problems. Some, like me, were the children of workers. Despite this we shared an egalitarian ideology. I'll never forget the evening our entire group went to Coppelia. Each of us was going to go in individually and, per usual, pay for our own ice cream. Spontaneously the group stopped. We said, let's all go in together and share. So the children of mamá y papá and the children of ordinary workers joined together.

'One of my friends said, "*Caballeros*, gentlemen, contribute whatever you can, one or two pesos, ten if you can afford it, regardless of what you order." I frequently tell this story, just telling it gives me pleasure. Everyone started chipping in; some of us didn't have any money but it didn't make any difference.

What was important was sharing. One student was from Angola and she put in the most because she had more money than the rest of us.

'We called over the waiter; at that time Coppelia still had waiters and lots more flavours. It was another era. Coppelia was really Coppelia; now it's a shadow of its former self. We began to order: "A salad for everyone, a *turquino* for everyone, a *vaca negra* for everyone, a cola," and so on. We kept ordering until we spent all the money on the table. Then we began to eat. Everyone ate the same food regardless of the amount of money they contributed. Some put in more, some less, some nothing, but we all ate the same things. When we couldn't eat any more we began to throw the ice cream. At that moment we were transformed into *una sola cosa*, we became one. It was a beautiful moment. For an instant there were no differences among us. It was something like socialism is supposed to be. From each according to their means, to each equally.'

The Coppelia story duplicates Mario's memories of *la merienda* with one important variation. The *merienda* story is set in the 1980s and recalls a time of economic equality. The Coppelia story is set circa 2000, a time of rising inequality. Significantly, both stories focus on food, Cubans' most elemental measure of equality and inequality.

'The neighbourhood is changing... Money has become everything.'

After graduating from university Mario designed pots and pans at an aluminium factory in Regla. He welcomed the opportunity to put his artistry into practice, and he wanted his pots and pans to be beautiful, functional, and durable – like Bauhaus objects. The salary was decent, and if he clocked in on time each day, participated in voluntary labour, and marched in the Plaza de la Revolución on national holidays he would receive a bonus in hard currency. It was a dream job, but Mario quit when his boss refused to adopt his designs. 'I was too young to start compromising my principles.'

After months looking for work, Mario took a temporary position developing websites at the Ministry of Industry. The salary was considerably lower than he earned before, but he saw the potential of getting in early on Cuba's opening to the internet. Mario had little knowledge of computers and had never accessed the web. Within a couple of months he was designing CDs and websites for major state organisations.

Mario had been working at the Ministry for two years when Lilia first interviewed him in 2006 and he said the sparkle was wearing off. He was unhappy about his low pay, collusion between management and the trade union, and the sluggish bureaucracy. He complained jokingly that voluntary labour was neither voluntary nor labour. He contemplated resigning but decided that working in IT had advantages. He was able to surf the web, which most Cubans didn't even know about, and while his generation complained of their isolation, he felt Facebook kept him in touch with international events and with his many friends who had left.

'Lack of freedom to use the web is one of the reasons young Cubans leave. They feel cut off. A person who surfs the web has an open door on the world. Access to the web transforms people, it changes the way you think, it expands your horizons. Most Cubans have never used the internet. They don't even know it exists.' Alejandro, also a computer geek, said the same thing.

Changes in his neighbourhood and among his friends were also upsetting him. 'For many people money has become everything. When I was young, people went to fiestas to dance and have a good time. Now they go to show off their clothes and expensive drinks. People used to enjoy being themselves. Guys hung out with you because they liked you, not because of what you had.

These emotions are getting lost. I wish our society would recover human feelings.

'The problem with youth is that although the Revolution offers opportunities to everyone who wants to better themselves, not everyone can take advantage of them. The material conditions of many families won't allow it. Take me, and I'm not trying to justify myself, I didn't have the best conditions. Nevertheless, I managed to better myself. These days young people don't see a future in studying, in self-improvement. They don't want to contribute to society. They want a job that pays in hard currency or one where they can steal.

'I shouldn't generalise. Some young people want to improve themselves, but the majority have lost faith in the future; they've lost hope. Think of it this way. It used to be that people wanted to have one doctor and one lawyer in the family. Now they want a butcher and someone who works in a company or a hotel. It doesn't matter if they are a driver or a chambermaid, what's important is they can steal. If they can't steal at least they will get tips in hard currency and the family can buy soap, detergent, and all the stuff you can only buy in dollars. That's the new mentality; people think about how they are going to feed and clothe themselves. In addition, young people's heads are stuffed full of illusions and desires. Many go so far as to forego food to get a gold tooth. For that kind it's all about appearances. They want to show off their money.'

It's ironic that Esteban, the feisty black marketeer, and Mario, the Communist Party militant, both bemoaned the decline in values. Nevertheless, it isn't surprising that Cubans who mingled with tourists and watched Hollywood movies yearned for glitzy clothes and gold jewellery they had never had. Hollywood's genius is its ability to create illusions and desires, and younger Cubans were particularly susceptible, having grown up in an era of savage austerity.

'The Party's principles are beautiful, but it was an illusion. It was utopian.'

When Mario's temporary contract at the Ministry became permanent in 2005, he advanced from the Young Communists to the Communist Party proper. He recalled his disappointment when he got to know the Party from the inside.

'I'm not like some Party members who seem like they're from outer space. I'm rational. I live. I suffer. I have feelings the same as everyone else. My motive for joining the Party was to struggle for change, changes like reducing somewhat the despotism and the hypocrisy, *la doble cara*. Do you know what I mean?' *Doble cara* is two-facedness. In Cuba *la doble cara* implies pretending to support the government and obey the law, when, in fact, you oppose the government and break the law. Many Cubans said *la doble cara* had eaten away at the moral foundations of society, and bred cynicism.

'I thought that as a Party militant I could help overcome all this. Now I'm on the inside I realise that…' Mario paused, maybe to figure out how he was going to phrase his criticisms, and what he wanted to say on a recording. 'There are many things about the Party that work badly because of the situation the country faces, the blockade and other things. There are also many things that work badly because of our own internal blockade, the way we deal with issues, many, many issues. I think that everything, everything, everything shouldn't follow a single Party line. There should be variations, modifications, angles and lots of flexibility.

'I believe many people are…' Mario stumbled, searched for words and started again. 'I have observed that many people are Party militants for their own convenience. I mean if you are a militant you enjoy a certain standing; you have a certain impunity. You can do certain things without drawing attention to yourself. If you are a militant you have a certain authority in your workplace and if you know how to take advantage of it you might get a trip abroad. If you are not a militant you have fewer possibilities. The Party's principles are beautiful. But it was an illusion. It was utopian. The principles don't relate to how things really are. When you apply these principles to the real world it isn't the same. For one thing times have changed. My parents' lives in the 1950s were nothing like my experiences of growing up in the 1980s.'

'Cubans today are not the same as Cubans back then.'

'I think a lot of doctrines don't adapt well to present-day circumstances, nor do they fit the Cubans of today who are not the same as Cubans were back then. In the past Cubans had a goal. They achieved it and they were proud of their achievements. Today's Cubans have different goals, different aspirations, and they want to achieve them come what may, regardless of the international situation. You see what I'm saying? I think that if I had understood all this before joining the Party, I would not have joined. I would be the same person I am now, and I like to think that I am not a bad person. I enjoy the work I do. I am a good, disciplined worker, and that would have been enough for me. I would not have had to join the Party, far from it. But these things happen,' Mario laughed nervously, 'and now I can't see a way of getting out.' Willingness to voice criticisms of the Party in a recorded interview epitomised Mario's honesty.

Beneath the radiant smile Mario felt increasingly disillusioned. He felt his job was becoming humdrum. He found the bureaucracy at work stifling. He couldn't buy basic food and clothing on his state salary. Sometimes he wanted to go dancing but he didn't have the money. He shared the same tenement room he had always lived in with his sister and her two children. He wanted more privacy, somewhere he could bring a girlfriend. 'Time is running out. I'm not that young anymore.' His neighbours who worked the black market or received cash from abroad were living far more comfortably. Perhaps Mario's disenchantment contributed to his candour.

What are your happiest and saddest memories?

'The happiest is the day they handed me my diploma in the Aula Magna of the University of Havana. It was the prize for all my efforts. The saddest is the day I lost my mamá. She was young, only fifty. Her death was one of those life-altering events that takes your breath away. She had advanced breast cancer. She went to the doctor, they did an x-ray and told her there was nothing they could do. They sent her home, nothing else. Watching her decline broke my heart. I was at her side when she died. It burned my soul. These things happen in life but they don't reduce your will to live. On the contrary, you begin to reflect and you say to yourself this is the hand that was dealt me for my time here on earth. Then you think, what if, in the time I am given, I work, I struggle, work, struggle, that's all I do. And yet, despite everything, I can't get what I want. Do you see what I am driving at? Struggle, more struggle, work, more work, an entire life of struggle and work. Then the end.'

Mario speaks a beautiful combination of prose and poetry that reveals his deepest feelings.

'Life has happy moments, though not many. There are moments when you feel good, more when you feel bad. As human beings we have defence mechanisms. You almost always forget the bad. That's how life is, neither black nor white but medium grey. Life is grey, and grey is not good. White is feeling you are fulfilled as a human being; you enjoy life's bounty; you see your dreams come true. Black is when everything around you is sad, very sad, dark, very dark. I think the day will come when life in Cuba is white again. Before that at least it will be yellow. The sun will rise every day. It will shine on us and warm us. The problem is knowing how to take advantage of the sun, of the opportunities you are given. Until now I've managed to take advantage of the opportunities that have come my way. When future opportunities arise I hope it won't be too late for me. I don't know if I'll be here; I don't know where I'll be, but wherever I am, I'm going to grab those opportunities. I won't let them slip away.'

Mario was determined to make something of himself but fearful that with Cuba's long economic crisis the opportunities open to him might be infinitesimal. He worried that his future would be medium grey. Despite his inner turmoil, Mario was almost always smiling a beautiful smile that spread happiness.

Mario ended his interview in 2010 on a hopeful note by quoting a famous line from José Martí. '*Quien tiene mucho adentro necesita poco afuera. Quien lleva mucho afuera tiene poco adentro.* (A person who has a lot on the inside needs little on the outside. A person who wears a lot on outside has little inside.)[9] These are my dreams, my yearnings. I hope they will come true.'

13

ALINA RODRÍGUEZ ABREU

San Miguel del Padrón, Havana

Backstory

The Havana International Film Festival is a starry assemblage of cinema, politics, entertainment and celebrity, with red carpets outside the capital's main cinemas. Its programme features blockbusters, arthouse movies and the occasional surprise. As I was standing in line at the Cine Yara in December 2010, a young Cuban man in front of me launched into a paean. 'You've got to see *Buscándote Havana*, chica. It's a heartbreaker. The director was just twenty-one when she filmed inside illegal settlements. She shows how migrants from Oriente really live, the open sewers and the flimsy shacks. When bulldozers flatten their piecemeal huts they get deported and then come right back. Alina caught it all on camera. They tried to stop her,' the man lowered his voice and stroked his chin (the sign for Fidel), 'but she was unstoppable. It got passed from hand to hand at first as no one dared screen it. Now it's a phenomenon. Everyone here is talking about it, it's the documentary that broke taboos. She won a bunch of awards. It's on tonight at midnight, one showing only. Chica, you've got to go.'

Cuban moviegoers usually shout, joke, and carry on conversations with the characters on-screen. That night the crowd was silent, they didn't want to miss a word.

'Guantánamo [where she came from] is very backward. There's been no progress. The economy fell through the floor and things are difficult, very difficult,' Maria says, in the opening scene. She is sitting in front of a wooden hut in a squatter settlement in Regla. 'In Guantánamo you get at the most five eggs [per month on the ration]; in Havana they give out seven or eight.'

Fidel, a serious forty-something-year-old, shows his home to the camera. A hodgepodge of cardboard boxes and metal from discarded refrigerators. Fidel left Santiago in 1989 in search of work. He has no home to go back to, no ties, he says, eyes piercing the audience.

'I am not allowed to work. I'm an illegal. I work whenever I can, whenever I can find it, riding a cycle taxi. I work to feed my family. I am persecuted because I am an oriental [from Oriente, the eastern provinces]. I am persecuted because I am an illegal. They [officials] think illegals are against the government. We are not. This barrio goes en masse to the marches in the Plaza of the Revolution to defend the principles of the Revolution. The whole barrio takes part in the Battle of Ideas. I don't receive food [on the *libreta*, the ration book]. My children go hungry. They cry from hunger. I am distraught. Life here is hard, very, very hard.'

Fidel turns away from the camera to hide his tears.

Between sobs, Lisbet, his wife, says, 'I fought the bureaucracy. The red tape, you just can't imagine it. Finally, an official at the Ministry told me, "In the eyes of the Revolution your baby does not exist. We can't give her milk because she doesn't have an identity card."' Wiping away tears, she says, 'I am sure, absolutely sure, that if Fidel [Castro] knew, he would solve our problems.' Her husband declares indignantly, arms flailing, 'I have revolutionary credentials. I was named after Fidel, and I named my son Elián, after the boy-hero of the struggle against Yankee imperialism. Here, in this house, live Fidel and Elián.'

Fidel and Lisbet had the audience weeping.

Juxtaposed with scenes of Fidel, Lisbet, Maria, and others talking of their plight, Pablo Rodríguez, a sociologist, analyses the migrant problem. 'The government has to regulate migration. Faced with longstanding economic difficulties, we simply do not have the resources to provide more houses, water, and sewage in La Habana.' But he also says, 'Socialism cannot allow itself the privilege of excluding a group of human beings under the law... Socialism is not a perfect society. The attempt to present an image of a perfect society goes against what socialism is. Socialism seeks to create something better, a social order of a different type, a world that is more humane.'

Alina said, in the interview, almost the same thing. That her generation is not demanding the impossible; they want the government to tell the truth. To stop trying to silence people who say out loud what everyone knows to be true.

As the film draws to a close, Ray Fernández sings 'Lucha tu yuca Taíno' in the background. It was young Cubans' protest anthem, and everyone in the audience sings along. The chorus has everyone chanting, '*El cacique tiene el power absoluto. Pero tu...Tu lucha tu yuca, Taino.*' ('The chief has the power, absolute power, while you, you Indian, you struggle for your basic food'.)[1]

The crowd lingered in the lobby, reluctant to break the spell. 'What with everything they've been through, those people's faith in the Comandante is amazing,' one young woman said out loud, to no one in particular. 'How can you be an illegal in your own country?' said another. 'The Palestinos are invisible in the media, hidden. This film makes us see them, forces us to pay attention to their problems.' A young man cried out, 'This thing is changing. I tell you, at last it's changing.' Some nodded tentatively. I asked him what he meant. 'Screening *Buscándote Havana* and *Memorias del Desarrollo*[2] here at the Film Festival signals a change. They're loosening the iron grip.'

Cubans wanted changes, though many feared they might lose more than they gained.

After Fidel ceded power to his brother Raúl in 2006, some felt the control they had become accustomed to was easing. The sudden, but hardly unexpected, succession created a sense of uncertainty, possibility, and for the leadership, vulnerability. A few writers and artists began to feel out how much criticism would be tolerated, how far they could go. Alina finished *Buscándote Havana* at the end of Fidel's rule when a sense of possibility was brewing.

In an outburst dubbed the 'Pavonato', named after a repressive Minister of Culture in the 1970s, a small circle of intellectuals turned up the heat. They denounced, in a flurry of emails to each other, the cultural crackdown that had taken hold three decades earlier. Writers who had been silenced, whose work had been deemed not sufficiently revolutionary, or revolutionary in the wrong way, revealed what it had meant for them, some for the first time. Their books had been banned. They had been banished to provincial towns, forced to work in lowly jobs, or they had been sent to rural labour camps for moral re-education. The Pavonato was cathartic, for those who divulged their secrets. The Cuban population as a whole didn't hear about these revelations, nothing surfaced in the official media. Yet saying what had been unsayable for thirty years was a liberation.

A hullabaloo of a different order contributed to the sense of change. Fidel emerged from retirement in September 2010 to tell a visiting US journalist that 'the [Cuban] model doesn't even work for us anymore'. Everyone knew it, they lived it, after all, but no one, least of all the Comandante, had ever said so that bluntly, or publicly. Highly placed officials implied this was an old man's blunder. A sign that Fidel was losing his mind. A more compelling interpretation is that his madness had a method.

The historic leader set the stage for his brother's pronouncement: 'Unless we change, we will be swept away.' The state sector is bloated and inefficient, declared Raúl Castro a short time later. 'We need to update our socialist model.' What exactly that meant was unclear, even to top government economists. Parts of the new policy seemed straightforward enough, for a time. Raúl announced the government's intention to lay off more than one million state employees who would be free to start small businesses. In the official vocabulary they would not be unemployed (*desempleado*); rather they would be 'available' (*disponible*). *Disponible* to open a cafeteria, say, or a barbershop, or a garage. *Disponible* to work for the new breed of petty capitalists. Raúl declared that food rationing would also be cut back.

Announcements of the reform coincided, as it happened, with the Film Festival, and with my interviews with Alina Rodríguez and other young Cubans. Everyone I met wanted to talk about the *lineamientos*, the guidelines, the official list of services, including manicurist, party clown and catering, which the state would leave to private enterprise. Publication of the *lineamientos* caused a commotion. Families got together around the kitchen table to pore over the descriptions of authorised activities, some ordinary, some comical. They talked about what kind of business they might open without state support, investment, or training. They tried to figure out an angle. Most of the young Cubans I interviewed were sceptical that they could make a go of a small business. They were also afraid. Afraid they would be one of the one million to lose their job, which meant losing their meagre but secure income. If rationing was to go too, they would lose the cheap food they relied on for half of what they ate.

The next morning I phoned Alina; a friend gave me her number. She sounded thrilled when I asked if I could interview her for a book about young Cubans' lives. 'Can you come tomorrow morning?' she shouted over the din of barking dogs and clattering dishes. 'I live far away. Catch a *camello* in front of the Cine Yara.

Get off when you see a giant billboard of Hugo Chávez grinning. You can't miss him. The *camello* takes more than an hour, better count on two. The stop is Sara's bodega in Barrio Obrero, San Miguel de Padrón.'

14

JUAN GUILLARD MATUS

Santa Ana de la Laguna

Having applied unsuccessfully to join the army after he dropped out of school, Juan was delighted to be called up for military duty at the end of the 1980s. He had always wanted to be a spy, and he thought the army would not only prepare him for his dream career but give him back his lost years. By the time he was discharged the world he knew had vanished. Cuba's international allies had perished, the country's economy was in crisis, and the system that incorporated Cubans into the body politic was disintegrating. State sector jobs were hard to come by and didn't pay a living wage. Juan came home to a community on the brink.[1]

Like every Cuban of his generation Juan grew up expecting to fill a slot in the state machinery that would provide a modest, but adequate, standard of living. Instead he had to invent a way of life. At the beginning of the Special Period, he and his best friend Leo looked for jobs so they could buy food and clothing. Eventually they found temporary work on the loading dock of a nearby hotel. Juan said it was a good job, implying he received hard currency in tips. A year later, when Leo was promoted, Juan was fired. Leo is white. 'Race might have played a part,' said a Cuban specialist on race. 'Many Blacks lost out on jobs in the tourist sector.' Officials felt that Afro-Cubans' *presencia,* appearance, did not project the desired image.[2]

After that setback, Juan held a series of manual jobs in the state sector, less to put food on the table, than to stay on the right side of the law. Most of his income came from selling chickens and piglets to his neighbours, who sacrificed the animals in Santería ceremonies before cooking them up for lunch.

Lacking food, clothing, and most importantly hope, many people from Santa Ana tried to flee the island on rafts. Like Mario's brother, Leo and his entire family joined the *balsero* exodus in 1994. Balseros hoped to be picked up at sea by the US Coast Guard and taken to Miami, or, failing that, survive the treacherous crossing. Rosa, our fixer in Santa Ana, told me that the township had the distinction of having more balseros per capita than anywhere else in the country. True or not, the *balsero* crisis prompted Santa Ana's town council to allow Juan to put on free discos twice a week in the defunct social club. 'It gave young people a place to go besides Miami… besides, it was my *trabajo voluntario,* voluntary labour,' Juan said, laughing. In another era, voluntary labour involved cutting sugar cane and picking coffee. To Juan's dismay, when the sound system broke the council asked a small businessman, a *cuentapropista*, to take over the disco, which he ran as a money-maker. The new private club was a spectre of things to come.

Changes underway

'When Leo and his family joined the scramble to leave, I was overcome by a sadness from hell. It was like losing my right hand. If you think about it that massive exodus was not, or not mostly, because of political problems. No one really cares whether Fidel gives the orders, or Almeida, or Lage [top figures in Fidel's government]. It's the economy. People always want to live the best they can. For instance, who wouldn't want a car. Just suppose I had to go to a meeting right now. Let's say I had to be there at one-thirty. A car wouldn't be a luxury; it would be a necessity. Or suppose I had to pick up medicine in Alamar [a huge housing estate east of Havana]. Most medicines no longer are available here; we have to go to Alamar. If I could go by car, I would pick it up and return in ten minutes. In ten minutes flat my car would be back in my garage. My only desire is to live the way I want, nothing more, like a normal human being, all easy and simple, with all the stuff.'

Juan's idea that he needed a car 'to live like a normal human being' was the product of ideological and material changes underway. Cubans had always admired American cars, but car ownership was rare, far beyond the reach of most people on the island. As private enterprise became more common, Juan began to dream the American Dream. Yet to appear reasonable he pretended he needed a car to carry out official work and pick up medicine. 'I wouldn't have to have a brand-new car, this year's model. But I need something to get around, even if it's nothing more than a puny little motor scooter.'

A puny little motor scooter was another fantasy. The government rewarded directors of research centres and heads of ministerial departments with motor scooters. Cubans at Juan's level rarely had a motor scooter or a car. Consequently, islanders refer to ordinary people as 'cubanos de a pie', Cubans on foot.

'For a poor person I have enough.'

Juan repeatedly described himself as a poor person. 'For a poor person I have enough. I have a place to live... I have a refrigerator, it's a family heirloom. I have a blender and a fan, both thirty years old. The Revolution gave them to my mother. Recently, I bought this battered up clothes washer, it's a Úrica.'

Úricas were made in the USSR and sold in the Gold and Silver Stores that Pavel remembered from his childhood in the 1980s.

Does it still work?

'Like a million dollars. I'm not in need of anything. I have a television, two in fact. One in colour, my ex gave it to me; it's being repaired. I have an air conditioner, but it doesn't work. Leo's family gave it to me when they left. You see, I have nothing to complain about. I live more or less. For a poor person I have enough. I have the essentials. I have music equipment.'

Although Juan frequently griped about low salaries and scarce food, he always tried to look on the bright side. He had a house full of equipment, though most of it didn't work.

How is the house in bad weather? Do you feel it?

'I've never left in a hurricane. I thought the trees were going to fall on the house, but inside I felt nothing.' When pressed, he admitted his roof and walls leaked, and he lacked running water indoors. 'I want to add a bathroom and a kitchen, and repair the roof and walls. I'm in the planning stage, but I get no help [from the state]. I am struggling on my own to make improvements little by little.'

Juan, would you ever leave Santa Ana for another place?

'No, I don't think so. My stepmother invited me to live with her in Havana, near the Hotel Cohiba. But I don't like Havana. I like the countryside. Here I breathe *aire natural*. I am in direct contact with plants and animals, with the whole world. I enjoy raising animals. I like all that. I could not adapt to Havana, to the noise, the cars, the smell, the fumes, the pollution... I would give everything I have in the world simply to be allowed to stay here on my little plot.' His stepmother inviting him to live in posh Vedado does not ring true. In oral history narrators can portray themselves as the person they would like to be, or the person they feel the interviewers would admire.

Santa Ana held more for Juan than tranquillity, clean air and a tiny homestead. He was beginning to feel accepted, at least some of the time. 'Here in this town I am like an idol. Bam, bam, [people say] this guy is one beautiful *negrito*. You see, I get along with everyone. I don't say but or why to anyone. Everywhere I go people like me. I don't know what it is about me.' Feeling a part of the community is important to Juan, maybe because he felt ostracised as a child. He talks a great deal about his acceptance, probably too much. It's constantly on his mind.

Miami vis-à-vis Cuba

When we first interviewed Juan most narrators avoided talking about exile. Attempted escape was a crime, and in official eyes anyone who left was a traitor. Victoria, however, ignored the taboo.

Tell me what it was like when your compañero *Leo came back to visit?*

'Ay, that. It brought tears to my eyes. The first time Leo came back he jumped out of the car shouting, "Brother, my brother, I don't want to leave." "Are you crazy," I said, "You risked your life. Now you're saying you don't want to go back?" Sometimes Leo says he doesn't like coming home because it's so painful to leave. He told me that after seeing the whole wide world balseros say, "Cuba is your country, it has the smell you love." Leo says, "It's incredible but when they come back, as soon as they smell Cuba they start to cry."'

Yes, it's like that.

'That's the truth. Our land has pull. Leo says, "Bam, it tugs at you even when you don't want it to. But can you imagine who would want to stay? The situation here is hell, the politics, the blockade, all the other stuff." How exactly does Leo put it? "If food, transport and housing were better you wouldn't have to leave."' My teammates got a kick out of Leo/Juan's phrase and they repeated it often. It became a sort of shorthand to sum up many of the interviews.

Juan combined Leo's voice with his own so frequently and so smoothly sometimes it was hard to distinguish which of the two supposedly was talking. It came naturally; many narrators adopted this sort of ventriloquism to guard against reprisals. Although Juan probably intended to camouflage some of his views, still my Cuban colleagues were amazed by his bluntness.

What is there on the other side that attracts? (The other side meaning the US, particularly Miami, on the other side of the Florida Straits.)

'Ah, it's development. Oh, I am speaking about them [my friends over there]. What with the hassle, no, no, no, I'm not talking about me. I don't want to leave, even if it were handed to me on a plate. I'd just like to visit.' (Juan did not want us thinking he wanted to emigrate as it might get him into trouble.) 'But they say that over there they have everything. You must work hard, but they have everything. Though some things they don't have much of; they don't have tranquillity like we have here.' Many young Cubans said that in US hard work pays off, you can even buy a nice car, while in Cuba hard work gets you nowhere.

'The last time Leo came back he brought his young daughter with him. Leo and I were sitting right there, inside the doorway, talking about this and that, drinking. The door was open, and his little girl was playing right there beside the fence. A boy walked past shouting something unintelligible. It totally unhinged Leo. "Catherine," he started screaming. "Leo, what's happened?" I said. "Fuck, for a minute I thought I was back there. There a child can't be outside like they can here," Leo said.

'Here you see young kids at the disco, eleven, twelve, even eight years old. The parents aren't worried. It's eleven something at night, and they're still there. There's no danger. Over there you can't do that,' Juan explained. 'Leo says you can't be outside. They'll either assault you or do this and that. He says, "Over there it's terrible. They'll kidnap your child and you won't see her ever again, never again." I'm telling you, over there there's lots and lots of violence, lots and lots. People get killed fairly often. Of course, things like that happen here too, but they don't show it on TV. It happens, though much, much less. Over there, it's a big, big country; they have a lot of liberty, and everyone carries guns. Over there they sell guns to anyone.

'Leo said, "Juan, every now and again you hear pam, pam, pam and when you wake up in the morning someone is dead. They killed several of our buddies, balseros, seems they were involved in drugs. Lazarito, you remember him, they put him in the trunk of a car. He wanted to come back here but he couldn't. They killed him. Over there, funeral corteges go past all the time." Leo said, "Over there I've got my car. I've got my job. I earn enough even for fun things. I have a TV that gets hundreds of channels. But despite all the things I have over there, I want to come back here. Well, what I really want is to come back here with my car and with everything I've got over there. This country is very tranquil, the climate is very good and everything. But the economy, it stinks. It really, really, stinks. Forget the notion that Cuba will ever turn into a developed country, an economic and military powerhouse. Just forget it."'

Juan pretending to be Leo tallied up the pros and cons of Miami versus Cuba. On the Miami side of the equation he included a car, a TV that gets hundreds of channels, hard work that pays enough even for fun things, but also out-of-control violence. On the Cuban side of the equation, he included tranquillity, personal security, a good climate, but an economy that really, really stinks.

But you, have you any plans to, err, leave? Or will you stay in Santa Ana?

Juan tried to wriggle out of answering, but Victoria persisted.

But you? Will you stay with this [Cuba]?

'Good or bad, I'll stay with this. *Bueno*, if tomorrow someone says, "Do you want to go to Canada?" Well maybe... I don't know what it is about that country that attracts me.'

Juan vacillated. Perhaps he wanted to leave but feared repercussions if he told them. My hunch, however, is that he was ambivalent about staying or leaving. Although 'having everything' was tempting, what he really enjoyed was breeding animals, socialising, listening to music and relaxing. Also, Juan might have feared Miami. If Leo, who is white, was terrified by the violence, how would he, an Afro-Cuban, cope? My sense is that Juan felt deep down that Miami was not for him. But Canada, well, it was a great unknown.

Race and sex

Victoria coaxed Juan to talk about his love life.

How is your life as far as girls are concerned?

'It's something else,' he replied jovially.

Tell us about it.

In the middle of a long, comedic story about his romantic adventures, Victoria interrupted Juan to ask,

Your partners, are they white or Black girls?

I flinched when I heard this on the recording. Would she have asked a white man that question? Juan instantly rejected Victoria's binary racial map, Black versus white, to portray most of his girlfriends in a spectrum of browns.

'I've never had a girlfriend of colour.' I think he meant Black. 'They've always been *trigueñas* [light brown-skinned, the colour of *trigo*, wheat] and *mulatas* [light skinned Afro-Cubans].'

Why?

'Because, well, I don't know. But the girls who know me say, "You like white girls." I reply, "That's because I haven't had much luck with…" You see, I fell in love with a young girl from Vedado, Marisel, a *prietecita* [a Black girl], shshsh [indicating very swish]. And with Mayté, who's blacker than me… Someone once said to me, "Black women aren't your thing. You don't go for Black women." It's true, I don't. The other day there was a Black girl from Alamar visiting in town, *una negrita que eso es una blanca echa a perder,* a Black girl so beautiful you'd think she were white.[3] She told me, "I don't like Black guys." *Caballeros* [addressing Victoria and Marisol], but the white girls, they just won't let go of me. One of the young guys I hang out with said, teasingly, "You're the boss man of white women." Forget that. Must be they go for me because I have *ashé*, charisma, or so people say.'

So white women fall for you?

'Yes, it makes me laugh, seems they go for this, my thing. That race, Dalmatian, a Black man with a white woman, that's fashionable now throughout the world. I used to think it was only in Cuba, but no, it's global… As for me, I'm very careful when it comes to partners…'

Most have been white?

'Some. Most were *trigueñas*. But the colour I like best is *indeado*, that oriental hue. That's the colour I like the best for breeding, as I say, for breeding, because it's the colour most…'

Don't you think you're being discriminatory, in a sense, regarding your own, towards people of your same skin colour? Don't you think so?

'No, I don't think so, because look at it this way, I don't like *negritos* with blondes. I don't like that race, too pale, too white. It doesn't grab me. Excuse me [apologising to Victoria and Marisol, who are white] but I'm not attracted to blondes. I wouldn't like that. The burnished, dark-skinned women, a little *mulata*, maybe that I could go for. But blondes and whites, no. My friends say, "OK, but you've had one." I have had one, but that was, in man talk, just one of those little adventures. For a real relationship, arm in arm and all that stuff, naw, I don't like it, I don't know why. I'm sorry. I don't like seeing a Black man with a blonde. I'm sorry, but it bothers me. I don't like that mixing. People say, "How strange, can you believe, a Black man who doesn't like blondes," and they carry on like that. I get along just fine with blondes. I fool around with them and all that, but not...'

Juan's riff on romance and race set off a storm in our team. Some colleagues felt he was playing stand-up comic, and the performance was a satire on sexist and racist stereotypes. A case of wanting to shock Marisol, Victoria, and people 'around the world', so they would not forget the cool Afro-Cuban dude. Others said his performance was a demonstration of sexist bravado. 'He personifies the sexism and racism of rural men... He is a very backward, very primitive, very sexist man,' said Diana, a fierce feminist. Talking to Juan over many years I think his performance was a mixture of his attempt to be funny and shock, and his machismo. Readers, you can listen to clips from Juan's interview and decide for yourselves.[4]

Juan's narrative of race and romance has another disturbing side. 'I don't like seeing a Black man with a blonde. I'm sorry but it bothers me. I don't like that mixing... I don't know why, but it bothers me.' You don't need to be Malcolm X to figure out why Juan feels uncomfortable when he sees Black men arm in arm with white women. He is all too familiar with the history of violence against African-American and Afro-Cuban men, and he experienced *en carne propia,* in his own flesh, the taboo against interracial couples, a taboo that endured long after Cuba's revolutionary triumph in 1959.

'If I can't be a boxer, at least I can be a ping pong player.'

Juan insisted he is an optimist, a doer. He said that while others whine about what they don't have, he always tries to make the best of things. 'You have to confront what life hands you. You should sit down and say to yourself, I won't be negative... Why should I hide myself in a corner? If someone who has less than me, or more, can succeed, why can't I? I believe that nothing is impossible except eternal life. Nobody lives forever. But nothing else is impossible; I say that to myself. There are people who say they are incapable of doing certain things. But me, I say, if so-and-so can fly a kite, so can I. It's true not everyone has the same knowledge, or the same mental abilities, or the same talent. If I can't be a boxer, at least I can be a ping pong player. If I can't ride a motorcycle; I can ride a bicycle. There is something I can do. I think that here on earth nothing is impossible. At least that's how it seems to me.'

As Juan became more expansive, Victoria probed his view of politics.

You said you don't like politics?
'No I don't. My stepfather used to tell me, "Don't get involved, politics is just like business."'

But you do go to the marches and light stuff like that, don't you?
Victoria was trying to pin him down, and at the same time

feeding him an appropriate response. Juan replied honestly – overly honestly. 'I participate in politics but only partially. I went to yesterday's May Day March, but not to march. I had a big responsibility. I had been asked to chaperone secondary school students. They [town officials] asked their teacher and me to accompany the students. They promised to give me *una merienda* and all that. I couldn't lose one, not even one; I couldn't let anything happen to them. After the teacher lost two students she refused to budge. We didn't leave Havana until after we'd found the kids, around three-thirty. You see, we couldn't leave anyone behind. Can you imagine returning to Santa Ana with one child missing. *Caramba.* The teacher was in an absolute frenzy.'

Juan could not resist joking about the May Day March, and it was just the beginning of an intriguing anecdote that revealed much about Juan's political views.

Juan, what does the Revolution mean to you?

Victoria's question came from a questionnaire the team had discarded when we decided to do non-structured interviews. Juan replied with a gust of laughter.

'Yesterday the Revolution drove me crazy, absolutely crazy. It turned me completely upside down. Yesterday's march in Havana, it was a scene, I have to say. The Comandante [Fidel Castro] was saying something. Lots of people wanted to listen. I caught a snatch. He said, "Reading from the pamphlet I have in my hand the general opinion is…" Well, if everyone thought the way the Comandante says we do it would be marvellous. The fact is everyone doesn't think the same. What a joke. Transport is bad here, bad there. He said something like he wants to improve this and that. But it is one thing to say, and another to do. It's all *un gran engaño*, a big deception. You hear this and you hear that about salaries going up, and I'm not denying that's what I want. Who wouldn't want salaries going up? Before, when I was a boy,

I remember my mother and stepfather would go out, we would all go out together and that's the truth. I can't complain about my childhood. We had everything. We could buy everything. Salaries were enough. We lived. We went to restaurants, we went to all the restaurants in Guanabo where we ate like normal people. Everything was in the same currency. But it's all changed, that's the truth. Everything has changed.'

With Juan in full flow, two neighbours breezed through his gate ostensibly to buy eggs. Perhaps their real motive was to see what was going on. Juan shooed them away. 'Can't you see I am in the middle of an important meeting with two women from Havana?'

As soon as they were gone Juan picked up the thread. Propelled by a rush of adrenaline, by frenzy, by who knows what, he said, 'A lot of people say, *coño*, it's late, too late. Maybe for some it's too late, but not for us, no, we are going to take some more. I say we're going to grab more, while we still can. I think so, yes, I think so. Before this comes... before this runs its course, because it is running its course, it has to. But listen to me, what the people of this country have lived through has not been easy. It's not been easy.'

Juan was amazingly blunt, given his audience. Perhaps he momentarily forgot who Victoria and Marisol represented. Clearly he forgot their recorder. '*Es un gran engaño*, it's all a big trick,' and his prediction that this – the Revolution – was coming to an end, was out-and-out subversive. When Victoria asked 'Juan, what does the Revolution mean to you?' she certainly wasn't expecting this.

As my colleagues, their heads reeling, packed up their papers to catch the bus to Havana, Victoria asked, 'Juan, do you realise how you have told the story of your life?'

'Yes, and I have enjoyed it. It would be wonderful if this interview travels around the world. I would be happy if people everywhere get to know me. Everywhere it goes I want people to say, "Listen to this cool Black dude." What I don't want them to say is, "Listen to this *negrón*, this big Black man, what a bore, always in a mess, always in trouble, getting into fights and this, that and the other." No, no, I don't want that. I always like to see the good in things.'

*

Several months later, in early 2006, I went to Santa Ana to interview Juan on my own. When I pinned a tiny microphone to his T-shirt he laughed with pleasure. 'It's just like the one Fidel wears on TV,' he said, glowing with pride. After some banter, he removed the microphone and clipped it to my long-sleeved, man-tailored shirt, part of the outfit I always wore to protect me from the burning sun. Juan said with a mischievous chuckle, 'OK, Liz, now *you* tell *me* the story of your life, from the very beginning.' For the next two hours, he quizzed me about growing up in Brooklyn, life in Great Britain, and why I was recording Cubans' life stories. Ostensibly asking me about Europe and the United States, he took pleasure in showing off his knowledge of world politics, geography and natural history. I asked where he learned all these things. 'From radio and television.' Juan joked a lot, and I laughed a lot, though often the joke was on me. Juan poked fun at my long-sleeved shirt, my large straw hat, and my ignorance of pop music and football. Although interviewees rarely mentioned my garbled Spanish-Brooklynese, Juan joked, 'It generates our mutual misunderstanding.' His routines about The Beatles, Manchester United and David Beckham were bravura performances. Thinking back on his controversial stories about race and romance I suspected his one-liners about Dalmatians, *chorongo* braids, *indeadas*, 'the colour I like the best for breeding,' were part of his regular comedy routine. Juan is a performer, and his impulse is to play his audience for a laugh. What better audience than academics, 'squares', from Havana and London who were hanging on his every word.

15

ESTEBAN CABRERA MONTES

Fontanar, Havana, 2005–06

'Memories are all I have left. It is my destiny.'

With American blue jeans increasingly unattainable and his relatives in Miami seemingly lost to him forever, Esteban began the 1990s ever more desperate to leave. Many of his friends had already left, which only made things worse, he said, partly as an appeal to Julia's pity so that she would help him escape.[1]

'Losing friends makes me tremendously anxious. With all the other pressures of living here, with all my personal shit, losing another friend would push me over the edge. I couldn't bear it. Lucky for them they're no longer here. I wish I were with them on the other side [of the Florida Straits]. I have memories of when we were together. Memories are all I have left. It is my destiny.'

How did they leave?

'They were lucky. All except one got out legally. My friend in the US – his first attempt wasn't so easy. He tried the usual way. He cobbled together a raft and threw himself into the sea. Same as me.'

'You?' Julia shouted over Nirvana's music.

Esteban had just turned up the sound to drown out his voice – narrators frequently did this. Although an estimated twenty per cent of Habaneros of Esteban's generation left in the 1990s, people were careful when they talked about leaving.

'Yes, me. I tried to leave in 1993, in the depths of the Special Period, a year before the flood of *balseros*. A lot of them died. I was barely twenty. I failed; I was unlucky, you could say. It takes a lot of courage to do it. There were just two of us, and we made a raft from six tyres, the small kind for cars, and a piece of canvas. We set off from Santa Cruz del Norte [a town thirty-five miles east of Havana] because my friend who lived there offered to help. He's in the US now; he won *el bombo* [the US visa lottery].[2] He hid our stuff until the time seemed right. It was all very dramatic. I said goodbye to my father. None of my friends knew, no one outside my family. It was pretty hard knowing you're taking such a huge risk.'

What did your father say?

'You really don't get it,' Esteban burst out laughing. '"Be careful, son. Son, take care of yourself."' Esteban imitated a cowboy's drawl. 'You've got to understand that here in Cuba throwing yourself into the sea on a raft is perfectly normal behaviour for lots of people, because so many do it. Lots have been lucky; others haven't. Cubans tend not to think about the negative. We always focus on the positive: if you make it, if you manage to reach that country, if you emigrate, your family's economic situation will change completely.'

Esteban's main concern, as far as we could tell, was his own wellbeing, but he seemed to think that invoking his family might elicit more sympathy.

'Getting back to my story, unfortunately I'm still here. Our raft was too flimsy for the rough seas and our provisions were swept overboard immediately. We hadn't made the raft strong enough. It wasn't a good model,' he summed up, laughing at his joke.

'We had to swim ashore in very cold water and hide in the bushes until morning, when we caught the bus back home. So much for my first attempt. Life carried on. I had to come back and face the reality of my country. I had to figure out how to confront my problems. I had to create a life.'

'Thanks to the blackouts I learned how to think.'

Most Cubans remembered the Special Period as the worst of times; Esteban remembered it as the best thing that had ever happened to him. A friend's parents and their friends got together during the nightly blackouts to discuss history, politics, literature, and to dance. Esteban joined the gatherings. He had dropped out of school when he was seventeen to support himself and he said the get-togethers gave him the education he had missed.

'Thanks to the blackouts, I learned how to think. I got to know interesting people, intellectuals and writers. I got into the habit of reading. Because I had left school early, that came as a shock. My intellect had been left behind, you could say. The gatherings helped me learn. My friend's mother was a professor of literature at the University of Havana. His father had been a writer but had stopped writing because it is difficult here to be a writer. All their friends were intellectuals. I remember that period very clearly, it was one of the most beautiful times of my life. Daily life was difficult; we had blackouts that lasted more than twelve hours; we had nothing, money was worthless. I lived through all that. It went on from 1990 through 1994, the year the people exploded [in the Malecón protest]. The next year, 1995, conditions improved a little bit.'

Ernesto 'Che' Guevara
cutting sugar cane.

A white dove lands on Fidel Castro's
shoulder as he delivers a speech to commemorate the thirtieth anniversary of the
Cuban Revolution in Havana, 1989.

Fidel Castro speaking at the Plaza de la Revolución,
Havana on Worker's Day, 1 May 2005.

Lined with shops, bars and galleries, Calle Opispo
is one of the busiest streets in Old Havana.

Paseo del Prado, a promenade that marks the division between the
Centro Habana and Old Havana municipalities of Havana.

A street in El Cerro, considered one of the poorest municipalities in Havana.

Miramar, one of the most affluent suburbs of Havana.

Downtown street in Old Havana.

Housing in Havana, photographed by the author while conducting interviews.

The 'camel' bus, the public bus network serving Havana.

The exterior of a small *mercadito* in Old Havana.

The Santiago de Cuba carnival, one of the largest and most famous carnivals in Cuba.

Cubans playing dominoes in the Havana streets, August 2014.

Village in the rural Pinar del Rio area, western Cuba.

Houses in the rural Vinales area, western Cuba.

An outlying neighbourhood of Santiago de Cuba, the second-largest city in Cuba after Havana, located in the southeast of the island.

'Those intellectuals discovered that the best way to pass the time during the blackouts was to party. They hooked up a lightbulb to a car battery, scrounged up batteries for a tape recorder, and played music from the 60s and 70s: The Beatles, The Who, Clearwater Revival. I learned a lot about that kind of music, about a lot of things. They sort of gave talks; it was all very attractive. Not only did they talk about art and books, they talked about their own experiences and frequently their stories were comical. When they started to talk, I moved closer and listened very carefully. After a while I tried to speak myself, I wanted to learn how to do it. This lasted for a couple of years. Those were marvellous years and I am grateful for having known those people. Their gatherings were the best thing that ever happened to me. My friends came to them too; they hadn't left yet. It was the most important moment in my life, and now it's gone. Life was shit before, now it's shit again.

'I remember those people saying they'd fought to make this revolution, but they'd been deceived. They'd participated on every front. They'd thought everything that was happening was for the good of society, but later their ideas changed. When the Revolution took a completely different turn, they decided it wasn't so good, not good at all. The system He imposed was very totalitarian and the Revolution hadn't turned out the way they had hoped. They felt He had not given them what they had expected. As the years passed, I often wondered what became of them. I never saw them again.

'They were deceived… He didn't give them what they had expected.' Esteban echoed the discourse of the Cuban exiles of the 1960s and 70s. *He*, of course, is Fidel Castro. As a precaution, in case someone overheard, instead of saying his name, Cubans used sign language. A tap on the shoulder signalled his epaulets; a stroke on the chin represented his beard. Esteban, even with Nirvana blaring in the background, was careful. It came naturally.

'I tried to speak myself.'

Esteban wanted Julia to understand that at one time he had been an activist, and organised gatherings to educate his friends. He implied that he had been part of the Varela Project, a pro-democracy movement the government suppressed.[3] Esteban may have exaggerated his political engagement. In telling your life story to a stranger you can inflate your importance, portray yourself in the way you want to be seen.

'We got together at a friend's house and I sort of... yes, I would talk about these things. But we had to stop because it could drive you insane. You can't go outside and shout, "IT IS NOT LIKE THEY SAY IT IS AND, PLEASE, WE NEED IT TO CHANGE!" We couldn't do that because we were only one, two, maybe three people. Others hung back... Let me tell you something... I created, umm...,' Esteban hesitated before correcting himself. 'I thought many times about creating an organisation. You see, sometimes you get so frustrated [he laughed nervously] that you look deep inside yourself and contemplate whether you should create an organisation, how can I put this, an organisation to bring about change. But it struck me as quite a difficult thing to do. No, not quite difficult, very difficult. I'm not talking about now. I thought about this years ago when the mood was more favourable, when people helped each other more... My friends had the same ideas, many of them aren't here any longer, but even they weren't prepared to...' His voice trailed off. Esteban wanted to be seen as a leader of sorts, an anti-hero.

'The young people coming of age now, the ones you see everywhere, they aren't interested in any of this. They grumble, yes. I've hung out with them; I've listened to their conversations and they don't know shit... Really and truly, they talk garbage, lots of garbage about consumer things. Their only interest is in having lots of stuff. They don't talk about other issues, and there is a lot to talk about. All they do is complain about not being able to afford to go to a disco. That's why I say it's garbage. I've listened to the young, the generation born yesterday, and I can tell you they are not going to do anything because they don't understand what this is all about. They don't think. I'm not saying every single one of them, maybe there are a few who do, but if there are, I haven't met them. Listening to today's youth has made me lose a little of my... err, what you'd expect.' He did not say what he'd lost, maybe his hope.

Esteban wanted Julia to know that he had a history; he wasn't a political lightweight who went around stealing in order to go to discos and buy sound equipment. He wanted her to appreciate that politics mattered to him. Most of all he wanted her respect.

'The Varela Project was founded in my neighbourhood by professors from CUJAE, Centro Universitario José Antonio Echeverria [Havana's technical university].'

He paused, perhaps weighing up how far he could stretch the truth, or what he shouldn't say.

'The Varela Project was founded to make peaceful change, to promote democracy. That's what these people advocated, nothing else. And what happened? They were sent to prison. Many were university professors, educated people who behaved in a civilised way. What I'm saying is that you have to find another way to make change here. We gave up because if that's what happened to people who tried to follow a peaceful path, can you imagine? It will have to be another way, taking to the streets, or who knows what, taking up arms, making an attempt on someone's life. But that's a very different thing and we don't have any part in that. We don't support that kind of thing at all, not at all. What we want is peaceful change, and we are confident the government will make that happen. Well, not confident exactly; we have a vague hope. That's the craziness of our country. It is not that we don't love our country. We adore it. I love the climate, I absolutely love the heat, and I dislike winter intensely.'

I suspect Esteban's riff on loving *la patria* was a satire on the leaders' repeated exhortations to love Cuba. Numerous older narrators told us they love Cuba; many sounded sincere. Cuba's deep vein of nationalism grows out of the country's long anti-colonial struggles against Spain and the US. Other narrators might have figured 'I love Cuba' was the right thing to say in a recorded interview.

'A US visa. The chance of a lifetime.'

In the summer of 2003, Esteban joined a crowd occupying the park in front of the US Interest Section in Havana.[4] Hundreds of people were drawn to the park by a rumour that the Interest Section was giving out visas. Esteban's account of the occupation is savvy and funny.

'My next-door neighbour came to find me. He told me the Interest Section was about to give out one hundred and some extra [residency] visas. The minute he told me I felt like – *bueno*, how can I describe it – like my soul had been reincarnated. I made up my mind there and then. We got to the Interest Section about midnight. There were lots of people, some had been there for almost a week. We tried to make ourselves comfortable on benches near the Anti-Imperialist Tribunal. The park is almost like a waiting room where people go for news of the visa lottery. There are always people hanging around there, waiting for announcements from the Interest Section.'

Cubans gathering at the Anti-Imperialist Tribunal for news about US visas is beyond satire.

'Everyone wanted to see what would happen at daybreak. More people showed up, you could see them pouring into the park. There was a mix of people who had come for the new visas, people who were always there for the lottery, which is a daily event, and state security agents. You could tell the security guys because they dress in civvies and have microphones in their ears. They were mixing with the crowd, listening to what people were saying, trying to figure out who was more and who was less. I mean more than just talking. People who were… err, you might say, the most absorbed of the group.' Esteban laughed at the code word he had just invented.

'In the daytime everything was completely normal. One or two guys from state security would read out a statement exhorting the crowd to leave. They said the stuff about additional visas was a total lie. They said nothing out of the ordinary was going to happen. I can tell you the date, it was a couple of days before our Comandante's birthday, the 13th of August. Yes, the 13th of August is our Comandante's birthday, so it must have begun on the 8th.'

It is ironic, but not surprising, that Fidel's birthday, celebrated every year with street parties and speeches, was Esteban's aide memoire.

'We were there several days, and every day was the same. The security guys would say, "We have been instructed to tell you it is a lie and…" But no one in the crowd got discouraged, no one believed it; they would never believe those people because this wasn't the first time. The same thing had happened years before.[5] Besides, no one wanted to believe it. People around me chanted, "We shall not be moved." I joined in and we stayed put. Things like that sometimes get sort of heated because those people [security agents] are arrogant. But nothing happened and that night we went to my house for an hour or two to shower and grab a bite, and then we went back.'

Did you get some sleep?

'Sleep? Of course not. We got back to the park about three in the morning. It was our only chance for a visa. It was the chance of a lifetime. A visa is what all Cubans have always wanted, or most Cubans. The days passed, every day the same until the 13th of August, our Comandante's birthday. I had predicted that the 13th would be the last day, and it was. It was the worst. We woke up in the park, just like every other day.'

What do you mean like every other day?

'Every night we slept in the park on cardboard boxes spread on the ground. We found them outside a cafeteria. Everyone did. We got used to it. We told stories, played games, cards. Some people played dominoes all day long. Dominoes and a bottle of rum, the usual. They hid the rum to look serious, and they didn't drink the whole bottle, just tiny sips. That's how we passed the time until the 13th of August, our Comandante's birthday. Then, as luck would have it, a hurricane blew in. Their people had organised it.'

Esteban never passed up a chance to crack a joke.

'When we woke up, they had already cordoned off the park. We watched as a brigade of workers from the electric company trooped in carrying chainsaws. I say electric company in quotation marks because there was no way of knowing if they really worked there. The park is lined by beautiful almond trees and when they began to cut back the trees we had to vacate the park. What a brilliant eviction strategy. Don't you see, it was all an excuse, thanks to the hurricane. They said that they needed to cut back the branches, and that everyone had to vacate the park. They tried to get everyone out; some left, not everyone. In fact, very few did. Most stayed right where they were. This led to trouble. When the agents saw their plan wasn't working and the people were refusing to leave, three trucks from the Ministry of Interior arrived. We were quickly surrounded by MININT [armed forces and the Ministry of Interior] agents who worked in groups. Five or so agents would grab a person, carry him away and push him into a van. We watched, but we didn't move, forwards or backwards. We stayed right where we were – at least my group did, my people.

'Then it turned a little ugly, the crowd got angry and the police too. The agents didn't show us enough respect. I don't know what people in the crowd were saying, but it really upset me seeing agents behave disrespectfully towards the elderly. An older man asked a security guy a polite question, very nicely, and the guy screamed at him in this nasty way, "Señor, you must leave this very minute, I don't care about…" You had to see it. Those guys are vile; they don't care about anyone. Things really heated up after that.'

Was the crowd mostly young, or were there people of all ages?

'All ages, a mixture, some young, very young. I knew a lot of them, though I hadn't seen them for a while. Lots of people go to that park regularly; they keep in touch; they pass messages, if you get what I mean. People spotted their friends and asked, what are you doing here? We were all there for the same reason. I click with those people; we're good friends. It is a place where you can talk about the system and other things without any fear. You can say what you are thinking and what you are planning to do. You might say you're ready to… to change this. You don't have to be afraid. That means a lot to me.'

Esteban's claim that you could talk freely in front of the US Interest Section reminded me of the popular joke: A dissident organisation had three members: one was a US agent, one was a Cuban agent, and the third was a fool.

'Now I don't have to devote my time to changing history.'

So, overall you say what you think? Is that right?

'Say what I think? Yes, yes, of course, obviously, I say whatever is on my mind. I always have. My father told me always, always tell the truth, and that's what I do.'

Esteban switched from sarcasm to cynicism.

'Sometimes, when I hear people say they support the government, I feel driven to state a couple of truths, though it's usually not worth trying because those people have a blind spot. They can't see what their lives are like and they don't care. It's best not to talk to people like that. All I do is state a couple of truths and quickly walk away. It leaves them thinking. I find it all a little depressing. I've lost some of my interest in all this, because I've seen it doesn't solve anything. I've lost hope that people here will decide to do something about it, will resolve to change it. I became more realistic and decided to pursue a different path. I turned to something else, a personal solution.'

Esteban's personal solution was to leave the country. It is the solution many Cubans turn to which partly explains why, despite growing impoverishment and inequality, there is almost no organised opposition.

'Now I don't have to devote my time to changing history,' he said, laughing, perhaps embarrassed by his own hubris, but perhaps not. Esteban exhibited little self-doubt.

'Nah, I am not interested in making history. I've realised that educating people is not going to solve anything. It's not the solution.'

After an uncomfortable silence he asked, 'Should I tell you how the protest ended? Well, to carry more weight, guys from state security went inside and brought out two – I don't know what you call them, the people who work in the Interest Section – two bureaucrats, both very American. If they had been Cuban no one in the crowd would have believed a thing they said. The bureaucrats came out carrying a sheet of paper and a loudspeaker. They said in no uncertain terms that the crowd had to disperse because the rumour about the lottery was false, there were no extra visas and no new agreements. "Please leave," they begged the crowd. Well, when the two Americans read out the statement the crowd had to accept it. They had to give up.

'The crowd was a sea of people. By then the state security agents had had enough time to identify everyone who was there, and there were a lot. There were more of us than them. When they saw how many people were there they became sort of jittery because, well, they are Communists, and they saw for themselves that lots of people want to leave because they oppose the system. That led to more problems. The security agents started taking people to jail. I saw it myself. They took people away for no reason. End of story.'

Esteban's story exemplifies the escape valve. The crowd in front of the Interest Section, instead of organising, devoted their energy to coming up with a way of leaving.

An insider's story of the black market

Esteban devoted part of his life to politics and a greater part to mammon. Recollecting the aftermath of his first attempt to flee, he said, 'I had to go to work and I took a job in a state company assembling Korean and Chinese televisions, but the salary didn't cover my expenses. The pay was very, very low. Salaries still are. Not knowing if this would ever change, I decided to leave my job and go into what we call the street life. The street, business, the things you're not supposed to do, activities that are frowned upon. It's an easy way of making money.'

What kinds of activities?
'Anything that doesn't involve stealing. I went into business, all kinds of businesses. Here in Cuba you can make money doing almost anything. People are short of just about everything, so anything can become a business. You sell the first thing that turns up. A sack of cement, computer parts, a camera. It's all the same. You go selling with a friend, you both carry backpacks. You can make money selling anything you can think of, women's clothing for example.'

Esteban did not actually use the expression, 'You can make money.' He said, *puedes resolver*. In Cuba *resolver* is a magic verb. It means buying, selling, bartering, borrowing, stealing – in a word doing whatever needs doing to survive well or survive badly.

But how do you... Julia started to ask. Esteban interrupted.

'Yeh, I know, I know. You want to know how I get my hands on the clothing and the other stuff I sell? Well, let's just say I know people,' Esteban laughed nervously. 'Eh, alright then, I'm not saying anything that everyone doesn't already know, am I? The whole world knows that in Cuba everybody steals from their workplace. Take cigar factories: workers steal cigars, put them in a box, slap on a seal, and flog the box to tourists on the street for ninety-five dollars. That's the cigar business. Take television factories. Workers steal parts – a condenser, a circuit board, whatever – and sell it to a repair shop, or to someone who works the street. There are people on the street who specialise in electronic parts.'

Esteban was clearly speaking from experience.

'Unfortunately, I won't trade in certain things. I won't touch anything stolen from a tourist or from foreigners leaving the airport.'

Esteban probably felt he had to say this, whether or not it was true.

'Living near the airport, I know people who follow tourists to steal their cameras or whatever. Sometimes I have buyers lined up and I could make a little money that way but first I always check the provenance. Pro-ven-ance, do you know what I mean?' he asked, using a Spanglish version of the English word.

He wanted to be sure Julia understood that he had morals. On a related note, many narrators repeated the popular joke, 'They pretend to pay me, and I pretend to work,' to explain why so many Cubans thought it was legitimate to steal from the state.

Stealing from the state became so common that officials had a euphemism for it: diverting state resources. In 2013, in a major speech to the National Assembly, Raúl Castro entreated Cubans to stop diverting state resources, and to inform on anyone who did, no matter how highly placed. Cubans I spoke to doubted the speech would deter anyone, and a few years later Mario said, 'Corruption has become part of our inner nature. It's in our veins.'

'Survival comes at a price.'

'Try to imagine how we have to debase ourselves to survive,' Esteban complained. 'Survival comes at a price. You get mixed up in a lot of bad things.'

Though survival was hardly the word for his comfortable lifestyle, he was hoping to elicit sympathy, and trying to get Julia to put herself in his shoes.

'I am the sort of person who tries to work things out. I am a survivor. You need intelligence to achieve the little I have.'

Esteban was not modest by nature.

'I steer clear of trouble on the street. I don't get mixed up with the wrong kind of people because it always ends badly. You might even go to prison. If I discover that something belonged to a tourist, or a Cuban, or came from somebody's house, I don't get involved because that could get me tangled up in big, big problems. Luckily, in my thirty-one years I've never been in prison. I don't know what it's like to be locked up, and I don't want to know.'

Do you have friends who've been inside?

'You mean in prison? No. It's like I told you, partly it's because of where I live. People around here are – how can I explain it, a little different from the people in Central Havana. In Central Havana they are more belligerent.'

Esteban is saying, without spelling it out, that the Afro-Cubans who live in Central Havana are aggressive and prone to criminality.

After the head of his neighbourhood branch of the CDR reported him to the police for not having a job, he worked briefly at an assembly plant. 'I learned a thing or two about electronics there, but I quit after four months because the pay was garbage. Garbage, I tell you. The salary was two hundred and some pesos per month plus *una jaba*. You know what I mean by *una jaba*? A plastic bag with shampoo, soap and some other bits and bobs they give you to buy you off. I did well at the beginning – ahhh, well, maybe not so well. The truth is I was just hanging out – *ahí tirando* as they say in Cuban – because I didn't have a choice. I had to take the job.'

In a later interview, Esteban retold the *jaba* story, portraying himself as a conscientious worker and daring rebel who was fired for talking truth to power.

'I am not a delinquent.'

'I'd been working in construction here, in the neighbourhood, on that house across the street. But I ran into problems with the police, because the head of the CDR reported me for vagrancy. One day she stopped me outside my door and said, "Why aren't you working?" "I don't need to," I answered. "I don't work because I'd be paid so little it wouldn't make any difference." Yes, I really said that. I told her the truth. "Besides, I receive money from abroad." "That doesn't matter, you must work," she replied. "Don't you know the law?" I was ultra-polite and said, "Excuse me, but…" She got a little pushy, so I told her that I'd try to find a job. Truth is, I'd be doing myself a favour if I got into her good graces. I'd get her off my back. They have me down as an anti-social, you see, but I'm not. I'm not a delinquent. I've never assaulted anyone. I've never robbed a little old lady in the street. I wouldn't do anything like that. I am the most peaceful soul you can imagine. They got me all wrong. They've got all of us young people cornered. It's a...' Esteban whistled. 'We know all about it, but what can we do; we live on an island.'

Esteban's story made me laugh. What he said, and how he said it, whistle and all, bears an uncanny resemblance to the song, 'Gee Officer Krupke!', from *West Side Story*,[6] sung by two gang members.

West Side Story meets Esteban's life story. Both feature petty criminality, male rebellion, and policing as social control with the protagonists portraying themselves as blameless victims of an oppressive system.

A few days after Esteban's run in with the head of the CDR, the police called him in. 'I spoke with Officer I-forget-his-name. He asked, "What do you do? How do you support yourself?" "I have friends abroad who help me out." He said, "No, no, no, don't give me any of those cock and bull stories. You must get a job. If you don't, you'll get into trouble." We went back and forth for quite a while. Finally, I agreed and I started as an apprentice making circuit boards. It was a snap. I passed all the tests. I was tops.

'I'd been working at the plant for four months when one morning I arrived early, with the usual spring in my step. The job was pure garbage, but hey ho, in life you've got to stay positive. When I arrived my boss called out, "Come over here. Look here, you missed a day's work." "Are you sure?" I replied. "Yes, yes, one day you didn't show up, and another time you arrived late." "Wait a minute," I said, "Missing work one day, that could be, but arriving late, it was only by fifteen or twenty minutes. You're not going to deduct anything for that, are you?" "I'll have to take away your *jaba*," he replied. "You're not going to get a *jaba* this month, because you missed a day." I said, "Shit, don't say that." Then I tried, you know, to sort of sweet talk him. "You've got to understand, it was only one day, and you know the *jaba* is the most important thing I get, and besides, I don't receive a *jaba* every month, I get one every other month." Then I mumbled something like, "Shit, how can this happen?" but I tried to keep calm. Then he bellowed, "You can't have a *jaba*, you can't, you didn't fulfil the conditions for a *jaba*."

'So tell me Julia,' he said in a voice dripping with sarcasm, 'why do they say communism is the most perfect society? My boss shrieked [Esteban mimicked], "You've lost the *jaba*, you've lost the *jaba*, you're not getting one." "Alright," I said, "Keep the *jaba* and keep the fucking job. You hear me?" I turned on my heels and calmly walked out, *muy facil, facilisimo*. I felt elated, as if I'd just walked free from prison. I said to myself, I'm never going back to work ever again. And I didn't, until two years ago.

'You know I am a bit of a radical [an extremist]. People say I'm an anarchist. Alright, then I'm a Cuban anarchist. *Perfecto*. And I know what anarchist means. I don't support the system, not at all. Anyway, I see it all as pretty absurd. There I was, obeying all the laws, working [at a state job]. I got up bright and early every morning and went to work like clockwork. But they gave me a hard time. Why? They threw this shit at me because of one day. The most important thing is to act like a human being. That's what this kind of system is supposed to be about. The system says we are all human and so on and so forth, but I don't see it working like that. Do you know what happened in the end? They took the *jaba* away, and I found out that my boss kept it for himself, on the sly. When I heard that I said, good, you keep the fucking *jaba*. You need it to survive, not me. I won't put up with this shit. I'm getting out of here and I'm not going to sweat it out in this shitty factory which doesn't give anything in return. What do I get? Two hundred and some pesos. I can't live on two hundred and some pesos. Can anyone survive on that?'

Esteban was defiant. He infused the *jaba* story with self-righteousness, and turned it into an allegory about the evils of communism, exploitation by the state, corrupt bureaucrats, and the absurdity of the entire system. To Esteban's way of thinking the episode – or rather, his rendition of it – justified not only his refusal to work at a state job, but his politics and his entire way of life. The story fitted his purposes to a tee.

After turning his back on state employment, Esteban worked his way up in the underground economy. He began peddling house to house, next he was an intermediary handling hot merchandise. Understandably reluctant to provide details of his work, he hinted that he was involved with a syndicate that handled just about anything stolen from the state. He explained that in his line of work there could be long dry spells, but if all went well he could make five or six hundred dollars a month – a fortune by Cuban standards.

Esteban attributed his success in business to his intelligence and his caution. I suspect his achievements rested on his brother's connections. Esteban's half-brother bought and sold houses on the sly ten years before Raúl Castro's government allowed a real estate market to develop. 'My brother does very well. He runs a problem-free business. It is legal, in quotation marks. Get what I mean by legal in quotation marks?'

Esteban explained that government officials closed their eyes and took a portion of his brother's profits. He grumbled that his brother was constantly nagging him to stop complaining about the government and stop plotting ways to leave. The brother was afraid that Esteban's behaviour would jeopardise his business.

Second failed escape

Esteban was deeply depressed after his second failed escape. When he had first attempted to flee on a raft in 1993, he had half-expected to be fished out of the sea by the US Coast Guard and taken to Miami. Then he would be home free. But US policy changed after the *balsero* crisis of 1994. To stem the flood of rafters, the US and Cuban governments agreed that only Cubans who reached the US soil would be allowed to stay; Cubans picked up at sea by the US Coast Guard would be sent back to Cuba. Dubbed the 'wet foot, dry foot' policy, it was a boom for professional traffickers.

In 2004 Esteban paid a trafficker a thousand dollars to whizz him across the Florida Straits in a *cigarillo*, a speed boat. A thousand dollars was approximately three times the average annual state salary. When Esteban arrived at the departure point, twenty people were trying to board a motorboat designed to hold ten or twelve.

'I began to get suspicious of the whole thing because, as everyone knows, if you're not very close with the people you're going with, they could throw you overboard. You could die. You must be very careful because it's happened so many times... It was a fantastic boat, but in the end it was all a lie... I had to go back home.

'At times I get so depressed, I don't even want to see my friends or go out. Here the bottom line is that you have no privacy in your life. There's always someone, if not two or three people, meddling in your personal life, trying to find out what you are doing, telling you what you should be doing. It's unpleasant. I'm thirty-one after all, and I try to live as independently as possible. Up until now I've more or less managed. But the CDR is a surveillance mechanism designed to intrude into people's lives. Intrude in order to inform.

'Picture this: A certain person gets a kick out of informing, maybe they get something else too, and you don't particularly get on with them. I'm not doing anything bad, that's the truth of it. I don't steal, but she and I don't get along. When she sees a police officer walking around she tells him, "That guy who lives over there is stealing or something. He's doing something wrong." Then the officer interferes in my life; he makes my life impossible. He can get me locked up for a year or two or three or whatever, under a law they've invented called the vagrancy law. Anyone who doesn't work is an outlaw. Kind of absurd, don't you think? Absurd, but people are serving time for it, for nothing. There was a demonstration in the Plaza de la Revolución, where I heard that mothers were protesting because their sons are in prison for this, for refusing to work for nothing... The way I see it, it's wrong to force me to work for nothing. I'm not a slave. That's how I see it, and I'm not the only one. Everyone does.'

Esteban talked himself into a frenzy, as if his life depended on it, and in a way it did.

After Esteban's second failed escape, the CDR head reported him to the police again. The officer said bluntly, "Get a job, or go to prison." Esteban found work at an assembly plant on the fringe of his neighbourhood, and boasted that during the probationary period he did so well his boss wanted him to stay. But Esteban failed the background check.

Why did you fail the security check?

'I don't know. I asked my boss the same question... and he answered, "You are a good worker, you fulfil the quotas, you arrive early every day. You missed work twice in two months, but apart from that, you did very well. The problem lies with state security; they gave you a bad report. I don't know why, but you can't work here." I told him the whole story: I told him the police chief in my barrio told me I had to get a job. "That's why

I'm here, so I don't understand why I can't keep my job." My boss told me, "Look, go back to the police officer and tell him what happened."'

Esteban acted out his story and the interview turned into a self-justifying – and very engaging – monologue.

'Well, it was still early, I'd got to work early, so I went straight to the police station. I explained the situation to the officer in charge. He said, "No, no, wait a minute. How is this possible? This is another one of your cock and bull stories. I told you, you have to have a job. You have to become *integrado* [have a legal job and participate in state organisations]. OK, so there's been a mistake."

'It was all pretty bureaucratic. The officer said, "Now go back to the plant and give them these two telephone numbers, they're mine. Tell them to call me; we'll work this out." I said to him, "Good, that's great. OK. I have your numbers. It will all work out." I thought to myself: Be a little bit positive and see what happens.

'The next day I got up early and went around to the plant. I saw my boss and I said, "Here are two telephone numbers for the officer in charge. Now you have not one, but two ways of getting in touch with him. All you have to do is call him and he'll tell you there is no problem of any kind, none at all. I don't know what this is about a negative report." He took the numbers and said, "OK, alright, go home and wait for me to get in touch." I did as he said, and that was three months ago.'

Esteban laughed so hard he could barely speak. He knew he had told a good story, and he seemed pleased with himself for capturing the total absurdity of the bureaucracy.

After the job fiasco, Esteban got back to business, illegal business. How could that be, I wondered, if state security had him so clearly in their sights? I don't have the answers but perhaps the security apparatus had bigger fish to fry. In a river full of piranhas

Esteban was a minnow. Maybe they regarded him as a nuisance, not a threat. Maybe his brother's connections kept the law at bay. Perhaps the police were incompetent, and many Estebans escaped their net. Esteban almost certainly exaggerated what had happened in his desire to portray himself as a reasonable man caught in a perverse system.

Slumming

As part of Esteban's charm offensive he explained to Julia the ins and outs of Havana street culture, and taught her a bit of slang. He acted as a kind of anthropological informant. His girlfriend was a British anthropologist and he seemed to like describing the local customs to foreigners; it gave him a sense of authority. I feel it was also part of his exit strategy.

'Working the street has been useful... I've come to know people of all sorts, like the ones we passed the other day, people of that class, street people, people living on the margins, people without culture. I've learned from them. At parties where the host invites people you have nothing in common with, you must talk the way they do. *¡Qué bola aseres!* How are you, mate? *¿No hay una patica por ahí?* Can I say it here [on the recording]? *Una patica* is a marijuana joint. Under certain circumstances you must speak that way. I am pronouncing this very clearly so you'll understand it later [when you listen to the recording]. The real thing is more vulgar.

'Remember that guy we passed we other day, I said to him, "*No hay cráneo* brother." It's street language, a mixture of Cuban and English. It means no worries; *cráneo* is cranium. It's not from now with the influx of tourists; its roots go way, way back from before the triumph of the Revolution, back to when the Americans controlled Cuba. They owned this country. Everything we produced belonged to Americans. In this mixture of Cuban and English, a refrigerator is *el freezer*. There are other street languages that I don't know. I don't speak them because they use very strong words, bad words, very, very bad words that I won't say. The words are very Havana, very inner city. They're not used in my neighbourhood. People in Old Havana are very different.'

Do you often go to the centre of the city?

'Mostly on weekends, that's when I have time to relax.' Working the black market was, apparently, a full-time job. 'When I was younger I went to Havana much more. I went to learn a bit about how to move in that world... I went to *toques de santos* [Santería/Yoruba celebrations of a person's saint's day]. They are very impressive. I like traditional Afro-Cuban music. It's fantastic. At those events I met those kinds of people [Cubans of African descent]. They aren't all negative, not at all. You can't judge a whole people. Some are very good people, but some are... Where and how they live sometimes makes them act a little bit hard towards the people around them. They are not very flexible. Well, as I said, for years and years I mixed with them, I went to *fiestas de santos* and all that. I played dominoes on the sidewalk outside a *solar* [tenement] in Old Havana until late at night. Dominoes and a bottle of rum: a very classic scene. You can't do that around here [in his neighbourhood]. In Old Havana you see it, you're in it, the ambiance comes from the noise, the people in the street. Suddenly a woman comes down the stairs screaming, shouting swear words, and a child comes running up. I like all that; I've drunk it all in. That's how I got to know all kinds of people, all classes. I enjoyed myself. But there were some very difficult moments because sometimes it's dangerous... they might attack you. They see you're a bit... or you're wearing a piece of jewellery, that sort of thing.'

Esteban relished his memories of slumming. He enjoyed the feeling that he was more refined, more cultured, classier, than Afro-Cubans of Old Havana. He was, in a word, condescending.

Esteban's story portrays many of the contradictions of Cuban life. His mother, a devotee of Santería, was a loyal Fidelista even though the government suppressed her religion. Esteban decried the racism in Cuban society, but was oblivious to his own racial stereotyping – despite or because he himself was of African descent. Often writers portray Cuban politics and ideology as smooth, like a bowling ball, when in reality they are full of cracks and fissures. Whether we empathise with Esteban or condemn him, or both, his life story complicates our understanding of Cuban society.

'No Cuban is a complete atheist.'

'I am an atheist. I go to *fiestas de santos* because I enjoy the music, the music has a tremendous beat. Afro-Cuban religion has a history, but I can sincerely say I am not interested. I am not a believer... That whole religion is pretty aggressive, with its animal sacrifices and all of that. I think it's better to eat the animals, don't you? I am an atheist, but not a total atheist. No Cuban is a complete atheist. Everyone is a believer the moment they need help and at that moment they always ask for help.'

Who do you ask?

'I only ask when I am alone, and in real need, and then I ask my mother. I say, *"Por favor, madre mía."* You understand what I mean? It's a spirit, or something you believe in. But I can assure you I am an atheist in relation to all other beliefs. Catholicism, I have no truck with that, or with any Afro-Cuban religion.'

In the next breath Esteban described the rituals he performs to bring him luck every time he leaves the house on business, and he demonstrated his routine by sprinkling cascarilla powder on the floor and tracing the sign of the cross.[7] He explained that when he needs extra protection, he wears Yoruba amulets under his clothes.

'Most of the time I approach life as a realist. I try to understand what is happening, how it all works. That's better, don't you think? That way you don't waste your time. But there are many believers in this world and I would never tell them they are wasting their time. I prefer to live in the moment. Going back and forth to church or spending time in a [Santería] sanctuary consulting a man or a woman, bringing them this, that and the other is a waste of time. Instead of doing that you could use the time *resolviendo*, sorting out, your problems… I think that's better; don't you? Not that I am criticising any religion.

'Whew. I think we've gone about as far as we can go in talking about my life. I'll wait to see what punishment I'll get.'

16

BARBARA VEGAS

Regla

Barbara was clearly reluctant to talk to us, but her desire to do her boss, the director of Regla's Casa de Cultura, a favour outweighed her misgivings. He had given her a big promotion, from night guard to head of administration, and she was grateful.

She listed the schools she attended and the jobs she held. 'I graduated from school with top grades when I was sixteen and was sent to a training school to become a transport technician. It didn't interest me so after a few months I dropped out. Growing up I always wanted a job where I could help people and they assigned me to a childcare centre. I quit after a couple of months. Then they assigned me to a health clinic. Then I worked with old people but I left that too. I discovered that I didn't enjoy working with infants, the sick or the elderly and I quit eight jobs in a row. I was too immature to take on responsibilities.'

Barbara's experience probably reflected changes in the conditions of labour. In the 1980s, the state guaranteed that every adult had a job and workers could seek employment that suited them. When the state phased out guaranteed employment, Barbara had to rely on herself to find a job. She discovered it was a frustrating business.

'Tell us about the discrimination you remember from school,' Daisy said. The question surprised Barbara, partly because she was in the process of applying for Party membership and suspected the interview was connected to her application, partly because the Party line was that racial discrimination ended in the 1960s. 'I don't remember any discrimination at school. No, there wasn't any. I was one of the best students in the class, the other was a white girl, and the teacher, who was white, treated us the same. She didn't show favouritism and we both got top marks.' 'Are you sure?' said Daisy. 'Yes, I'm sure.' Barbara stood up to signal the interview was over. Racism was a taboo subject. 'My life has not been eventful. I've led a normal life.

'My mother died two years ago and from that moment everything changed, changed totally. Since then I feel that I am alone with my son. My husband. My brother helps me out a lot but I feel alone, like I have no one. No, I have no one, no one. We are two siblings, that's all. From the time my mother died I have had to face life alone, without anyone, without a mother-in-law to help me with the child. I have tried to do the best I can with no one to support me. There isn't anyone I can turn to for help. Everyone is struggling with their own difficulties. That's the way it is.'

Barbara lived in the same house her entire life, and I felt that her intense isolation was a measure of how much society had changed in the post-Soviet era. Some things changed less, others more. Often Cuban women told us that Cuban men did not change.

'I have to keep pushing my husband. Do this, do that, watch the child. When he was young he did not have to help around the house. His mother did all the chores and he spent his time having fun. His life was all about music and fun. We've been together going on five years. Five years and he still hasn't gotten it into his head that he is a married man who is supposed to do something around the house. It never occurs to him that a husband needs to work alongside his wife. Five years and he still doesn't understand. When I get home from work I don't have anyone to help me get things done. I do everything myself.

'I've managed to more or less to stay afloat, more or less. I know that I'm the one who has to wash the clothes and do the cooking. I try to get a little ahead of things, a jump on what I have to do. I try to do a little the day before so that when I get home in the afternoon I'm not completely overwhelmed. Every morning I try to do the washing, put the beans on to soften and prepare a little of the meal before I go to work. My husband does what he can but you know how men are.'

Barbara's story is a working woman's story, an everyday story about making sure to put the beans on and get a start on the evening meal before going to work; the burdens of housework and living with a husband who doesn't understand that he has family responsibilities. It is a story about the patriarchal structures of Cuban society. A story about the Cuban Revolution.

Barbara discovered that talking about her misery was cathartic and she began to confide in us. 'Unlike many people in my situation who take medicines to relax, antidepressants, I haven't taken anything, not one aspirin. There are days when I am very anxious. I am besides myself when my child cries. I feel I am going crazy. I tell myself that I must pull myself together without resorting to pills and so far I've been able to get myself under control. I've made it through.'

In Cuba talking about mental health tends to be more a woman's instinct than a man's. It is a mark of intimacy, of sisterhood. After the collapse of the Soviet bloc men said that Cubans were suffering a collective depression, and many said it was a reflection of the breakdown of communist ideology.

17

PAVEL GARCÍA ROJAS

El Cerro, Havana

'We don't really have any memories of the end of socialism in the USSR.'

With his encyclopaedic knowledge of Soviet armaments, his love of the army and military culture in general, his happy conviction of Soviet superiority, Pavel was no doubt like lots of Cuban youngsters at the end of the 1980s. The fall of the Berlin Wall changed everything about the society he grew up in, and yet no one realised, or knew anything about it, at the time. Pavel remembered a silence, a void.[1]

'On thinking about it, I realise we Cubans don't really have any memories of the end of socialism in the USSR. It simply was not part of our narrative. What I mean is we weren't told what happened. Fidel gave a speech in which he made clear that it wasn't going to happen here. He spoke very badly about the leaders of the Soviet countries. But what had happened? We were never told. I understood the speech, it was 1991 and I was fifteen years old. If what had happened had been explained to us I would be able to tell you. What I remember is that one day my grandfather was watching television and said aloud, "They should just leave the two Germanys alone to decide for themselves. If they decide to unite it won't be under capitalism. They will form a socialist country." My grandfather was no fool; he was a man of considerable education and knowledge. He was not a communist or a revolutionary extremist. What he was saying must have been what people had been told. I am telling you this because it shows how much we were conditioned, how little understanding we had of what was happening in the world. Everyone in the world knew that the two Germanys were not going to form one socialist country. Everyone in the world knew except us.

'If you look at how our newspaper and TV reported those events it makes you uncomfortable. I have no doubt the coverage was minimal… It is unbelievable how much our media can ignore transcendental events. I am not talking about manipulation of the news; I'm talking about outright ignoring it… I remember my mother subscribed to the newspaper *Novedades de Moscú* [*News from Moscow*], and the magazine *Sputnik*, which was similar in format to *Selecciones* and *Reader's Digest*. With the start of Perestroika these demonstrated a new way of thinking, and she got into the habit of saving the magazines. One day out of the blue the Cuban government suspended their sale. I remember my mother, and probably public opinion in general, suspected it was because of the articles they carried. At the time of Perestroika, the articles dismantled the myths of socialist justice and liberty. I can't recall whether the Cuban government made statements that gave weight to people's suspicions.

'Before the fall of the socialist bloc, we had a Soviet Film Festival here every year that received lots of media coverage. From a very young age I would read about Soviet films in *Sputnik* magazine. Then films began to turn up at the festivals with themes that reflected Glasnost and Perestroika. I remember people talking about those films in my house. I was too young to see them at the time. Much, much later I watched some of them, *La pequeña Vera* [*Little Vera*], *El mensajero* [*The Messenger*], *El frío verano del 53* [*The Cold Summer of 53*], *Ve y mira* [*Go and Look*], and especially *Arrepentimiento* [*Repentance*], a supercharged story of the difficulties of the Stalin years.

'As for Tiananmen Square [the 1989 Beijing protests and massacre], I knew next to nothing. Perhaps I recall hearing something about it at my father's house, overhearing him and friends. I didn't see the photo of the man in front of the tank until many years later.

'There were, of course, some opposition movements in Cuba at that time, for example movements of Christian Liberation, like the one started by Oswaldo Payá, the man who died a strange death several months ago. He founded his movement in 1988.[2] There were movements, important debates, questioning by the opposition. But it was invisible.'

Black humour and the Special Period

At the time of the collapse of the Soviet bloc, Pavel was on the verge of entering pre. His heart was set on going to a pre in Vedado that specialised in music and art, not because he hoped to go into the arts. He was attracted by its reputation for nonconformism. Pavel explained that his mother managed to get him in despite his lacklustre grades. It wasn't the same school Mario attended, but seems to have had at least one thing in common: parents with pull.

Pavel described the difficulties of getting to school in Vedado after the Russians stopped supplying petroleum. Instead of belabouring the hardships, he underscored the humour. 'Buses were rare. They sped around with people hanging out the doors and windows, clinging on for dear life. I had to run a block or two and leap on to a fender as the driver swerved to avoid the bus stop. Stopping at the bus stop would have created havoc as there were crowds of people waiting.' Remembering made him laugh. 'Everyday was an adventure. Cuba is not a country for old men, like in the film title.

'Crime went through the roof. We don't know the statistics, of course, but we know theft was rampant. Everything got stolen, bicycles, everything. People got killed for their bicycles. Here in this second-floor apartment in El Cerro I hung my bathing suit on the balcony to dry. The next morning it was gone. The thief must have stripped naked and run away wearing my bathing trunks because he left behind his underpants.

'Desperation led to situations which, telling you about them, sound comic. The cats of Havana suddenly disappeared. People ate them. Blackouts lasted ten to fifteen hours in Havana – in H-a-v-a-n-a,' Pavel chanted slowly. 'Remember, I'm talking about Havana, and Miramar, where people don't face half the problems those living elsewhere on the island have to endure. All of a sudden, certain foods disappeared from the ration, and the portions shrank. At first you don't notice, it doesn't seem like a big deal because you've never had food in abundance. You're already accustomed to living on little.

'In the depth of the Special Period Fidel handed out bicycles. Many people died in bicycle accidents because the streets were very dark during the blackouts. My mother has two colleagues whose sons died riding bicycles. My sister's best friend, and a classmate of mine at pre, all died in bicycle accidents.' Pavel's matter of fact, 'Fidel handed out bicycles,' surprised me. I wondered whether he had actually seen Fidel giving out bicycles, maybe on TV, or whether the phrase 'Fidel gave' came naturally to him, as it did to so many Cubans, even though he criticised Fidel's paternalism.

Pavel's privilege

Pavel's account of the difficulties mirrored other peoples' stories. Just about everyone we interviewed described hardships and growing individualism in the Special Period. Pavel took a different tack; he emphasised his privilege. 'I've never been without water. The fact that I can say, living in Cuba, that I've never had big water problems verges on the incredible. Of course, once in a while the water went off for some minor reason, but that was nothing. Cuba as a whole, and Havana in particular, has extraordinary water problems. Also, my entire life I've had a telephone. That too is extraordinary.

'Many people cooked with *luz brillante*, kerosene, which is very dangerous. The father of one of my good friends died from burns after their stove exploded in the kitchen. They also lived in Miramar, but they were poor. The house next door to ours burned down. *Luz brillante* is like that, all of a sudden it explodes. It's impossible to control. I never had those kinds of problems, nothing like that.' Pavel's family cooked with bottled gas, which was a luxury.

Pavel's life story demonstrates that the advantages of being middle class and white survived fifty years of revolutionary upheaval. Yet, in the Special Period his Fidelista family, like everyone else, had to figure out a way to make money on the side. For this, the location of the red brick house – one block from the large Carlos Marx Theatre – was fortuitous. In the absence of public transport people cycled to the theatre, but they had nowhere safe to leave their bicycles. Pavel's family converted their spacious lawns into a bicycle parking lot, and charged a few centavos per bike for the evening. Every centavo helped.

Sex work

Before 1959, Havana was famous for prostitution and gambling. On coming to power the revolutionary government outlawed gambling and ran programmes to 're-educate' sex workers. A short time later Fidel announced that the government had eliminated the oldest profession in the world. In the Special Period sex tourism flourished as women and men turned to sex work to buy food, clothing and luxuries.[3] The government did little to discourage it, and Fidel bizarrely boasted that Cuba's sex workers were the best educated in the world. Since sex tourism brought in foreigners and dollars, Cubans concluded that the government was not averse to it, and Cuba soon became known as a global hot spot.

Recollecting his adolescence, Pavel described how prostitution affected his generation. 'Prostitution really came alive with the onslaught of tourism in the Special Period. It was part of my everyday life at pre. The tourist signified money, which meant prostitutes could have things most of us didn't have, things as basic as food. The huge wave of tourists, at a time when we had shortages of everything, caused prostitution to skyrocket in a terrible, terrible way. The brutality of prostitution really shows the depth of the crisis of the 90s, the debacle, the disaster. The head of the Young Pioneers in my grade school, I remember her from when I was eleven, became a prostitute when she was fifteen. Who would have thought?

'Another childhood friend, the only person to support my application for membership of the Union of Young Communists, was a prostitute. In the mid-90s, when I was in pre, I applied to join the Union of Young Communists. My family expected it. What with Perestroika and all that I was totally mixed up. I was someone who defended the Revolution, defended everything, everything. I was an ultra-extreme defender, but I was also saying things I shouldn't have said. I vividly remember my membership interview. I was in a large hall full of Young Communist militants. The room was dark, the only light was a dim shaft coming through a high window. The atmosphere was ominous. It was like a scene in a film. I began speaking and I said that I supported a multiparty system. I talked the nonsense of a mixed-up adolescent because

I didn't understand all sorts of things. No one said anything but it was clear they did not like what I was saying. I remember that the only person to come to my defence was a Young Communist in my class at pre. She was a prostitute. She was a prostitute but we had been friends since infancy. She defended me because she knew I was passionate. Everyone else was silent.'

In mid-sentence Pavel went very still. Remembering seemed to upset him. He continued in an uneasy voice. 'At my school the figure of the prostitute was so powerful it became a positive role model. Female students who weren't prostitutes tried to imitate their way of dressing, their conduct. The behaviour of the women students was *muy fuerte*, very extreme. Among male students the model of the male prostitute wasn't so extreme. The men tended to preserve, what should I call it, their integrity. But among the women, their behaviour was quite deplorable. I felt that the women wanted to appear sexually free, without moral restraints.

'Can you imagine, Liz, all this happening in a country where on television they keep telling you our country is the greatest, the best in everything, renowned for social justice. I think the situation [in the Special Period] generated a collective insanity. Everyone in Cuba lived through it. It defines our historical moment.' Many younger Cubans said that in the Special Period their generation suffered a collective breakdown.

'Experiences are more or less traumatic, depending on your personality. Without doubt, I escaped the worst of them.' Pavel went on to explain that he had had an exemption from obligatory military service and *la escuela en el campo*, rural pre-university schools, because his father arranged for a doctor to certify he had asthma. He described the rural boarding schools as 'barbaric places where adolescents' privacy was regularly violated… Those schools had long-lasting effects on teenagers' concept of intimacy, and on their consciousness.' He speculated that girls at those schools who had suffered sexual traumas were more prone to engage in prostitution. Pavel's view of *la escuelas en el campo* was widely shared. Mario remembered his school as a violent, frightening place.

Pavel wanted to study history at the University of Havana for as long as he could remember. He applied to the programme but was rejected, as his grades were not high enough. It came as a shock. His father had been an important figure at the university and he had always assumed he would follow in his footsteps.

Pavel found himself adrift. It was 1994, and the Special Period had settled in. At eighteen years of age he was neither in education, nor employment. Most Cubans in a similar predicament had to earn an income. They might try pedalling food and clothing door to door, or working illegally in construction, as Esteban did. But Pavel didn't need an income. He was looking for a calling.

Pavel's father, who had left Cuba temporarily to teach at the University of Barcelona, decided not to go back. He sent money to his son, with the proviso he oversee the care of his elderly father and aunts in the El Cerro apartment. Pavel moved in and remembered enjoying the arrangement. 'You could say my father assumed economic responsibility for the household, and I was responsible for their physical needs.'

In the Special Period, Pavel's politics and emotions were in flux. He had lost faith in Fidel and socialism. His political disillusion, combined with a sense of academic failure, brought on an emotional breakdown. 'It was my belated crisis of adolescence. I went from being a believer to a non-believer, and the transition was traumatic. Politics didn't interest me in the least. I figured I would leave Cuba, and I couldn't care less about what was happening here. I didn't participate in anything political. I was neither for, nor against. I was completely apathetic.' Instead of devoting himself to politics, as he had done in the past, he explored the meaning of life. 'What am I doing here? What have I done? What will I do? Where am I going? I pondered all those strange and difficult questions.'

Pavel studied theology at the Episcopalian Church, where he met his wife. He took up aikido, describing it as a peaceful martial art, and ceramics. He started an economics course at an institute for workers' education, but decided he didn't have a head for it and dropped out. His father arranged for him to study English at the prestigious Instituto Superior de Relaciones Internacionales [Advanced Institute of International Relations], Cuba's training school for diplomats and spies.

'In a period of several years I did a lot of different things. So many that I can't remember them all. They are lost somewhere in the back of my mind. I felt like I was spinning in circles. My memories of those years have disappeared because I wasn't involved in formal state institutions, and I didn't have to earn an income – my father provided. If I had had to work, I would be able to fix my memories around a chronology of jobs. But no. I would wander around striking up acquaintances with people I met on the street. I never took drugs, but I was going through a period of insanity or something like that. I would come and go, exploring places, entering doorways and alleyways, getting to know different kinds of people.'

Almost every afternoon Pavel went to the movies. He said he became addicted to the cinema. The dark theatre, and the stories on the screen, helped him forget his personal problems and the societal breakdown he was living through. 'Going to the cinema was almost like psychotherapy.' Many members of the post-Soviet generation felt alienated and depressed, but few could afford the luxury of dropping out completely.

Prior to the 1990s, at a time when Cubans had more faith in their government, and their government had more power to enforce their rules, Pavel would have found it difficult, if not impossible, to fall off the official radar. After 1990, that began to change. Increasingly, people lived in the shadow of the state because state-sector jobs did not pay a living wage. Many narrators said that ironically their miserable wage made them feel free for the first time in their lives – free to speak their mind – because it didn't matter very much if they were fired. A greater irony is that in public Cubans continued to hide what was on their mind.

When the University of Havana started a distance learning programme Pavel got his life back on track. He said the programme was his salvation. For three years he juggled studying, caring for his relatives, and going to the movies. By the time he graduated with a degree in history he had decided to turn his passion for film into a career, and applied to the International School for Cinema and TV in San Antonio de los Baños, outside Havana, to study film direction. Unlike every other educational institution in Cuba, the International Film School was privately funded and charged hefty fees. Unsurprisingly, most of its students came from overseas. Being Cuban, and having the means to pay, Pavel was an exception.

The politics of the Film School

When Pavel first narrated his life story, in 2012, he heaped praise on the Film School. 'The school was a great change, a great moment in my life. It had a completely different atmosphere, a completely different way of life from anything I had encountered here in Cuba.' Pavel said the international students talked politics in ways he had never heard before. 'They thought for themselves and said what was on their minds.' He attributed the school's open ambiance to its private funding and its open-minded director. 'It is largely independent from the state,' he kept repeating. Three years later, when he was fired from his job at the school for participating in anti-government activities, he discovered another side of the apparently independent school and its director.

'The Cuban ethos is to leave.'

'The Cuban students also talked, they said things like, "The system doesn't work," and some acted on their principles. But mostly their attitude was why make trouble, we won't be living in Cuba much longer. The Cuban ethos is to leave. Unfortunately, this is the Cuban reaction to anything a person doesn't like about living here, whether it's that members of the army enjoy privileges, or that some Cubans live very well from remittances, or that they themselves have lost hope that their life will improve. I can't tell you why exactly, but the general mindset is to leave. All of my friends have left, are in the process of leaving, or are plotting ways to leave. In short, younger Cubans fall into one of three categories: those who have already left, those on the verge of leaving, those trying to figure out a way to leave.' At film school, Pavel presumed that soon he too would leave.

On the day his daughter was born in 2005, which was a day or two before he graduated from film school, he had an epiphany. Her birth transformed his worldview. Holding his baby daughter made him resolve to remain in Cuba and fight for democracy.

18

ALEJANDRO ESPADA BETANCOURT

Boyeros, Havana

Alejandro Espada Betancourt was twenty-seven when I first interviewed him in 2012, but I had met his mother Olga Betancourt seven years earlier. Marisol and I had interviewed her in 2005 and 2007, before she emigrated to Miami.[1] Alejandro lived in her house, a spacious but rundown modern affair on a quiet, leafy back street in the Altahabana district of the buzzing Boyeros suburb. As a youngster Alejandro was a computer geek, and he went on to graduate first in his university class in industrial engineering. He had a desirable job at a top state company, and with bonuses his salary came to four to five times the pay of most state workers. But still he could not live the way he wanted to, and he sold pirated digital entertainment on the side. In the Cuban context Alejandro's business was state of the art.

Alejandro was always in a hurry; there was a lot he wanted to accomplish. Fair-skinned, grey-eyed, broadly built, he is six feet four inches tall. A giant by Cuban standards. The youngest of the narrators in this book, he claimed to speak for his generation when he said he felt he had had enough. 'We want to be able to plan for the future, to harbour hope. I no longer have dreams… No, I can't go on like this.' I last interviewed Alejandro in Cuba in 2015, and there was always this tension; could he stay and live the life he wanted, should he leave? I interviewed him in Miami in 2016.

The geopolitics of cancer

Alejandro's mother, Olga Betancourt, was raised in Santiago. 'The culture in my house was *Life* magazine and *National Geographic*.' Her mother was a school teacher and an ultra-Fidelista. Her father worked in a cafeteria. He was from a wealthy business family but they were estranged. Inspired by Frank Pais, a leader of Fidel's 26th of July movement, who taught at her private Baptist school, Olga became a Fidelista. She recalled that from a young age she spoke her mind, which created lifelong difficulties.

The Revolution tore Olga's family apart. In 1966, two uncles, Jehovah's Witnesses, were interned in Military Units to Aid Production (UMAP), labour camps, where the government sent gay people, religious believers, dissidents and nonconformists for 're-education', including the singer Pablo Milanés.[2] Olga's uncles emigrated to Miami on their release. In that same year she won a scholarship to study Russian in the USSR. En route to Moscow, during a stopover in Havana, she broke her leg, fell in love with the doctor, and abandoned her Russian-speaking career. She remained in Havana and taught English at CUJAE, the José Antonio Echeverria Polytechnic University.

Alejandro's father – not the doctor – was the director of the Institute of History in Havana, a research institute linked to the Central Committee of the Communist Party. Part of the time he lived with Olga and Alejandro, the rest of the time he lived with his wife and their children in Vedado. It was a very Cuban arrangement. Alejandro had few childhood memories of his father.

Born in 1985, nine-year-old Alejandro was diagnosed with lymphoma at the beginning of the Special Period. Despite dire shortages of medicine, he was treated in Havana hospitals. But his doctors had no way of knowing whether the treatment was effective because the hospital could not import chemicals for scanners after the United States government tightened the embargo. In desperation, Olga got in touch with her Miami uncles, the Jehovah's Witnesses. 'My husband was a Communist Party militant and we were not permitted to have any contact with the US, not by letter, nothing. But in that moment of crisis I found a way.' Olga took Alejandro to Miami for scans, also so that he could eat properly. 'Remember this was 1995, a very difficult phase of the Special Period, nothing was easy.'

—from Olga Betancourt's perspective

'The trip to Miami was an odyssey.' Olga recalled that after months of pleading with the Cuban and US governments to grant her permission to travel, she and Alejandro boarded a plane to Miami with humanitarian visas. The Miami League Against Cancer had agreed to pay the medical bills. On her arrival at the Miami airport, she was beset by journalists from Radio Martí, a station funded by the US government, who were expecting her to denounce Fidel Castro. She refused. 'They continued to harass me by telephone. "We will give you fifty dollars, take you to breakfast, pick you up in a car, drop you back home." My uncles threatened them until finally they stopped. I was put under a lot of pressure. I was also under pressure from Cuban officials from the Interest Section in Washington. They never understood that my trip was for humanitarian purposes, because of my son's illness. They continued to charge me every month for extending our visas, as if we were tourists visiting the United States. My Miami family had to pay. That is another event in my life that marked me: the lack of comprehension by the authorities of my own country.'

Olga recalled that soon after arriving in Miami she phoned the League Against Cancer. They told her their offer was conditional on her defection. 'That was disgusting; it was blackmail. It was so low, how can I put it. I have experienced many strange things in my life that left their mark. When my family realised the promises of the Cancer League were false they went into ruin. They paid all the hospital bills. They were not rich people. My uncle worked in a hardware store. My aunt did not work; she was a housewife. They mortgaged all their property, their house, their car, everything, to pay the bills. A complete blood analysis cost a bit more than one thousand dollars. I've kept the papers; let me show them to you. All this deeply affected Alejandro, and I had to take him to a child psychologist. She charged something like two hundred dollars for the first consultation. My family dug into their pockets. They gave money. They gave more money. In four months they spent everything. They had nothing more to give. But there were more tests. We wanted the boy to be put inside a very large apparatus that looked like a space capsule. It would check him millimetre by millimetre. That test was very important, but it was very expensive.

'I sent letters to everyone I could think of. A woman in Iowa suggested I contact the Willy Chirino Foundation. Chirino is a famous Cuban singer who left Cuba in 1961 in Operation Peter Pan.' Operation Peter Pan, organised by the Catholic diocese of Miami, airlifted 14,000 Cuban children to the US between 1960 and 1962. Some stayed with American and Cuban-American families, others lived in foster homes. The Cuban community in Miami was certain that Fidel's government would not last, and the children could go back home as soon as Castro was overthrown. Some of the Peter Pan children did not see their parents again for thirty years.

'I called the Willy Chirino Foundation and the secretary told me, "We only help children who have emigrated." Well,

1995 was a difficult time, there were many Cuban children at the Guantánamo Naval Base who had tried to emigrate in the *balsero* crisis the year before. Willy Chirino was helping to secure their release from Guantánamo and bring them to Florida. As Alejandro was not an emigrant he would receive nothing. It was hard on me; we were halfway there, but we found ourselves stuck. Everyone must take responsibility for what happens in their life, and my problem number one was the life of my son. I had to do whatever it took, except if it went against my principles. I would not give up.

'Another woman suggested I go to the Catholic Church. I went and talked to an ultra-reactionary priest who had a TV programme. He said I should come on his programme and afterwards we would discuss the hospital bills. I told him, "I did not come to Miami because of political problems. I came because of my son's illness, and no one will get me to change what I say."

'I went everywhere I could think of. I left no stone unturned. I went back to the Willy Chirino Foundation. They said no, we can't do anything for you. I felt that that was my last chance. I was very depressed, and I began to cry. I called a lady in Oklahoma, an American, who suggested I go to the Miami Children's Hospital, the one where Alejandro had been treated, where my uncle had paid the bills, and speak to Cubans who worked there. She said I should appeal to them as a mother. It had never occurred to me; I was so wound up in my own problems, in my own suffering. I went to the hospital and I found a Cuban woman on the staff who had a good heart. She helped me... *Vaya* [good God], I won't name names or anything like that, but she helped me. Then I found a Cuban doctor, a specialist, who saw my son for free.

'You know, Liz, for us here in Cuba, this is normal. Not for them there, with their capitalist mentality. But those Cubans had been raised here; although it's true that by then they were not so Cuban. The point is that that doctor treated my son for free.

For me it was a tremendous achievement, and not only that, he gave me his card. He said, when I was back in Cuba if my son should have any problems I shouldn't hesitate to phone him; I should call collect, and he would pay the charges. He said that he would continue to help us even though we were in Cuba. That was a real accomplishment. It was a beautiful thing from a humanitarian point of view, don't you think? Another Cuban doctor, a woman, helped us. Cuban exiles are not all bad. Those people were raised here in Cuba, educated here, formed here, and the truth is they helped me. The two doctors and the Cuban woman were beautiful people.

'Well at last Willy Chirino himself phoned to say his foundation would pay for the final test which cost I don't know how many thousands of dollars. After he paid he invited us to a Christmas party for all the children he had helped. It was in a large park in Miami adorned with decorations and lights. Alejandro and I went; it was the polite thing to do. *!Que pasó!* It was a circus. There were I don't know how many TV cameras and radio journalists. All the children from Guantánamo he'd brought to Florida were there. He was going to throw a big party and give out presents in front of the cameras. We arrived early so my son could go on all the rides for free. We went on the rides together and we were having a good time when I saw the children from the Guantánamo Naval Base filing in in front of the TV cameras. I said to Alejandro, "The party's over for us. Let's go." He began to cry, he wanted a present. He tried to get in line with the children waiting for presents. It was all being filmed for TV. I said to him, "No, you will be so embarrassed. You who are a Cuban child, who will return to your country, standing on line with children who have emigrated with their parents. The presents are for the child émigrés, not for you. Do you understand?"

'He did not understand. "But mamá, I want a present." I told him, "We are going to get you a present, but you cannot stand in this line. You will be embarrassed when back home in Cuba your friends and family see you on TV with these children." Well finally my son agreed to leave. I got him away just before the circus began.

'In December, when we had finished with everything, we came back here [to Cuba]. I had a job bringing him back. He didn't want to come. My son had become accustomed to living in luxury: having electricity and running water all day long, and food, toys, a car, all kinds of things. Over there everyone gets around by car, even poor people, your normal worker. But coming back to Cuba, knowing we were in the depths of the Special Period, without food, without running water, without electricity, without who knows what.

'The first fifteen days were hell, absolute hell. I had to see a psychologist, I had to seek help, I could not cope. I could not help him; I couldn't even help myself. To a child it was incomprehensible. It was as if I had dragged him out of a palace and brought him to live in a hovel. I could not talk to him about principles, morals, any of that. I could not talk to him about anything. Well, finally things settled down. My son was saved.'

—from Alejandro's perspective

Alejandro's memories of the entire saga were completely different from his mother's. While Olga remembered coming back to shortages, difficulties obtaining food, and constant anxiety, Alejandro remembered the fun he had playing on the Nintendo he brought back from Miami.

'I have no memories of my family facing tremendous difficulties during the Special Period. Nothing like that... My father raised animals – chickens, turkeys, rabbits, guinea pigs – in the garden. My mother grew vegetables and fruit. Besides, my father was director of the Institute of History. He was an important person in the Party and in the government, and we always ate well. I do not remember ever eating anything unusual. We did not have to eat the strange things others ate in the Special Period, like fried grapefruit rind. I do not remember anything like that. In fact, I grew and grew. I grew taller than anyone else. I am taller than my father and my mother. I have always been the tallest in every school I attended.' When Alejandro and I walked around Havana people constantly remarked on his height.

'I was in the fourth grade when I had my operation. It was the depth of the Special Period. I remember my mother frantically rushing around, always on her bicycle. I have no memories of my father. No, I don't remember seeing him when I was in the hospital. I should tell you, I have always gotten along well with my father, but it was not the relationship I had with my mother. She took me everywhere.'

Alejandro's lack of memories of his father may reflect his parents' living arrangements, as well as the gendered division of labour in his household. Domestic roles changed little in revolutionary Cuba. Women continued to do the bulk of childcare and housework, even though most women had jobs and community responsibilities.

'In 1995, when I was over there [Miami], everyone was talking about the *balseros*; that whole thing was still a big mess. As a child it didn't really interest me. A distant relative of mine had left Cuba in the 1994 exodus. He had been picked up at sea [by the US Coast Guard] and taken to the Guantánamo Naval Base. I met him after he arrived in Miami. That's all I can remember.

'My first real memory of Miami is a helium balloon. I had never seen one. What an impact. I clearly remember my uncle's car. Yes, the car stands out in my memory. My uncle gave me a first-generation Super Nintendo, a games console that had just been invented. My passion was role-play games, watching films and a thousand other things. I was in another world... I went to Disneyworld in Orlando. That is something I will always, always remember. We were there three days and we visited three parks. That had an enormous impact on me. Just imagine, a Cuban child at Disneyworld.'

Did you want to return to Cuba?

'My mother never asked me. She made the decisions and I did what she said. I was just a kid. If she had asked me, I would have said I wanted to stay. But her mother was here, and she was still married to my father.' In fact, as Olga explained, she was never married to Alejandro's father.

'The roots of the little business I have now distributing TV series, go back to when I had lymphoma. Since then my head and my heart have been in computers. I returned here with my Super Nintendo and a PlayStation, the latest models, and I brought all the games back with me. They were a sensation. All my friends came to my house. My mother imposed limits: no gaming between this hour and that; only x number of children at one time. I swapped games. In Cuba people fabricated new games. They were constantly inventing. My PlayStation wasn't compatible with the pirated disks, so I got into upgrading, inventing, and all that stuff. I sold the Nintendo and bought another PlayStation. That is the story of my youth. I played some in the street, but mostly I played games on the console. I got to know people through games networks. Many of them are still my best friends.'

Were there girls in the games networks?

'*No, es cosa de hombres.*' No, it's a man thing.

Ten-year-old Alejandro was in the vanguard of Cuba's tiny computer-literati. With the dire shortages of the Special Period, compounded by the US blockade, only officials at the highest levels of the Party and the army had access to computers back then in 1995. Until 2008, Cubans were not allowed to buy computers. No wonder Alejandro's gaming consoles were a sensation.

'It was a time you don't forget.' A struggle that pitted David against Goliath.

Alejandro was a top student at pre and aspired to becoming a world-famous engineer. He joined the Union de Juventud Comunista (Union of Young Communists, UJC) thinking it would advance his career.

'People tell you that if you want to have an important position you must be *integrado* [involved in official organisations]. Some people told me you have to join the Juventud Comunista, others said no. I figured it would enhance my standing in relation to others, so I joined and I am still a member. I could have quit any time, but the fact is I think the UJC isn't really anything. It's nothing. Honestly, I never wanted to get involved with any of that.'

Alejandro recalled that despite his political apathy, he threw himself into in the campaign for Elián González, the child rafter. Six-year-old Elián was on a tiny makeshift boat that sank while crossing the Florida Straits in 1999. His mother and ten others drowned. Fishermen rescued Elián and turned him over to the US Coast Guard, who took him to Miami. When Elián's father in Cuba petitioned the US courts for custody of his son, Elián became a cause celebre in a propaganda war that pitted Cuban-Americans against Fidel Castro. At the end of a two-year legal battle, the US Court of Appeals granted custody to Elián's father and the boy returned to Cuba.

Alejandro remembered participating in the campaign demanding Elián's return. 'It was an important moment in my life.' He recalled his sense of purpose, and throwing himself into collective work. 'During the whole Elián thing they called us up for voluntary labour. They recruited young people at pre. We built the Anti-Imperialist Tribunal' – where Esteban and fellow discontents hung out hoping for US visas. 'We spent entire nights working and joking. At school we had to do what they called social work every month. It was part of the Battle of Ideas. We worked very hard. I remember when the Anti-Imperialist Tribunal was nothing, nothing was there. I remember building schools that now are famous. I worked day and night. I have happy memories of all this because despite the hard work, the manual labour, we were doing something worthwhile. We felt we were essential to the success of those projects. Our group developed strong bonds. We were together day and night joking and working. I really enjoyed myself.'

Curiously, Esteban also described developing strong bonds at the Anti-Imperialist Tribunal – but of a different sort. He remembered the camaraderie generated in the heat of the protests against the government.

'At the time of the huge marches for Elián buses picked us up at dawn,' Alejandro recalled. 'In the beginning I went to all the marches, later on to only one or two. The rest of the time we snuck away and headed for Coppelia. It was a time you don't forget; the marches were enormous. Multitudes marched. They organised us into contingents, they called out your name, ticked you off a list. They kept a record of how many marches you went on; I was at five. I lived all that nonsense. Yes, I lived all that nonsense the year I was in tenth grade.'

Alejandro clearly enjoyed recounting his passion and sense of purpose, the feeling he had played a part in the Elián campaign. At the same time remembering the marches seemed to make him a bit uncomfortable because he had become very cynical about politics. 'I lived all that nonsense.' Many Cubans of Alejandro's generation who like him felt alienated from the government recalled the fervour generated by the Elián campaign, and said they were glad they had played a part.

A rising star

After graduating from pre, Alejandro, like all students expecting
to go on to university, had to do military service before starting
their university course; or, if they had an exemption, a form of
alternative service. His mother arranged for him to do alternative
service in the IT department of the technical university where she
worked, and where he was enrolled to study industrial engineering.
'Some people do their social service spraying mosquitos. Others
are sent to work places. I was fortunate. Although I had never so
much as touched a real computer, and had never even seen the
web, I was assigned to work in the IT department where I got to
know the world of computers... I learned mountains of things.
Everything I know now I learned there. It was an exceptional
year. The following year I got my first computer.'

Industrial engineering was Alejandro's alpha and omega.
'What we in Cuba call industrial engineering in other countries
is business administration. At university we learned how to create
a business, provide leadership, manage the company. We learned
the entire process. When I was a student I visited state enterprises,
analysed their systems, and recommended ways to make them
more efficient... *Bueno*, ever since graduating I have been working
in this entrepreneurial world, right here in Cuba.'

Alejandro was very ambitious. At university he calculated how
many As, how many teaching assistantships, how many meetings
of the Juventud Comunista, how many marches he had to go on
in order to graduate first in his class. 'If someone with the same
number of points as you holds a position in the Juventud, or goes
to every single march, he will be ranked first. Honestly, I never
wanted to get involved in anything like the Juventud, but I did.'
At that moment Alejandro's mobile phone rang.

'Sorry, Liz, that was a friend of mine. A mutual friend is coming
from Pinar del Río bringing food to sell. He brings lobster, fish,

cheese and ham and sells them at affordable prices. My friend was calling to place an order for two packets of lobster. We don't talk about that kind of thing on the telephone, but he speaks in code to get his message across. I adore lobster and shrimp. I can't afford to buy very much, but every month I buy some. The guy also sells pork fillets without too much fat, and amazing, wonderful ham… I don't like eating cheap stuff. In the evenings after I get home I like to eat well. My priority is eating.' Alejandro giggled, maybe partly because he owned up to enjoying expensive food, partly because he was talking about illicit activities.

'Umm, where was I when my phone rang? Oh yes, no, I never held office in the Juventud. But to accumulate points I signed up to throw a javelin in the University Games. I'd never thrown a javelin, but it gave you points. I joined the chess club to get points. It matters because the students with the most points get their first choice of jobs. I graduated with more points than anyone else in my class. I graduated number one.

'Graduation was both the happiest and the saddest day of my life. Happy because I became an industrial engineer, and I won the *titulo de oro*, the gold medal for being the top student. Sad because no one from my family was there. Everyone else, all my friends, had their parents. I had no one. You can understand how I felt. It was very, very hard. My father could have come but he didn't; nor did my half-sister on my father's side. My mother was in Miami. Not having anyone was very painful. The sad reality is that I have no family here that I can count on. Not having anyone has pushed me to get ahead on my own, to live as best I can. To my mind I have achieved an enormous amount. I have been very successful.'

'The great divide in Cuba is economic'

Many of Alejandro's friends had to drop out of university. 'To study at university, you need to have economic resources. You must pay for lunch, transport, other things. Many people had to drop out because even though there are no fees, they couldn't afford to continue. Some were brilliant. It can be very difficult, especially if you're expected to help support your family. When you are studying you have no income.' He could have been talking about Mario.

Alejandro described the lives of several close friends who had dropped out of university because of poverty. 'I have one friend who I really, really admire. He stayed and graduated despite the desperate situation in his household. They never had a TV. He never had a girlfriend because he has no privacy at home, and he can't afford to take a girl out or anything.' Again, this echoes Mario's predicament.

'The great divide in Cuba is economic. Differences in purchasing power determine how people live. If your family has more buying power, more money, it conditions how you think. It's like the refrain, "Tell me how you live, and I'll tell you what you think." The truth is because of the way most Cubans live, because of their poverty, they know nothing. They don't even know Facebook exists, or the internet. Their lives are totally divorced from all that, and it is a very large group. On the other side are people who have the economic resources to go to university, and pay a fortune to go online for fifteen minutes.'

To Alejandro, a major indicator of inequality was internet access. This seemed as true of Cubans in 2022 as it did in 2012, when Alejandro railed against the high cost of going online. The Cuban government has gradually expanded internet access, but at a price. Internet use is rationed via money, as are most things in Cuba these days. If you have money you can access the internet on your smartphone or in your home, but only the better off can afford this. The internet remains the playground of the affluent.

'How much more you enjoy what you have when you have earned it through your own sacrifices.'

Alejandro fumed about the growing gap between Cubans working in the private versus the public sector, and was angry that university graduates who spent years studying and did important jobs were not well paid. To him, in the ideal society a person's salary would reflect their educational attainment. 'If only my sacrifices counted for something, but in this country they don't. It makes me furious that people who have done nothing, who have never studied or anything, have greater possibilities than me. Eighty or ninety per cent of university graduates share my feelings. In the way our country is run, someone who sells *churros*, fried doughnuts, on the street, or works in a shop, earns more than a person who has devoted five years of his life to studying at university. That really and truly hurts.'

Alejandro dreamed of living *decorosamente*, decently. He said that if he could live *decorosamente* he would not leave. He rolled the word around on his tongue and the sound conjured up comfort and respectability. 'If only they [the government] gave me the opportunity to live *decorosamente* and have the basics. All I want is to live normally and be able to go out from time to time. It would feel good to earn a living from your own sacrifices. Take me, a mountain of people came to my house asking me to do this and that until I had enough money to buy an air conditioner and a washing machine.' 'This and that' meant his digital side-line. 'I saved little by little. It took me about a year, but I did it. How much more you enjoy what you have when you have earned it through your own sacrifices. You value it much, much more than when it is given to you. That's my opinion.'

Raúl Castro's denunciation of egalitarianism and praise of individual initiative struck a chord with Alejandro, who criticised universal social provision. Alejandro was not alone. Mario said egalitarianism had eroded Cubans' work ethic, and Pavel, always the bluntest, said 'Cuba has become a nation of parasites.'

'"I no longer have dreams."'

What are your dreams for the future?

Alejandro shot back, 'To each according to who he is,' a very deliberate reworking of the Marxist tenet, 'To each according to his needs.' 'An engineer should have the means to dress nicely and go out on the town, do things a person who sells *churros* would not be able to afford. It would be the normal way of life for a person who has really and truly struggled to secure a good job that requires education and mountains of studying. You should be able to live the way you want without constantly having to *inventor* – do a little something on the side. I dream of inviting my friends, me the engineer saying to guys who have not been to university, or who work in a shop, "Hey guys, I'll buy you a drink." Now it's the other way around, it's they who invite me. They have money, I don't.' Cuban social scientists are calling this phenomenon 'the inverted social pyramid'.

'I would like to fix up my house and build a pretty fence. But that costs. I would like to have a decent job and earn a decent salary that would allow me to enjoy the pleasures of life, just like any normal person. I would like to travel abroad and come back. I think this is the dream that now, in 2012, most Cubans cherish. It's the same dream that Cubans had in 1990 and maybe in 1980 too. But they are just dreams.'

'Have you seen *Suite Habana*, the film by Fernando Pérez?' Alejandro asked me. 'Remember when he asks the *señora*, "What are your dreams?" And she replies, "I no longer have dreams." It's like that. At the end of the day you are left without dreams.'

Do you dream of leaving?

Alejandro's immediate response was that he longed to see his mother, whose face he could no longer visualise. 'What I remember are the photos... I don't know if I want to leave, but if conditions here do not improve... I don't want to live in a country like this, a country where you can't plan, where you can't dream. A country where there is no hope for the future; where everything you do is for right now, for today. It is true that they [the state] gave me every opportunity to study. But in the end where did it get me? I have many great friends, and it would break my heart to leave them. But I can't go on like this. I think thousands of Cubans are in my same situation. That's why emigration by young people is massive. We don't see a future. We don't see our lives going anywhere if we stay here.

'Older people can say, "At least I was able to enjoy it when it was good." I like this country. I would like to be able to stay, but I have certain requirements, economic requirements. Politics I don't care about. I don't mind who is in charge. I don't keep track of them, or any of that. I would like to stay, but only if I can really make something of my life, build on what I have studied, become a professional of some importance, become a somebody. I do not want to dedicate my life to pirating TV series and films for other people. I don't want to have to do this in order to live. I am an engineer, and not just any engineer; I am an engineer with a gold medal. So, my answer is that if I am given the opportunity to earn well and live well on my salary I would stay. I would never even think of leaving, except to visit my mother, and then I would return... If they gave me back my dreams, I would not have to leave, not I, not anyone. The truth is that in this country, well maybe there are some murders and a little bit of violence, but generally I can walk anywhere with complete confidence that nothing will happen.

'If I can't live decently, if I can't become a professional of some importance, if that does not happen, then I am going, but going

with a heavy heart because I would be leaving millions of friends.
Do you understand how I feel? Really, if doesn't change here, if
the changes that are happening do not affect my life, if they help
others but they don't help me, well that is the problem. Let me
say, if someone appears today and tells me I can leave tomorrow
and never return, I would go.'

Cubans once dreamed of making history, of participating in
a socialist revolution that inspired the world. Many Cubans no
longer dare to dream.

PART 3

INEQUALITY, 2006-20

'We must change or we will be swept away,' Raúl Castro declared on succeeding Fidel in 2006. Fearing the Fidelistas at the top of the Party would oppose his market reforms, he banished them from public life before announcing the plan to *actualizar el modelo económico*, update the economic model – the government's euphemism for rolling back the state's economic monopoly and loosening restrictions on the private sector.

It seemed, at the beginning, that Raúl's government would radically transform the economic system. The Central de Trabajadores de Cuba (CTC), the Cuban Workers' Trade Union Federation – in lieu of Raúl himself – announced a mass layoff of state workers, and the government simultaneously increased the number of sectors open to private businesses. The direction of change seemed clear: the state would play a smaller role in the economy leaving space for a larger private sector, mostly small businesses. To fend off resistance to the layoffs, and encourage newly unemployed workers into self-employment (the official term for private business), Party leaders admonished that no one should rely on the state to guarantee their livelihood; they should rely on themselves.

Reactions to the changes varied. The evening the list of sectors open to private enterprise appeared in *Granma*, I returned to my B&B to find my landlady sitting at the kitchen table poring over the newspaper – not something she normally did. She looked up, smiled, and asked if I thought she should open a tapas bar in the garage, or a party planning business. She had been looking for ways to invest her earnings from the likes of me, and in the meantime kept her dollars and euros wrapped in bundles in the safe behind her bed.

Alina Rodríguez viewed the changes differently. She said the idea of officials going around telling workers threatened with layoffs they would end up better off made her cry. She scorned the idea that a half million Cubans with no money to invest, no business experience, and no government assistance would blossom into petty entrepreneurs.[1]

In short, Cubans with hard currency welcomed the changes and opened businesses. Cubans without hard currency, the majority, tried to patch together a living working at a mix of state- and private-sector jobs.[2] The next year the government introduced more market reforms by lifting restrictions on the sale of houses, car ownership and travel abroad. The measures eroded the egalitarian foundations of the Revolution and intensified inequality.

The urban property reform enacted by Raúl Castro's government fundamentally transformed the nature of housing. When Fidel ruled, Cubans were allowed to swap but not sell their house. Consequently, the value of a house was not calculated in money, but in how well or badly it suited a family's needs. Houses had a use value, not an exchange value. With the changes, a house was more than a home. It had a market value; it was a financial asset and a store of wealth. The new housing market transformed Cubans' consciousness as they saw their home as an economic opportunity. The commercialisation of housing gave rise to a property revolution that altered the streetscape of Havana. Estate agents opened offices and dilapidated houses were renovated and sold by islanders – often fronting for Cuban-Americans – to the newly affluent petty bourgeoisie, or sold *por la izquierda,* under the table, to foreigners.

The clash between Raúl's policies and the founding principles of the Revolution came to a climax at the 2011 Congress of the Cuban Communist Party when his followers voted to remove egalitarianism from the Party's Statement of Principles.

The most popular reform, the one all Cubans had longed for, eliminated many restrictions on overseas travel. From the 1960s, when the state imposed travel regulations, Cubans needed official permission to leave the country. Following the migration reform travel was regulated primarily by the market. If a Cuban had the money to pay for a plane ticket and a passport they could travel overseas; if not they stayed put, or left illegally – and had to be prepared to pay with their lives.

*

The success of Raúl Castro's economic strategy hinged on improving relations with the US government and an end to the blockade. The market reforms prepared the ground for a US-Cuban rapprochement. Castro let it be known through back channels that he was willing to negotiate with President Barack Obama and after high-level secret meetings, and a last-minute papal intervention, the two governments re-established diplomatic relations in 2015. This loosened but did not end the US blockade, as that required an act of Congress.[3]

When Obama visited Havana he made it clear that the purpose of the détente, from his perspective, was to promote a US-style democracy and free market system in Cuba. 'In the United States, we have a clear monument to what the Cuban people can build – it's called Miami,' he said, rubbing salt into history's wounds.

After issuing a mild rebuke to Obama, Raúl Castro announced that the state planned to step up the economic reforms and would allow small businesses to expand.[4] Fidelistas, poorer Cubans, and a large part of the *inteligencia* objected to the changes on the grounds that they would accentuate the emerging class divide.

In the latter days of Raúl Castro's presidency, the geopolitical situation facing the government went from moderately favourable to terrible. In 2017 President Obama was succeeded by Donald Trump, who tightened the blockade and vowed to topple the government in Havana. The Venezuelan leadership, facing a severe economic crisis and US sanctions, reduced oil shipments to Cuba, and a right-wing coup in Brazil removed Castro's allies from office, ending Brazilian investment in the Mariel Economic Development Zone which Raúl Castro had described as Cuba's most important infrastructure project since 1959. The triple blow had a devastating effect on the economy. Rising food prices and widespread shortages eroded most Cubans' already precarious standard of living. With Raúl Castro turning over the presidency – but not his power– to his protégé Miguel Díaz-Canel, and dissatisfaction growing, the leadership decided to put the market opening on hold. It was not the moment to stir up class-based discord.

Covid turned Cubans' economic difficulties into a disaster as tourism virtually stopped, closing down the government's prime source of foreign exchange. People went hungry; supermarket shelves were bare, and the state scaled back the ration as it simply could not import enough food to feed the population. Hoping that market measures might alleviate the situation, at least for some, President Díaz-Canel, the leader in name, announced a return to a pro-market strategy. Unlike in Fidel's era when Soviet support underpinned a paternalist arrangement that, to put it crassly, provided food in exchange for allegiance, by 2020 the Cuban government had nothing to offer, and growing discontent was met with growing repression.

If there is one enduring lesson from Cuba's thirty years of post-Soviet economic devastation it is that when US politicians set out to destroy a Latin American country the likelihood is that they will do anything to succeed.

19

MARIO SÁNCHEZ CORTÉZ

Old Havana

'The thread of equality is broken.'

Mario was feeling disillusioned and stuck.[1] It was 2010, Raúl had been in office more than two years, and Mario had been working at the same low-paid job in the Ministry for what seemed like forever. Now the guys in the neighbourhood were taunting him. '*Compadre*, you've spent a mountain of years studying. Where did it get you? Why all the sacrifices? Why not make something of yourself and earn decent money?' Mario's salary, the equivalent of one dollar a day, did not cover his food and clothing. Rarely did he have money to buy a beer. He almost never went out. 'My life had been very difficult for twenty years,' he said, as he expressed outrage that Raúl Castro's government was expanding opportunities for small businesses while laying off state workers like him.

'The achievements of the revolution are disappearing… Certain people have *poder adquisitivo*, purchasing power. Let's put aside how they got it, maybe via *jineterismo*, sex work; it's their life and they can do whatever they want with it. But let's just say that on Teacher's Day the son of a *jinetera* gives his teacher x dollars and the worker's son doesn't because he can't. The teacher is poor.

She does not earn a decent salary and she needs new shoes. Let's also say the worker's son is smarter and harder-working than the son of the *jinetera*, but the teacher gives the latter higher grades because he gave her dollars. At that instant the thread of equality is broken. The *jinetera*'s son, because he has dollars, will get into a better school. How can I keep telling my nephew that if he studies hard he can achieve whatever he wants, he can accomplish his dreams? I can't because he sees what goes on.

'That's the reality and it's very crude. I'm telling you what really happens, without prettifying it for foreigners. A few weeks ago I went to the doctor. To get better treatment I gave her a soda and a ham sandwich which was all I could afford. What the hell, I know that her lunch is terrible and she doesn't get a *merienda*. She smiles. I tell her the food is to make her feel better, that kind of thing. I made a sacrifice and bought her a genuine soda [a soda sold in hard currency], the kind I never buy for myself. The doctor says, "How nice, lucky me, I can have a *merienda*," and she devotes a lot of time to me. She becomes my friend. She smiles and blah blah. In walks a man who doesn't have a regular job but he has *poder adquisitivo*, purchasing power. He doesn't give her one bottle of soda and one ham sandwich; he gives her a carton of sodas and a whole box of delicious sandwiches. The next time I go to the doctor I'm waiting in line and he walks right past me to the front of the line. We are supposed to be equal, but... you know what I mean. There is corruption at every step. If the doctor were paid enough to cover her needs she would say to him, "Keep your box of sandwiches. When I want a ham and cheese sandwich I will buy it myself. Now go to the back of the line and wait your turn."' Mario was shocked that healthcare, one of the Revolution's great achievements, was tainted by corruption.

'Who is keeping an eye on this? What are they doing to stop it? The emerging class is gaining power. Now they are a petty bourgeoisie but with the new economic policies they will grow bigger and bigger. They will be allowed to invest more and own bigger businesses. Workers don't have the same possibilities. The first lot can drop twenty-five CUC [Cuba's convertible currency] just to get into a club.[2] I'm not saying clubs are high-culture places, but I can't choose whether or not to go to one. I simply can't afford them. That's what I mean by inequality. We are seeing it grow. That's what I mean by the emerging class. In the medium term *bisneros*, business owners, are going to have a lot of economic power. In time they will wield political power as well... Our revolution was founded on the principle of equality. Why isn't the government putting an end to all this?'

When Raúl Castro began liberalising the economy Mario was passionately opposed to the new measures.

'It's not fair that someone living right next door gets ahead from one day to the next, legally or illegally. You know what I mean? What I believe is to each according to their work, to their contribution to society. It's in the documents we studied at Party meetings, but they haven't upheld that principle' – the ubiquitous they.

Mario objected to *empresas mixtas*, companies jointly owned by the state and foreign companies. 'Think about it. Take a man who works for an *empresa mixta* who receives part of his pay in *divisas*. First, he fixes up his house; next, he buys a car. Before you know it he doesn't even bother to pick up his food rations. The crowning blow is that you had been friends and now he looks at you with disdain. The changes have been gigantic. I'm not against change. I'm not against foreign investment, but they told us everyone would reap the benefits.' Fidel and Raúl had said that to keep the economy afloat the country needed tourism and private businesses, and the profits would be equally shared. Mario felt betrayed.

'Liz, make sure you put this in your book.'

Mario saw the government pandering to tourists and it infuriated him. 'In Cuba tourists ride around in luxury buses, the kind with air conditioning. They step out of their air-conditioned bus to walk around Old Havana and take pictures to send back home to their friends, a memento from Cuba. None of the inequalities shock them; they don't even notice. They don't understand Cubans; they don't understand how we think and feel; they don't understand our problems. Liz, make sure you put this in your book.'

'Don't worry. We're not about to take away free healthcare.'

Mario talked us through the last meeting of his Party branch where the head had given a talk on what was wrong with egalitarianism. Mario said the presentation confused him, and he began to repeat word-for-word what he could remember. I stopped him. 'Are you sure you want to tell us this; aren't Party meetings supposed to be confidential? Remember, I am recording this interview.' Mario laughed. 'Liz, if they didn't want me to be part of your project they would have told me long ago. By the way, [pointing to an imaginary device on the ceiling] if you lose one of the recordings let them know and they will replace it.'

Clearly, Mario took for granted that the security apparatus saw and heard everything. Several times he said the leadership was old, out-of-date and dictatorial – that was his word. Either he figured the government tolerated harsh criticism, or he got carried away. I think the latter more likely, but whatever the cause, Mario rarely seemed to censor himself.

'In the branch meeting we discussed children's heart operations. The head gave us this topic because we're always hearing on

TV that in Cuba we perform x number of heart operations on x number of children, that each operation costs x amount, and they don't do free heart operations in other countries of the world. We talked about how that's grand for the mother [Mario said nothing about the father]. The operation is the most important thing in the world for her. For the baby too; it saved his life. Let's say the operation costs twenty-five thousand dollars. For the mother that's OK, but what about for the rest of us? We discussed how everyone thinks public health is free, but in reality we all are paying for it. We pay for the operation by not getting paid enough for our labour to cover our basic needs. Part of the money I do not get paid goes for public health, for operations like this one that costs twenty-five thousand dollars.' Mario said the meeting ended with a heated discussion about whether healthcare should be free for everyone.

I was, quite frankly, shocked to hear that the Cuban Communist Party was discussing the pros and cons of free healthcare. Seeing my astonishment, Mario tried to reassure me, 'Don't worry, Liz, we're not about to take away free healthcare. That really would be the end of socialism.' Mario's account of Party meetings prefigured Raúl's criticism of egalitarianism.

'It was beautiful because we were equal, but it wasn't egalitarianism.'

Mario said he mulled over the discussions they had in Party meetings, trying to make sense of them. Material equality had always been his moral compass, his North Star. 'When I was a child folks had little, but we made do. It was beautiful because we were all equal. But it wasn't *igualitar*, *igualitarismo*, egalitarianism.' He stumbled over the word. 'You know what I'm trying to say. No, they didn't just give us everything, but we all lived pretty much the same.'

In December 2010, the same month Lilia Campos and I interviewed Mario, Raúl Castro gave a speech denouncing egalitarianism. He said, 'The Revolution adopted an excessively paternalist, idealist and egalitarian focus to achieve social justice. It was wrong and unsustainable... These erroneous concepts became very entrenched in large sectors of the population. For this reason, we need a change of mentality among the citizenry and the leadership.'[3]

The speech was a watershed. It overturned the Revolution's commitment to promoting equality. In official circles egalitarianism became a dirty word, and the state media launched a campaign denouncing it.

At first, Mario's words puzzled me. 'We were all equal... but it wasn't egalitarianism... No, they didn't just give us everything...' When I heard Raúl's speech the penny dropped. As a Party member Mario knew what was coming, and it shook him to the core. Raúl's speech turned everything he believed in upside down, and he was struggling to reconcile his good memories of economic equality with the new Party line.

Four months later, in April 2011, the Congress of the Cuban Communist Party deleted egalitarianism from the Party's Statement of Principles, replacing it with a pledge to provide equal opportunities.[4] The Congress, in effect, declared the anti-egalitarian ideology was the official doctrine of the Party. Cubans who followed the ins and outs of Party politics – and there weren't many – saw Raúl's condemnation of paternalism, idealism, and egalitarianism as a thinly veiled attack on Fidel. Fidelistas, for their part, opposed the change and argued that equality of opportunity is not a softer version of egalitarianism, but its antithesis – a means of justifying inequality.

'Almost everyone above me was under investigation for corruption.'

Mario's life took a positive turn two years later. In 2012, he sent me an email saying, 'My fortune has changed. I want to surprise you. I will tell you when I see you.' When I arrived at Lilia's apartment Mario was leaning back on the sofa. He had an irrepressible smile and was practically dancing with excitement. 'There have been changes in my department... The Party asked me to become the director. Almost everyone above me was accused of corruption.'

When Mario's department moved to the suburbs twenty-five brand new Vietnamese computers – still in their boxes – went missing. His boss, the ex-director, failed to report the loss. The judge at the trial ruled that even if the director and senior staff of the IT department were not accomplices in the theft, they were guilty of criminal negligence.

'There's a tremendous amount of corruption and bribery. At the end of the day your salary doesn't cover your needs, so you get drawn into it. It's the only way to get by. You don't care if you lose your job; you'll get another one that doesn't pay. It's the same story over and over again. You aren't interested in the work. You go to the office to see what you can steal.' Mario explained that he was promoted to the top job because he was the only senior staff member who was entirely free from suspicion. Mario was much too modest, as always.

To illustrate the inevitability of corruption, Mario repeated one of his favourite stories. A friend was flying home from London with overweight luggage stuffed with merchandise he planned to sell. When he offered a bribe to the check-in attendant at Heathrow Airport the man replied, 'If I take your money, I might lose my job. If I lose my job, I won't be able to pay my mortgage. On my salary I can pay my bills. With the money I would take from you I wouldn't be able to.' 'Here it's the opposite,' Mario said. 'If you don't take bribes, if you don't steal from the state, you can't get by; you can't pay your bills.' Mario made it clear he was talking about ordinary workers. Top officials who used their power to accumulate wealth were a different kettle of fish.

Mario reluctantly accepted the directorship, but not because his salary would increase by much. 'I still don't earn nearly enough to live on. At the weekends I repair computers *por la izquierda*. My only perk is a motor scooter.'

Did you manage to pass the driving test?

'Yes. Now I have a license to kill... I never aspired to a managerial position. I am a web designer, and my dream is to become an intellectual. I have a list of one hundred great books I want to read before I die.'

Heading a department nicknamed the *sala de embarque*, the departure lounge, turned out to be more challenging than Mario had anticipated. He counted on his fingers the colleagues who had emigrated, but soon ran out of fingers. What Mario disliked most about the job was the need to police his staff. 'I tell them not to enter prohibited websites, but they get carried away by curiosity. It happens easily because they don't have internet at home. They are human beings after all. I understand their craving and I look the other way. Many go to pornographic and counterrevolutionary sites... So far, I've not actually spotted someone on a forbidden site. I'm sure they are, but not when I am looking. Frankly, I would find it very difficult to inform on a *compañero*. They would face a trial and maybe lose their job.'

Mario recalled his first unpleasant experience. 'After rumours reached Havana of shenanigans in our Santiago office I had to carry out an urgent inspection.' 'So you flew out there?' I interrupted. 'No, I took the bus. It was one of those dire trips, a voyage to kill. Getting there was an ordeal, it took thirty hours.'

In a narrative befitting García Márquez's *One Hundred Years of Solitude*, Mario described two surreal bus trips to Santiago. Eventually the cyber police discovered that the Santiago office was selling internet time and phony passwords. Mario said it was an innovative scam. The mastermind was jailed, and the local director was fired for criminal negligence.

'When I took this position I didn't have any idea of what I was getting into. From my vantage point, at the bottom of the ladder, I never imagined, I couldn't see the big picture. You see what I'm saying. I was a web designer. I had never even served on the management committee. When I discovered what the job entails I said to myself *Candela*.' *Candela* is one of Cubans' favourite expressions and it means anything from 'hot stuff' to 'what a disaster'. The literal translation is 'on fire'. 'But I enjoy challenges and I don't like to lose face. As a result, day in and day out I am putting out fires.'

'Youth don't identify with the Revolution.'

After his promotion, Mario moved up a notch in the Party hierarchy. 'That's the way it works. Now I am the Second Secretary of my branch, responsible for recruitment, and that's another challenge. Our primary goal right now is to increase Party membership. The historical generation, the cohort that made the Revolution, is passing, and we need to replace them with younger members... But the reality is that youth don't identify with the Party, they don't want to be part of it. They have other... let's just say they are indifferent. Besides indifference, they lack commitment because at the end of the day being a Party militant doesn't get you a house or a car or money, quite the opposite. Youth are interested in...' Mario stopped mid-sentence and chuckled, 'I'm talking as if I were not young myself. The fact is I'm still very young.' He was thirty-seven.

'It is very difficult to recruit young people into the Party. In their eyes the state lacks credibility. To an extent they're right. Because of attitudes, decisions, arbitrary forms of rule, youth don't identify with the Revolution. I mean most don't, but you can't generalise. Some young people are integrated into the ranks of the Party, most aren't. Things have changed. Times have changed. The historic leaders have aged; their ideas have aged too... Today's youth think the state is incapable of solving their problems so they say to themselves, if they can't improve my situation, if they can't provide me with what I need, I won't believe in them.'

'Since youth do not identify with the revolutionary process they develop independently, if you see what I mean. They think along different lines. They go their own way. I think the Revolution, like everything, needs renovation. For things to work the Revolution needs new goals, real things. I think that's how it should be. We used to think that everyone should support the Revolution. Everyone should be integrated, but real life doesn't work that way. In every other country of the world some people support the government, and some oppose it. In those countries they put the two parts together and they arrive at a consensus. I think the solution lies in consensus. That's reality.'

Some people we interviewed were cautious. Mario took risks. I was surprised that someone in his position advocated consensual politics, particularly as he took it for granted that Big Brother was listening. Mario prided himself on being independent minded – a trait the Communist leadership did not encourage.

To your way of thinking what are the most important issues facing Cuba today?

'Listen, what I am about to tell you is very important. The most important issues are secrecy and silence. While it isn't like it used to be, we still have a long way to go. Secrecy is very pernicious. Most Cubans feel free to talk one-to-one, but in official places they won't. Consequently, you don't know what they're thinking. I believe everyone should be allowed to say whatever they think, good or bad, within reason of course. To be able express ourselves openly and completely is a right that belongs to all of us. It won't harm anybody. It's what we need; it's what people want, especially the youth who want to go so far as to debate issues. We [Party members] need to sit and listen to them. I think things should not be done dictatorially in the sense that THIS IS HOW IT IS. No, people, like animals, have different colours, different shades. The grass should be allowed to grow so it provides different food for different animals according to their different developmental needs. Do you follow me?

'We should not pretend there is *un pensamiento único*, a correct way of thinking. We are not all identical at birth. In school they taught us to think; they said thinking is good, so they shouldn't stop us from thinking later in life. That's the reason a lot of Cubans leave. They leave for economic reasons, but they also leave because of... let's say... they don't see the way they think, their concerns, reflected in... and I'm not talking only about solutions. At least if they received an answer, if someone said, "It is not possible to solve your problems," at least people would feel that they, their ideas, had been taken into account. I am convinced of this... But to ignore people, to disregard their ideas and what they say, no, it's not right. Inevitably it allows antagonistic differences to grow. Difference is part of human development. The recognition of differences could strengthen us, make things better here.'

Mario insisted on speaking his mind and what he had to say challenged the official doctrine. He believed in openness, rights, free debate, consensual politics, accountability and difference – all the things Cuba's leaders regarded as subversive.

Do you think the government is allowing people to express themselves a little more? Is that beginning to happen?

'It's happening, it's happening, but not enough. It's happening but not at the level of...' Mario broke off. 'By insisting that everything goes through proper channels [inside the Party] lots of things get stuck in the chain of command... Middle-ranking cadre [Party members] do not want the higher-ups to know what rank-and-file members are really saying because many complaints are aimed at those very people, the middle cadre.' Mario subscribed to the Good Tsar Syndrome.

'Many, no, most youth don't identify with the revolutionary process because it hasn't found a way to solve their problems, their basic needs, their housing, food and clothing, the ABC of socialism. It hasn't solved their education problems, their medical problems, they have to wait to see a doctor. The state would like to make improvements, and to a certain degree it has, but not enough. Youth is by nature nonconformist, and not only politically. Right now, most young people in Cuba don't want to go to university. They don't see a future in becoming a professional. They don't think it will solve their economic difficulties. A few go that route, not many.'

'Some Cubans have advantages. Just like everywhere else it depends on the cradle you were born in.'

Explaining how he tries to inspire youth in his neighbourhood to go to university, Mario tells an anecdote he had told before. But he gives the story a different meaning.

'I tell them every one of us faces many hardships, but you shouldn't let your necessities crush you. You shouldn't use it as an excuse. Don't let your poverty stop you from becoming the person you want to be... Some Cubans have advantages, just like everywhere else it depends on the cradle you were born in. I tell them that when I was at university some of my *compañeros* arrived by car. Their parents gave them money, twenty, thirty, even forty dollars to buy snacks and lunch – and that didn't cover their clothes and shoes. They got more for that. They went to Varadero for vacations. They ate at restaurants. They had life on a plate. *Muy bien. Felicidades por ellos*, lucky for them. The bottom line was that we were all in the same classroom and we all had to pass the same exams.'

When Mario told the story in 2006, and Fidel was still in charge, he stressed the injustice of inequality. 'When I was at university... universities had already become very elitist...' After Raúl Castro's market reforms altered the country's economic structures and Cubans' consciousness, Mario stated matter-of-factly, 'Some Cubans have advantages, *just like everywhere else it depends on the cradle you were born in.*' By then Mario viewed inequality as the new normal and he modified the story to fit the times.

'What inequality looks like.'

After Raúl Castro's administration relaxed restrictions on the size of Cuban-owned businesses and allowed people to buy and sell their houses, Mario gave me a guided tour of his barrio. He wanted to show me what the new inequalities looked like. At first glance the buildings on his street all looked dilapidated to me, but Mario opened my eyes to the signs of prosperity. 'People with money live there and there,' he said, pointing to two newly painted pastel-coloured houses with bars on the windows, water tanks on the roof, and heavy curtains to stop people peeking in. He told me a Cuban-American had recently purchased the rundown property across the street via a proxy who lives around the corner, and there were rumours it was going to be an Airbnb. Although the gap between rich and poor was small by international standards, to Mario it loomed large.

Back in his windowless apartment with water seeping through the walls Mario explained the workings of upward mobility. 'A few families moved out [of the neighbourhood] and now they live in Vedado in nice houses with big gardens and patios. They might own a *paladar*, a restaurant, or several cafes. They might buy a couple of *almendrones*, big almonds [Cuban slang for classic American cars], hire drivers, and presto, their money multiplies and keeps multiplying and they become part of the emerging class, the petty bourgeoisie. The government is licencing more types of businesses and this gives the emerging class more opportunities to invest. The new laws favour them and the inequalities you now see will grow. People in the emerging class almost always have family overseas who send them money. They're the ones with the most opportunities.'

'The economic changes haven't gotten to the root of the problem.'

How have the recent economic measures affected you and your friends?

'The changes haven't touched people's hearts yet. Take the measures allowing people to buy and sell houses and cars and travel overseas. How many can afford to do this? The real issue for most people is still the ABC of socialism: housing, food and clothing. That's what people care about. Market liberalisation, well it's happening, *muy bien*, we watch it, but it is not going to solve our problems. The long and the short of it is that most people are sceptical. The vast majority of Cubans don't have a house or a car to sell, and can't afford a plane ticket. The economic changes haven't reached our level. No, the economic changes haven't solved the problem for us. I suppose you could say that it's a long process and that in five or ten years it will begin to bear fruit. Finally, people like me might begin to...' Mario's voice trailed off.

Mario's prediction was optimistic. Several years later the economy tanked and Cubans by and large faced hardships redolent of the Special Period. With tourism and remittances squeezed by President Trump's fierce blockade and then by Covid, even the emerging petty bourgeoisie was suffering.

What impact are the measures having on equality?

'What can I say? Inequalities are increasing. They are growing, but the group that stands out for their wealth isn't very large... People who work in the tourist sector, and I don't mean to belittle that kind of work, they earn more than a professional. Maybe they can afford to buy a car, a good house, food and clothing. Maybe even a mobile phone, which is a luxury.[5] Professionals do not have those things. The people who work in the tourist sector are part of the emerging class. They are becoming powerful and their purchasing power allows them to negotiate. Do you get what I mean? From a social perspective these people are, well, they may not have the highest intellect, but they are doing very well economically. This is the inequality around me. These are the people who can pay twenty-five thousand CUC/dollars or more for a house. But the truth is, many people buying houses live abroad. They send money to a Cuban who buys a house in their own name. I think they [the leadership] are selling off the country, though of course there are laws to prevent this. This is the emerging class and they are accumulating economic power. Some state functionaries are also living very well. People in my barrio believe some of our neighbours are diverting state resources [the official euphemism for embezzlement], but the government couldn't prove it. At the end of the day what possibility does a simple

Cuban worker have to buy an apartment, even to add on a room for his expanding family?'

'The last thing you lose is hope.'

After a long silence Mario said in a cheerless tone, 'At the end of the day the last thing you lose is hope. Hope is the last thing to go as you grow older. As you age hope changes colour.' He added, with a sardonic laugh, 'I hope many things will change. I also hope I will travel someday, and all that mess... I hope to prepare a... what should I call it, a platform for those who come after me.'

'We are not the same Cubans we were before.'

The next time we met, two years later in 2014, Mario started talking even before I managed to switch on the recorder. He was impatient to tell me how much Cubans had changed. 'Liz, if you had come here to interview in the 1970s and 80s and you asked young Cubans, "What do you want to be when you grow up?" they would have answered, I want to be a professional, a somebody, or, I want to become an engineer and build buildings, or, I want to help improve people's lives, or, I want to contribute to world peace... If you ask today's Cubans their response will be, I want to make a lot of money, fix up my house, and improve the welfare of my family. If you ask, "What are your dreams for the future of the world?" they will answer, I want to emigrate to a country where I can make a lot of money. When I was in my teens my friends wanted to be doctors or lawyers. If you ask my nephew's friends what they want to be when they grow up they will say, I want to be a tourist.

'Cubans have become individualistic. They think only about themselves, not about others. We are not the same Cubans we were. For example, just a couple of years ago *bisneros*, business people, were looked down on. Now they have status. Young people admire them because they make money. They don't admire me for the sacrifices I made to study or for my contributions to society. Compared to the *bisnero*, I am viewed as lowly.'

'We are not the same Cubans we were' was, in the noughties and beyond, a popular saying that summed up people's feelings about changes in the national character.

'Let me tell you what is wrong with egalitarianism.'

Several years had elapsed since the Party overturned its commitment to egalitarianism and I asked Mario how he felt, in hindsight, about the change. His response surprised me.

'First of all, we have to put egalitarianism into the present context. Professionals like me and many other workers know that our salaries do not cover our basic needs. Even if we don't always do our work very well, we contribute to society. Take nurses, often they don't attend to you as carefully as you would like, but they are there when you get ill. Think of the doctor who gets to work in a *camello*. Probably she faces lots of problems. When she woke up there wasn't any water; the tank was broken, and she had to fetch water in pails. But she got to work. She may not smile when she sees you, but she takes your blood pressure and says, "Stick out your tongue. Ah, you have tonsillitis," and gives you a prescription. It's true, the doctor might be stealing medicine, and the construction worker might be nicking cement blocks. It's true they might not be doing their job as well as they should, but that's because what they are paid for their labour does not cover their essential needs. It's a social problem, a problem we have to solve, and it will take us many, many years.

'Let me tell you what is wrong with egalitarianism. These people get up and go to work every day, rain or shine. Their work might be poor, or it might be good, but they are doing jobs that are necessary. They are contributing to society and their work benefits us all. A lot of people don't do that; they live on the margins of society. No, it's even worse, they are parasites, yet they receive the same as the rest of us. They have the same rights as the person who gets up every morning and goes to work. There are a lot of people, youth especially, who don't work, or study, or make any contribution at all to society. Yet they receive the same as the rest of us. That's what's wrong with egalitarianism. I say, to each according to their contribution, to their work. If we don't apply this principle we'll have paternalism, total paternalism. That was one of our errors, now we're seeing the consequences. My point is that people should not receive more from society than they contribute... I'm telling you how I see things, what I believe... But what do I know? Sometimes I don't know what to think. But there is one thing I know. It is necessary to renew the leadership of this country. The historic leaders can stay, but it's essential they embrace new ideas.'

The structure of Cuban society had changed, the official ideology had changed, and so had Mario's ideas and memories. A few years earlier he said his childhood was 'beautiful because we were equal... We all lived pretty much the same way'. But in the new Cuba his egalitarian perspective jarred with the new Party line. Mario's criticism of paternalism not only echoed Raúl Castro's speeches, it also echoed, and this I find unsettling, the voices of conservatives in the UK and the US who rail against the workshy and argue that government provision is a disincentive to work.

'To tell the truth the changes are bad.'

I was in Havana in April 2016, a few days after President Obama's visit. In contrast to the many Cubans who were sizzling with optimism that the Cuba-US détente would make them better off, Mario was feeling low. He did not foresee his life improving. 'My number one problem hasn't changed.' I knew Mario fairly well by then, and understood that his number one problem was housing.

Mario and his girlfriend had just broken up. They grew apart, he said, because they had no privacy. She lived in a small apartment with her extended family; he shared one large room divided by curtains with his sister and her two children. Mario wanted to start a family and feared time was running out; he was forty-one. We were meeting at Lilia's old apartment because Mario said his place was, as usual, full. Lilia had moved to Miami the year before, and Manuel, her twenty-six-year-old nephew, was living there.

How are the changes affecting you and your friends?

Mario shook his head. 'The economic measures haven't improved things at my level. To tell the truth the changes are bad. Take housing, you can buy and sell properties but at prices that are unaffordable for most people. The price of cars is even worse. Maybe the market reforms benefit some people, but only a very, very small group. Most of the people who own businesses are Cuban-Americans who live abroad; they've been out of the country for a very long time. When they come to visit they stay in the houses they bought, the rest of the time they rent to foreigners. Their properties produce money.

'We are selling off our national patrimony. I assume we have laws protecting our, what should I call it, our point of view. But to tell the truth I don't really know. The short answer to your question is that property ownership is far beyond my reach, and that goes for the great majority of Cubans. I repeat, the changes have not affected my kitchen table. They have not brought any improvements to my life. As for the barrio, maybe two or three families have moved to better neighbourhoods and are enjoying a more comfortable life – people who have relatives abroad, or who embezzle but haven't been caught. Corruption is getting worse. It's in our veins.

'People who advance through their own work, well there are very, very few. A couple of artists, and I like to think that's the result of hard work combined with talent. Many artists who left have done well. Their work fetches good prices. When they come back they have money to buy cars and houses. Thanks to the new economic measures, they go into business, real estate, cars, all sorts of things, and not always doing it the way one might wish. All the changes have pros and cons. They have opened up possibilities, though only for a tiny minority.'

Do you think the general population will benefit from laws allowing better off Cubans to buy houses and cars?

Mario paused, then he repeated the Party line. 'Yes, I think so, because however you see it, it is money invested in the country. It brings in hard currency. As you know, Cuba does not have access to international banking, so although this doesn't help individual Cubans, it helps the country as a whole. The government is repairing hospitals, buying equipment... But, as I said, most households do not feel any improvement. We are still waiting.' Mario was incapable of hiding his own views.

'Look, regarding the future I am highly uncertain. They can try to regulate private businesses, but once they [the leadership] have opened the door, maybe they can close it the littlest bit, but not more. It escapes their control. The emerging petty bourgeoisie goes against the principles on which the Revolution was founded, as well you know. So, you're running a risk. You don't know what the benefits will be, or the long-term consequences. You just don't know. You can't calculate the social costs it will unleash over time. I think it's good that things which have been controlled for such a long time have been loosened up. It had been too closed... It's better to be flexible than end up destroying the system.' Mario was wrestling with the national dilemma: how to build an economic system that was equitable and viable.

How would you describe the new petty bourgeoisie?

'Let's see. There are two groups. The sons and daughters of politicians, they have the education and *la prebenda*, the perks and the inside track. They have a different way of life. Then there is the new rich... I'm neither the son of politicians, nor of the pre-revolutionary bourgeoisie. Everything I have achieved comes from my own sweat and tears. We all might have equal opportunities, but we don't have an equal capacity to grab opportunities. That's the way it is...' Mario's barb about equal opportunities made me wonder whether he was growing disillusioned with the Party's advocacy of equal opportunities, maybe with the Party itself.

Mario's sister and her boyfriend had just rented a room in the tenement next door to have some privacy. I asked how they could afford it. 'Her boyfriend pedals a cycle taxi and he charges in hard currency. He earns much, much more in a day than I do. I could do the same thing. I could quit my job as director of the IT department at the Ministry, leave it all behind and pedal tourists around Old Havana. It wouldn't solve all my economic problems, but it would take care of a lot of them. I could rent a place of my own. But it shouldn't have to be that way. Driving a cycle taxi wasn't my life's ambition. I am still trying to get by doing the things that give me satisfaction.' Mario's economic situation vis-à-vis a bici-taxi driver encapsulated the problems of Cuba's dual currency economy.

You seem to have retained the values you had growing up.

'That's probably true. I say to young people... I don't have enough to cover my necessities, but I have the satisfaction that I have achieved what I set out to do. I say to them, maybe to you that doesn't mean much because what you think about is that you need shoes. Shoes wear out and you throw them away. But who you are, what you carry inside, nobody can take that away, nobody.'

What do you think Cuba will look like in five years?

Before contemplating the future Mario reflected on the present. 'There has been a certain opening to raise subjects that before were taboo. But freedom of expression in newspapers, magazines, on TV, it's still a big problem. These things need to change to reflect reality, to address what people are really thinking and talking about.'

Do people feel they can say out loud whatever it is they are thinking?

'It all depends on the context. In one context people won't say what they're thinking, in another they will. People will say what they think when they're in a bar, on their second drink. When they're sober they won't.' Mario seemed to say pretty much what he believed when he was sober and his words were being recorded.

'People are afraid of saying what they think,' Manuel, Lilia's nephew, chipped in, as he pulled up a chair. 'Once, in my first year of medicine, when I was on my way home from school, I complained about the uniform. Chatting to my friends I said, I don't understand a country that gives every student a huge uniform and then requires them to come to school in one that fits. The *señora* standing next to me at the bus stop said, "Don't complain. Your education is free." I replied, "My education isn't free: first, I will have to do social service; then, from the day I graduate until the day I retire I will work for the state and they will pay me much, much less than I should be earning given my training. So rather than receiving a free education, I am paying for it." My classmates said, "Hush, be careful or you'll end up in jail. You can't say those things." You see what I mean.'

Mario nodded, 'Or someone will come up to you and say, "*Oye, te va a embarcar*, listen, you're going to get yourself into trouble." It's true, a lot of the time it's like that. That's how we live. Maybe someone goes to a meeting of the trade union, stands up and says, "I think such-and-such is bad because of this and that." Some people would say that, but very, very few. There is not a lot of, what's the word, let's just say spontaneity, to say what you think. Then again, as I said, it depends on the context.'

Cuba's security apparatus encouraged people to police themselves and each other. Many narrators said this was one reason most young Cubans were politically apathetic.

'Inequality is here. Now we have to learn to live with it.'

'Let's see, I don't think that in five years we will be eating at MacDonald's or Domino Pizza. I don't think that is going to happen, but we must be very careful. We need to remember what happened in the Soviet Union, and not make quick changes... In the space of five years I don't think we will see many things change. Five years isn't enough to make a big difference in the food Cubans are able put on the table, in our way of life... It will take more time. Here everything works very, very, very slowly.'

What do you think will happen to inequality?
'Inequalities will increase. Inequality is here to stay and we need to learn to live with it. Inequality will always be part of who we are. It is utopian to think you can live in a society with full equality. It's impossible. What is possible is to have less inequality, where the range from the top to the bottom is much less.'

Dissidents and machismo

Mario and I had been talking for three hours and I was hot, hungry and tired. As I started to doze off, Mario and Manuel chatted quietly. 'Did you hear?' Mario said, 'In Villa Panamericana one of the Damas de Blanco [Women in White], was nominated for *delegada* [municipal councillor].' My ears pricked up; this was surprising stuff. Las Damas de Blanco is a dissident organisation famous for its Sunday processions demanding freedom for political prisoners and democracy. The police often disrupted their protests, though it was rarely reported in *Granma*. The government accused the group of receiving money from the US – which they did. Consequently, many Cubans felt they were US stooges. 'I think it would be a good thing if she gets elected,' Mario said, laughing. 'I doubt she can solve anything. Then again, maybe she can because the *delegada* there is...' I began to listen carefully, surprised to hear this from a Party militant. Manuel interrupted, 'The thing is the *delegadas* suffer more than anyone else. They are rejected by people who expect they will solve their problems, and they get the blame because the higher ups don't give them resources.' Mario agreed, 'He can't do much more than listen to people's complaints and try to prod the government into doing something.'

He or she, I said too aggressively.

'Every ewe has its ram,' Mario joked. 'Yes, Liz, you're correct to insist on he or she. I heard on television that many directors of state enterprises are women. I don't know the percentages, but in some ways the situation of women has improved. Women's gains are one of the achievements of the Revolution, but people don't pay much attention.'

It's marvellous that women have made gains, but at what cost? Do men share the housework? Or do women do housework, political work, and also direct enterprises? Do women do it all?

'I think there's been some change,' Mario replied.

Really?

'Well, not too much,' he laughed. 'Cuban men are very *machista*,' Manuel said. 'Cuban women are also very *machista*,' Mario added. 'Just imagine a househusband. "*Oye, socios*, mates, let's go for a drink. No, *mi socio*, I can't. I need to go home to do the ironing, the laundry, and whatever else."' Mario's routine had us all laughing. 'I've got my own theory: when the woman calls the shots *es candela*.' Mario gave me a look. 'But then every ewe has its ram. Imagine the guys. I mean if women have good jobs, an income, are *dirigentes*, leaders, it would take a lot to put up with them. *Cuesta trabajo*, it would be hard work. Those women almost always have couple problems.' I wanted to argue, but hunger and heat had worn me down and I suggested we postpone our debate about machismo and go have something to eat.

'I would quit my job tomorrow and try to make a go of it in business.'

Over lunch, Mario told me he had been invited to study business management at the ultra-prestigious Advanced Institute for Communist Party Cadre. Not only was it a tremendous honour, but it was a stepping stone to a high position in a state company. My first thought was that Communist Party courses in management, though perhaps long overdue, were a measure of how much was changing in Cuba. When Mario told me that only two Cubans of African descent had been invited to join the course, I took it as a sign of how little had changed when it came to racism and racial exclusion.

A year later, and several months before completing the course, Mario and I were standing in the street outside his tenement, idly chatting. I was leaving the next day and we were talking about this book. 'If someone offered me a thousand dollars I would quit my job tomorrow and try to make a go of it in business,' Mario said in a hushed tone; it sounded like a confession. He seemed nervous, perhaps he felt he wasn't living up to my image of a good communist. With people milling around it wasn't the moment to turn on the recorder and ask why he wanted to give up his career and go into business.

I could guess. Mario was frustrated. He had been complaining that he couldn't eat or dress decently on his state salary. He couldn't afford to go dancing or buy a beer. His biggest problem was housing, and he felt it stood in the way of having a girlfriend and starting a family. I knew other Party militants had managed to finagle themselves a decent house. Mario hadn't tried to work the system, it was not his way. Many Cubans who ran businesses lived far better than him, and he was tired of making sacrifices.

I recalled what he had said some years back, meditating on the meaning of life: 'What if, in the time I am given, I work, I struggle, and that's all I do. And yet, despite everything, I can't get what I want. Do you see what I am driving at? Struggle, more struggle, work, more work, an entire life of struggle and work. Then the end.'

'Most Cubans' lives have not improved.'

In 2018, the last time I interviewed Mario, he still was working at the Ministry, and moonlighting as a motorbike taxi driver/ courier to supplement his pay of around two dollars a day. He hoped to develop another side-line, and was thinking of making crafts for tourists. 'I continue to work in the Ministry because

I am a coward,' he joked. Five years earlier he had said he remained at the Ministry to contribute to society.

We ate lunch at a fancy restaurant a few steps from his house. Mario was the only person in the room who wasn't either a tourist or white, and it goes without saying he had never been inside the restaurant before. Explaining why inequality was disproportionally harming Afro-Cubans, he said, 'What is happening is that the owners of private establishments like this restaurant can hire and fire at will. The managers of state enterprises can't do that.' Cuba has laws prohibiting discrimination by race, gender, sexuality and age, but they are not being enforced.

'Most Cubans' lives have not improved. We still face tremendous uncertainty regarding food, clothing, all of our essential needs. We are still hoping that things will improve.' Mario remained a Party member but with the economy stagnating, the population disaffected, corruption rampant, and many Cubans leaving, he feared for the country's future.

20

ALINA RODRÍGUEZ ABREU

San Miguel del Padrón, Havana

After months laying the groundwork, Alina let herself believe that filming the documentary would run smoothly. She and her team first went to Santiago and Guantánamo for a week to film in the neighbourhoods the squatters had come from. 'The question we kept asking ourselves, with conditions so terrible here in San Miguel, was why did they come? I had never been to the eastern provinces so I didn't know whether I would find a palace or a bird's nest.'

On their first day of filming, the team in Guantánamo was arrested. She had permission to film in Santiago, and with only one interview in the adjoining province she had decided it would be a waste of time to apply for another permission. The police kept them until nightfall, so they lost the entire day.

The following morning in a poor rundown neighbourhood on the outskirts of the City of Santiago they were filming out in the open when the police arrived and arrested them. They took away their camera and told them to go back to their hostel and stay there until they phoned. 'By the next afternoon we hadn't heard anything. We were worried because the camera was rented, so we went to the Party headquarters to ask for a meeting. We talked with the cadre in charge of ideological formation in the province and this… this person asked us pretty aggressively why we were filming in such an ugly place when there were beautiful things like the policlinic that had been built as part of the Battle of Ideas. He talked bureaucratic, political gibberish, and there was zero understanding between us. He told us we could not film anywhere in Santiago Province but if we returned the next day we could collect the camera.' When Alina did so, she found that almost everything had been erased. 'We lost everything important. We never received an explanation, nada. How could they do this? We were totally crushed, completely defeated.'

By the time Alina and her crew returned to Havana they felt more defiant than anything. They learned always to be prepared for the worst. 'I knew what I was doing was extremely sensitive. I might have been naïve, but I was no fool. Making a film about illegals would be tricky… After that nothing surprised us.'

Alina's family was frightened and begged her to stop. She convinced them that they had to stand up for their beliefs. 'Like it or not the environment in the settlements is hostile. Most of the population is Black, and I am *blanquita, rubiacita, chiquitica* – white, blonde, tiny and female. I was always the focus of attention from the minute I arrived so my mother came along to protect me. Now she's totally on my side.'

Alina's team had known nothing about life in the settlements. 'They live in Havana, but they did not know that here in Cuba, in Havana, places like that exist, places where people live in unsanitary conditions, with dirt floors and walls made of cardboard boxes, surrounded by rats. Places where the children are not allowed to go to school, because legally they do not exist. When the team learned about the people in the settlements, they identified with them. Identified so strongly that no one quit for fear that they might be jailed, that their student card might be taken away, that they would end up a marked person. No one. Everyone on the team supported me completely. They were just

HOW THINGS FALL APART

as committed as I was, and despite my fears, despite all of the problems, I never considered abandoning the documentary. We developed a bond with those people and if they had the courage to speak out on camera, we had to have the courage to present what they said in the film.'

Alina explained that what makes a person illegal is the fact that their identity card doesn't have a Havana address. Even if they had been living in Havana for twenty years, according to their identity card they lived in Santiago or Guantánamo and they could not change their address. As illegal immigrants they did not receive food on the ration, have access to schooling, healthcare and housing, or permission to work. 'If you think life in Havana is difficult, imagine life in the provinces where there has been no development. People don't have dollars and you need dollars to survive. It is complicated. Do you recall the sociologist in the film? He helped me understand that these people have been marginalised for so long that they have become psychologically damaged, and they [the leadership] cannot put it right simply by giving them a place to live. There are many contradictions in our system but they try to hide them and that's not right. Of course we don't have a perfect society, no society is perfect, but we are not allowed to say it. They want us to believe that what we have is perfect. This goes right to the heart of this country's problems. Do you understand what I'm saying?'

Alina spent the next five months visiting squatter settlements in Havana and getting to know the residents. 'If I wanted them to open up, I had to win their trust. They had to be confident that I would never do anything that might harm them, at least not intentionally. I needed to build trust so they would talk freely about their situation, their everyday problems which necessarily implied criticism of the government. It was very hard and very complicated. I talked with hundreds of people. Many illegals confided in us, those who wanted to do honest work. The more marginal people, the delinquents, we never won them over. They remained suspicious. We did our best not to manipulate anyone. Of course, there is always some manipulation but we tried to be as honest with everyone as possible.'

Alina's plan was to film in four municipalities: San Miguel, because it had the most settlements, and she lived there; Regla, just below the huge statue of Christ, where almost every day police arrested and deported migrants; Playa, where the government more or less allowed the squatters to pave the streets and erect houses; and Guanabacoa, where the settlement was 'legally illegal', because the squatters received food on the *libreta* and paid for the electricity they took from the grid. After Alina was prevented from filming in two of these places she abandoned her original plan.

Alina wanted to begin filming in the settlement she knew best, the one at the end of her street, where many of the residents trusted her. But when her team arrived two state security agents were waiting for them. 'We had told people to expect us, and besides we had permission. It was not like we just turned up. I had permission from the government of the City of Havana and the provincial government. I had a pile of permissions because we were trying to do everything completely legally.' When she had applied for permission she included the script, a timetable and the addresses where they would be working. 'Well, the two security agents dressed in civvies took us to the municipal offices where the president of San Miguel was waiting. Fortunately, he no longer holds that post; he was ousted. He was one of the many opportunistic bureaucrats we have in this country. After I showed him the letters of permission, he said, "Those documents are not valid in my municipality." In *my* municipality, as if he owned it. I knew at once we were not going to be filming in San Miguel.'

After the setback in San Miguel, Alina altered her strategy and applied to local functionaries rather than to important officials. 'Miraculously, most of them gave us permission, even in Regla which is known as the most violent settlement with prostitution, drugs, everything. Getting permission to film in Regla was truly amazing.'

Alina's team coordinated the film shoots in Regla like a military operation. They would show up early, film only inside homes and make a quick getaway. But it wasn't possible to hide seven women and men toting two large cameras and bags of equipment.

'In a repeat of our experience in San Miguel, when we left the settlement in Regla a police car was waiting for us and took us to the police station. They crammed us and all of our equipment into two police cars. When we arrived the president of the municipal government appeared all of a sudden along with the police chief, two security agents, and an unidentified man. They were there to question us. I showed the president his letter granting me permission. He said [she put on a treacly voice], "Of course we have confidence in you, and we are going to allow you…" I explained our intentions, said we are students at the film school and that if we were filming it, it was because it existed; we weren't inventing anything. Can you believe, it's not like we were from the BBC, or Channel 23 [in Miami]. We are Cubans and we should talk about our… We tried to reason with them but of course they weren't interested. They had already decided to give us permission to film, but not because of anything we said.'

The following day the team worked quickly. They discarded the script, improvised and left the settlement early. They did not want a repeat of the previous day. 'After I got home the president phoned. He told me we were not permitted to do any more filming in Regla. Fortunately, we had done two days of shooting. If we hadn't, there would be no documentary. We really needed a third day but he flatly refused. For the second time I was stopped in my tracks.'

The team encountered a different problem in Playa. The day before they were scheduled to film, police evicted a number of families and bulldozed their houses. 'After that, the people we had lined up to interview were unwilling to speak with us. They were afraid. They probably thought that if they talked to us their home would be razed, so everyone kept their mouths shut.'

Some migrants were keen to cooperate and gladly showed the terrible conditions in the settlements. Others did not want to have anything to do with the film. 'We came across everything. Some people had confidence in us and trusted us to respect them. They were keen to explain their problems and they showed no fear. They were people who wanted to work and would take any job, even if it was illegal. But we also wanted to interview more marginal people. If you think about it, the people in the film express themselves pretty well. The delinquents wouldn't talk to us. No way.'

Alina lamented that she had had to leave a lot of footage out. Some of the scenes showing solidarity and cooperation ended up on the cutting room floor. Afterwards some people criticised the film for its shortage of images. They said it had too many interviews and not enough shots of daily life. 'I am not justifying what I did, but I was dealing with a very complicated topic, and I had to convey a lot of information that people here do not know. If this were a subject that people knew about and had seen on TV, I could have made a more artistic film. But I had to explain everything; if I hadn't the audience could not understand the situation. I am sorry I was not able to include more scenes of how people live, of their everyday illegalities, but it was out of my hands. I had to change the documentary radically from my original design. I think it turned out pretty well for the people in it, and it demonstrates our commitment to them.'

Alina planned to show the film in the settlements but said that in the end things got crazy and she wasn't able to. Instead, she gave out DVDs. She wanted to hire a bus to bring people from the settlements to the premiere at the Chaplin movie theatre at

INCAIC, the film institute, but she ran out of money. 'We invited them, some came and it was super-emotional for them to see themselves on the screen. It was beautiful. For many, seeing the real truth on the screen was a very important moment.'

After they finished the film, everything became very difficult for Alina and Nomar González, the producer. The film programme refused to allow them to submit the documentary as their thesis. 'After everything the school had done to help us, they turned their backs. Nomar needed to submit the film to graduate but they censored it, a documentary that no one had been allowed to see because it was too controversial.'

Alina was not permitted to enter the documentary in the 2008 Havana Film Festival; nevertheless, it shared first prize. 'This demonstrates that in Cuba things are not what they seem, or something like that. The film is not brilliant, it is not out of this world, but generally here you cannot say the least little thing.'

Finally, some of her professors spoke up for the film and the school allowed Alina to submit it as her thesis. 'At least they got to watch it and saw that it was made with sincerity and that my purpose was not to destroy or criticise anyone. My aim was to acknowledge our problems so that we can try to solve them.' Remarkably, the official organisation of writers and artists, UNEAC (Union Nacional de Escritores y Artistas de Cuba), named *Buscándote Havana* the best documentary of the year. 'I know the film was discussed by municipal officials and in the Party. I am not really sure but people told me it was shown at the highest levels, and the Minister of Culture acknowledged that it shows an aspect of our reality. As for Raúl, I am not sure whether he has seen it or not, but others have. Of course, it has never been shown on TV, and I don't think it ever will be. I was interviewed on TV but they did not allow me to talk about the documentary. At least some people know it exists and they pass it around clandestinely [on external drives].

'It is really important to understand the moment in which my documentary was made. We were part of the first wave of young filmmakers. At another time I would never have been allowed to film all this. In Cuba, the government had absolute control of all these things, and even though there was a tradition in film, that tradition has lost its way. What I am saying is that I am not special, nor do I have some great ability. I'm saying that there were conditions that allowed me to do it; conditions that emerged at one moment in time, and that have not gone nearly far enough. There is a lot we cannot do, like voice criticism on TV; that has always been forbidden. What I am saying is that now there is a space, but it is mostly underground. Beyond the underground we cannot do much. My documentary appeared at an important moment, a moment when people felt it was necessary to speak out.'

'Alina, something puzzles me. Why in the title, Buscándote Havana, *is Havana spelled the English way, and not the Spanish way, Habana?'*

'I wanted to play around with the idea of selling Cuba to tourists. Here they sell the Havana you see on postcards: the Capitol, the quaint streets of Habana Vieja, the beautiful, dilapidated buildings. That is why the film begins with shots of touristy Habana, the Habana everyone in the world recognises, the city foreigners come to see. I wanted to explore the reality behind those idyllic images. Foreigners come here to see the Capitol, but if they walk two blocks into the barrio they will see another reality, one that has nothing to do with pretty picture postcards. They will see behind the façade. In Cuba, like everywhere else in the world, no one sells their city by showing off its ugliness. In New York City they sell the Empire State Building, not the violence.'

I asked Alina whether the documentary had made life more difficult in the settlements. 'No, on the contrary it helped some people. In the settlement close to here there was a sort of mini-revolution. The squatters learned things; maybe it had something to do with the documentary, maybe not. Maybe it was because the president was completely dysfunctional, totally retrograde, and he's not there anymore. Although very little has changed, so far the changes are mostly positive. People were given plots to plant food, and now they are allowed to build houses with their own materials.

'Do you remember Fidel, the man in the film with the son named Elián, the cycle taxi driver? Thanks to the film, people offer him help, stop him in the street: "Aren't you Fidel from the film? Tell me what you need. Come to my house and I will give you milk for your baby." On a personal level people who have seen the film show solidarity and want to help.'

Having said most of what she wanted to say about the film, Alina began talking about her hopes and dreams, her difficulty trying to imagine Cuba's future and her own, her ambivalence about leaving or staying, her aesthetic aspirations, her confusion. Her words poured out in a stream of consciousness. Alina seemed to personify the exuberance and passion of a young artist.

To her way of thinking the Cuban Revolution represented a unique historical moment, a moment that will never be repeated, and she feels that Cuban exceptionalism has been especially good for artists. The contradictions in Cuba created conditions for artistic creativity.

'Cuba is a country that is so different. Probably it is the last country in the world with a system like ours. It won't happen again, not even if it were to come about completely differently. What exists in Cuba is not going to happen anywhere else, ever again. It won't happen because it was the product of a unique moment in history, and nobody knows how it lasted until now. For all these reasons the Cuban reality is incredibly rich and incredibly complicated, rich because it is complicated. Rich, complicated and different. For these reasons it is good for artists. Good because we are living in a historical moment that will never be repeated. The Cuban Revolution will never be repeated. This moment is good, at least it is good for me. Cuba's difference is what nurtured me. But now I have other needs.

'My personal search is driving me to do something else, not that I want to turn my back on society, not that I am uninterested. On the contrary, I suffer because I feel I have so much crammed inside. Doing film is very expensive and very difficult. Making films is hard in any country in the world, but it is also a luxury. Just think, under our conditions where most people spend most of their time figuring out what they are going to eat that day and where are they going to sleep, with all of Cuba's economic and social problems it is remarkable that filmmaking exists at all. Filmmaking is difficult everywhere in the world and making a living from it is almost impossible. But we all have to dream.'

Turning to the current situation, 'What we are going through now, the supposed updating of the economic model; I say supposed because we have been through economic restructuring umpteen times before. Not me, I am only twenty-seven, but my parents, who have been part of this process [her way of saying they were Party members]. How many times have they lived through restructuring? How many times have they heard: "We are going to rectify our errors", and then things go back to how they were? I won't believe in this restructuring until I've seen real deeds, successful outcomes. I think the new leadership [Raúl and his allies] is getting off to a bad start. They are making the same errors as they made before. Everything is absolute. This is absolutely good, that is absolutely bad. You have to understand that this country is mired in an economic crisis, and you cannot resolve the crisis from one day to the next. It's absurd that what is illegal today is legal tomorrow. Do you understand what I am saying? The truth is I am very, very sceptical about these changes. I hope I am wrong; I fervently wish they will work, but our problems are very deep, and they have been piled one on top of another for a very long time. Oh, excuse me. That's my cell phone. I can't hang up. The hang up button is broken. I will simply let it ring.

'All of these problems make me very sad. Sad because I have so much hope that people... that we won't have to leave our country, that young people won't have to leave, that we can stay and struggle and advance right here in this country. But there has to be a willingness, an understanding. They have to stop doing things that are indefensible. Stop claiming to uphold values that once we all upheld but now no one does. Take healthcare, it is not what it used to be but they insist it is. They tell us healthcare is untouchable, a sacred achievement of the Revolution, but if you go to a hospital you will see what is really happening. Education is not the education we had. Social welfare does not live up to the social welfare we had. If only they would stop turning everything into politics. If only they would really and truly struggle for what this country needs, then maybe, just maybe, we could solve some of our problems.

'To me, part of the solution is to stay. Staying is doing something. It's easier to leave for some, but once you've left it is not easy. Leaving is heart rending, but sometimes you get to the point that you are saturated. Many of my friends say: I am tired of struggling, being here exhausts me. Me, I feel that just being here is doing something. Although we have lost many of our values, people need to try to stand up for whatever it is they believe in. It's not easy. If only people had a little more consciousness, if only they would safeguard what they have. It is all interconnected. The government isn't to blame for everything. People here are completely apathetic. They are completely alienated and they want to remain that way. They don't care about anything. They don't want to think. They are indifferent. The Cuban Five,

Afghanistan, the hole in the ground outside their front door, it's all the same. People are tired of struggling, tired of being here, just tired. Despite this, and even though life is difficult, you do not have to leave. This is the hand we have been dealt, the time we have on earth. It is very difficult because there is so much corruption, corruption at every level. With what is going on at the top, how can we root it out at the bottom? I just don't get it, I really don't. To tell the truth I think they are playing with us, the people. They manipulate us all the time as if we do not understand what is going on. It is amazing they can think that. They made sure we got an education, made sure we learned to think. But then. What I think is that, in this country, things need to change, really and truly change. Only then will this country be able to move forward. Do you understand what I'm saying? Many young people, because when it comes down to it young people are the future. Older people have had their moment. Take my parents, they struggled for this. My father went to Angola. He went voluntarily. He wasn't drafted. He fought and when he came back he worked his ass off, and then what? He has nothing, nada. He is fifty-five. At sixty he will retire with nothing, with a pension of 230 pesos. Everyone knows you cannot live on 230 pesos. They [the leaders] know, but they ignore it. I don't have the solution. I don't know if there is a solution.

'The first error was to take away the liberty to do whatever you want with your life, when you want, how you want. You end up believing they will give you everything you need. But the moment comes when you feel you want to live well and you want to try to do as best you can. Yes, I believe this.' Alina emphasised that she really believed this because it went against everything she had been taught. In the official ideology, Fidelista ideology, doing whatever you wanted, when you wanted, how you wanted, and wanting to live well were hallmarks of bourgeois individualism. A negation of socialism.

'As for me, what I try to accomplish, I do on screen... I try to help people spiritually. It is not that I am uninterested in our reality, I am very interested. But sometimes you also have to fill people's hearts and nourish their spirits with something other than politics. In Cuba, for the past twenty years we have been living day in and day out with the same things. You scratch around for pesos. You worry about what you're going to eat, what you're going to do. I don't know for sure but I think sometimes it is good to get away from everyday reality. Not avoid it, but at least think about something else. Enjoy life a little. That helps people and that is what I can do.

'In this country we are walking a tightrope. No one knows what will happen tomorrow. Worst of all, we the people are the ones who always get hurt because that is how the system works. Everywhere in the world, the better off have power and the rest of the people do not. The fact is people with power do not care about us.'

While Alina analysed power and the meaning of life her grandfather got up and went downstairs for lunch, and the dog continued to bark.

'Wow, I've been talking a lot. I'll tell you why. It is not because I think of myself as an intellectual, not at all. In INCAIC we had real intellectuals in the 1960s and the 1980s. They were sharp and said what they thought. Ordinary people have to spend all of their time thinking about what they are going to eat today and tomorrow. Intellectuals should be thinking about how to solve our problems. In Cuba we have professors of philosophy, Marxists who have a largish following, and they are not saying, let's have capitalism, let the Americans come back. They are saying that we need to build on our accomplishments and overhaul this so that it works. But we are not allowed to hear what they have to say because they are people who think differently in a country where the government does not allow people to think differently.'

Although Alina was deeply critical of the leadership, she agreed with Raúl Castro's repudiation of equality. 'Socialism should stand for equal rights, not for everyone living in the same way. All people should not have the same status.' She said this from the comfort of a tidy sitting room in a pastel-coloured house. I wondered whether the squatters living at the end of her street would agree.

Two weeks earlier, after a major outcry, the government made a new announcement: the numbers would be reduced but the state would be laying off half a million workers over the next two years, and it urged people who lost their jobs to start little businesses. The announcement marked a watershed. It was the first clear signal that the leadership planned to reduce the state sector and expand the remit of private enterprise. Alina dismissed the government's assurances that half a million Cubans could become *cuentapropistas*, microentrepreneurs, as a cynical ruse. She was furious that officials were going around telling people threatened with layoffs that they would be better off working for themselves. 'Uff, it's ludicrous. Who do they think we are, a bunch of idiots?

'We Cubans won't put up with these layoffs. People are gradually losing their fear of saying what they truly believe. The government might lose control. If they lay off lots of workers this whole thing might get out of hand. Workers who've been at the same job for thirty years will get three months' severance pay. Three months' pay for thirty years. It's absurd. I don't know how this will end up. When a lot of people lose their jobs and find themselves out on the street with no money I don't know what will happen. The notion that we'll all buy licenses to sell pizza is a crazy, utopian idea. And now they're creating another layer of the bureaucracy to sell licenses and draw up regulations governing what you can and cannot do. A year from now, probably less, in three months, I hate to think, but people will be out of work and with the little money they have left they will buy a licence and soon they will discover that they can't make a go of their little business. This is capitalism in its crudest form. It's hard and brutal.

'Right now I have a contract with ICAIC. I'm not properly employed, almost no filmmakers are on the state payroll anymore. We're all on temporary contracts. The trade union at ICAIC called a meeting to tell us about the reforms, the layoffs. They said we would not become unemployed; we will be *disponible*, available. In this country no one is ever unemployed; they are available. Available, ha, ha, available for what I can't imagine. Available to hawk fried yucca in the street, to sell peanuts? Well I wasn't at the meeting but I heard that a young man stood up and said, "I just don't understand. You are our trade union and you are supposed to represent us, protect our rights. Now you're justifying why we should be fired. Worse, you are the ones firing us." The room erupted into chaos because one person was courageous enough to say what he believed. He simply said this whole thing is wrong.

'Politics is a very dirty business and I don't consider myself to be political.' I was astounded to hear this woman who had just risked her career for what she believes say she wasn't political. 'Well come to think of it, maybe you could say that by making films I am politically involved. The future rests on my generation. Now it's our turn.'

21

JUAN GUILLARD MATUS

Santa Ana de la Laguna, Artemisa Province

One hot March morning in 2014, Marisol and I went to Santa Ana to interview Juan. In the four years since we last talked with him most Cubans' lives had changed for the worse.[1] As we approached the township I noticed the surrounding countryside looked poorer and more neglected than I had remembered, the road was more potholed, and most of the fields had been abandoned to weeds. In contrast, on the outskirts of town I got glimpses of large, half-built houses hidden behind wooden siding. Juan told us that Cuban-Americans were illegally purchasing land and building second homes, but construction had stopped because building materials were scarce.[2] As we drove into town I saw that unlike Havana, Santa Ana had no new restaurants or bars, no glitz. Everything looked dusty and dilapidated.

We called at Juan's gate. No one answered, and seeing no sign of Juan's animals, we went looking for Rosa, the Party veteran who way back had said he would be interesting to interview. Rosa tried to keep track of her neighbours, but not because she was nosey. She seemed like a throwback to the early days of the Revolution. She had a strong sense of community and at the age of seventy-six she was a one-woman municipal improvement committee, constantly pressing the authorities to repair the town's broken-down infrastructure.

As we approached Rosa's old-fashioned stone house on the main street I feared she would say that Juan had gone to Miami, but no. 'Ah, Juan, *un personaje* [a larger-than-life character],' she said with a guffaw. 'You'll probably find him outside the market chanting, "Íntimas *para las mujeres*, Íntimas *para las mujeres*," sanitary napkins for the ladies, in his snazzy way.' After hurried hugs she sprinted out the door bellowing, 'Juan, Juan,' and waving her arms to attract attention.

We went to look for Juan in the market, a mostly empty building in what passed for the centre of town. Across the road was Santa Ana's only restaurant which served tasty food but was always swarming with flies. Outside hovered a batch of young men passing the time. They already knew we were looking for Juan, and hollered in unison, 'Juan, Juan.' Just as we were getting into our car, Juan ran up shouting, '*La inglesa, la inglesa*,' – the English woman – and threw his arms around me. I was momentarily disoriented as I never think of myself as English. Although I had moved from the US to Britain in 1990, I still feel American, and never more intensely than when I am in Cuba.

Juan, President of the Committee for the Defence of the Revolution

Juan's house had grown in the four years since we last sat on his porch. In the corner of his small front yard, where he used to breed chickens, he was building a tiny kitchen and bathroom. A small sign beside his front door, said 'President of the CDR, Committee for the Defence of the Revolution'. After extending my congratulations, I asked Juan what the post entailed. He looked pleased and smiled, but ignored my question. I wondered whether he would be as outspoken as before.

In the Revolution's heyday the president of a CDR exercised local power. When Fidel Castro founded the organisation in 1960, he declared, 'Committees for the Defence of the Revolution will be the Revolution's eyes and ears... They will be a collective system of revolutionary vigilance... so that everyone knows who lives on every block, what they are doing, with whom they meet.'[3] If the president of a CDR suspected a person harboured anti-government views, they informed state security. In addition, anyone applying for a job, Party membership, admission to university, or permission to travel needed a letter from their CDR.

All that changed in the Special Period. CDRs withered when Cubans en masse turned to the black market to survive. With the government's credibility in decline, people were less willing to take on the position, partly because the organisation had become an empty shell, partly because it was popularly believed that anyone who agreed to head the neighbourhood watch was facing difficulties of one type or another, and viewed the job either as a useful vehicle or a convenient cover. Knowing Juan, and knowing how much he craved approval, I assumed he must have felt the post conferred prestige.

Talking with Juan about the CDR reminded me of my interview with Ofelia in Old Havana the day before.[4] When Ofelia told me she was president of the CDR in her *ciudadela* I nearly fell off my chair. CDR president did not fit her profile. The first time I interviewed Ofelia she said matter-of-factly that she was a *jinetera* and when business was slow she worked as an illegal hairdresser. The subsequent interviews were largely devoted to her many grievances against the state that went back to her childhood. In 2012, her seventeen-year-old son was imprisoned for eighteen years for killing a teenager in a *West Side Story*-esque street fight. 'Being head of the CDR can't hurt,' she said. 'It might get my son better treatment. I am praying to God they will let him out before he serves the full sentence... In any event, they [the state] give me a few centavos to put on parties to celebrate the 26th of July, and the other holidays.'

Just when Marisol and I had managed to balance ourselves on Juan's wobbly stools, he offered to show us around his half-built extension. Thinking the new economic policies, or his CDR position, might have facilitated his home improvements, I asked whether his life had changed since Raúl took over. 'Very, very little,' he said, shaking his head.

'What they [political leaders] are doing is all for the good. I think the team working on these things... is good. The thing is, we citizens want changes now, right away. Everyone wants a single currency now, but you can't have that if the world economy is doing badly. We need to make changes one step at a time. As Raúl says, "*Sin prisa pero sin pausa;* Without haste, but without pause."'

'*Sin prisa pero sin pausa*' was Raúl Castro's mantra, his pledge to slowly but surely open up the economy. The slogan was purposefully ambiguous because Castro was trying to appease Cubans who opposed market measures, and those who wanted to liberalise more quickly.

Juan resumed, 'The same applies right now to relations with the United States. We need to go along with them, but cautiously, very cautiously, because the United States isn't easy. They know what they want to do, and what they cannot do. But as you don't know what's behind all of this, you have to take it very cautiously.' Barely three months had elapsed since Presidents Castro and Obama had agreed to restore diplomatic relations, and Juan was repeating official policy.

Juan's measured words bore little resemblance to his zesty anecdote years earlier, 'The day the revolution drove me absolutely crazy.' He sounded more like a government functionary on *Mesa Redonda* [*Round Table*], the TV programme that was the quasi-official mouthpiece of the Cuban Communist Party, than the young, comedic maverick who had bowled us over almost ten years before. His CDR presidency, his praise of Raúl, his indoor plumbing, suggested that Juan had changed. But the iconoclastic side of Juan soon resurfaced.

'So everyone can live.'

What do you think of the updated economic model?

'This country needs major changes in food and housing. These are the most problematic sectors.' Then, adopting Fidel Castro's habit of reciting long lists of numbers, always to two decimal places, Juan reeled off statistics on prices, imports and production quotas. 'I think the objective should not be to raise salaries. If salaries go up, prices will rise, which will only feed *la mano negra*, the black hand – the black market. The objective should be to make things available at low prices to the entire population, affordable to all, so that everyone can live. There's no point raising salaries if we have shortages. What happens is sellers of cement, beef, pork... The state has already said it cannot provide for the needs of the population. It simply does not have the resources and as a consequence we have major shortages. That's when private entrepreneurs move in. The black hand takes advantage of all this. That's what is happening to food and housing. It's the main problem facing our country.'

Despite quoting Raúl – perhaps a precautionary measure – the changes Juan wanted to see departed radically from government policy. Juan's priority was to provide food and housing to the entire population. 'So that everyone can live.'

I asked Juan to say more about the impact of the new policies on his way of life. At first he was evasive. 'I live OK for a poor person.' Unsurprisingly, he didn't want to say, with the recorder running, that he hawked sanitary napkins, socks, panties and nail polish his friend Leo sent from Miami. Juan was a tiny player in an illicit trade, a spinoff from Raúl Castro's new economic project.

'There is no room to give.'

Suddenly Juan abandoned caution. Assuring us that Raúl Castro encouraged people to speak out, he said, 'Ah, I will tell you the truth. People can't bear this any longer, can't put up with it. I hope things improve. They have to improve because there is no room to give.'

Would you prefer not to continue talking about the economic situation?

'No, no. Raúl gave people the chance to express themselves. People say, and I agree, it doesn't matter whether it's Fidel or Raúl in command. What people want is improvement. People don't bother saying any more, "*Fidel es loco.*" They just don't bother [the interview was two years before Fidel's death]. What they want is improvement. Friends who left say they don't care if Fidel, or Raúl, or Machado Ventura [the then-eighty-five-year-old First Vice-President of the Council of State] is *jefe*, chief. They want improvement. People are saying, and I am telling you the truth, "There isn't any food in the *bodega*, the ration depot." When they say, "There's nothing in the bodega," I reply, "No country is perfect. I say, do all 370-something million people in the United States like Obama? Do the 2 million and something Russians like Putin, or Maduro [president of Venezuela], or Li Keqiang [premier of China]?"'

Juan's delivery made this sound like a comedic riff. To his way of thinking the country's biggest problem wasn't fear, it wasn't a lack of democracy; the biggest problem was the lack of food, and most Cubans we interviewed agreed with him.

'A little while ago they announced on television that they were going to repair the roads, the potholes, the leaking water pipes, everything. Nothing happened. Everything carried on just the way it was before. Everyone began to talk, blah, blah, blah, because we all read, we all listen. We are not stupid or mentally retarded. People are informed about the change in the currency, about ETECSA [corruption scandals at the state telecommunications company]. People won't accept any old story. They meet in the street. In the street you can hear every opinion. Some people talk sense, others talk nonsense. But fear, no. People are no longer afraid. Or they don't reveal their fear as angrily, as violently, as they used to. Here in this town at least, you no longer see such viciousness. You no longer hear such vile things [about the government.]' Juan was attempting to balance his duty as CDR president to defend the government, and his inclination to tell us what was really happening.

Would you say that here in Santa Ana there is a sense that the system isn't working?

'I hear where you're coming from, but let me explain. The problem isn't Fidel or Raúl. The problem is the lower functionaries… Here the problem is the relationship between the functionaries of the municipality of Habana del Este [East Havana] and the town of Santa Ana…' Juan went on to tell a classic Good Tsar story about local bureaucrats hiding inconvenient truths from the country's leaders who were devoted to the good of the people.

Juan explained why his neighbours feel alienated from politics. 'Often people don't want to participate in meetings. They don't want to go to marches. They don't want to do anything because it's all *un engaño*, a fraud. They feel deceived and they just want to throw everything into the garbage. They object to getting involved in anything. People in Santa Ana feel abandoned, depressed and sad. When people feel like this it's ugly. One rotten potato spoils the barrel. Officials must listen to the people because the people are everything. Without the people the state is nothing. That is why leaders must listen to the people. If the people oppose the government nothing will happen. The truth is that here in Santa Ana the people are somewhat abandoned, yes, they are abandoned.' Many narrators, especially outside Havana, said that people in their community felt abandoned.

Juan is a self-taught, grassroots activist, a sort of popular philosopher. Like a Gramsci-style organic intellectual, Juan advocated a non-hierarchical, communitarian form of politics.[5]

With municipal elections coming up is there a possibility of electing some new delegates? Marisol asked.

'Yes, they're working on it. But a lot of people don't want to be a delegate [municipal councillor]. They say, "Why should I, if every time I say something it goes plop? They will want to cut you off, get rid of you, ask you to change your mind. They'll tell you there's no money in the budget. If you ask for that; they'll say you can't have this. If you ask for this, they'll say you can't have that because they don't have any money to spend." Many people are saying it's all nothing but lies. People are fed up with lies and more lies and more deceit.'

This sounded like the Juan we'd met years earlier, though his involvement in local politics accentuated his frustration.

What do you think will come of people's dissatisfaction, and what can you do about it? I asked.

'The Cuban people are *muy luchador*, real fighters. The people will take care that nothing ever happens here. Even if they talk and talk, nothing [will come of it]. *Cosas del pueblo*, it's the way people talk. They will say this is hell, but they will protect their Revolution. They would never want anything to happen to it. But they want to see improvements. They feel the hardships, and the hardships annoy them, make them angry...' Is this Juan, the CDR president, talking, or Juan the realist approaching fifty? In 2005, he was confident the Revolution was coming to an end. Almost ten years later he was certain it will survive, or he felt obliged to say it would.

'El Cubano [the Cuban man], what does he think of? Food. You hear on the bus, "*Coño*, when I get home, I've got to sort out what to make for dinner." [Instead of el Cubano, Juan should have said la Cubana, the Cuban woman, because in Cuba women do virtually all of the cooking.] A Cuban's greatest drama is worrying about what's in the fridge, what to cook for dinner. It's not the same as if you were to get home, open the fridge and there is chicken, shrimp, fish, eggs, beef, and cooking oil. Then you'd have no worries. But when you don't have anything, when there are scarcities, you say, "What can I do? What can I *inventar*, come up with, to stop my boy from crying? What can I put on the table?"... The Cuban people love food, partying, *bachata*, dancing and music. Take that away, and bam, you've got very little left.'

'I believe things are going to get better. With all these changes the state is moving in the right direction. I see that right now Raúl is very interested in making improvements. Many people don't agree, they say Raúl is a military man. But he has a good team and they're working *sin prisa pero sin pausa*. They're taking things one step at a time so there won't be a disaster, so we won't fall into another hole... Yes, I think we will keep this going.'

Juan's politics seemed contradictory – perhaps because we were recording the interview. He advocated a kind of popular participation at odds with the political system. He said he supported Raúl Castro and his government, but added that Cubans were fed up and hinted that he was too. He was confident the people would continue to back the government, or at least that they would do nothing to bring it down. It didn't compute, but why should it? Averse to losing his smidgeon of importance, Juan tried to say the right things, the things the authorities wanted to hear, should it come to that. At the same time, he couldn't resist telling us what he really thought. Ergo, his politics comes across as a mishmash.

'I am the salad to the meal.'

How would you describe your life right now?

'My life? It is not how I would like it to be because people are always thinking of their material needs. When I talk with the younger generation they say, "Here in Cuba we don't have anything. You can't live well in this country. You can't go anywhere. We don't have cars." I believe we live far too much for material things. Partly this is real; it is very real. As for me, despite the difficulties this country faces, the difficulties each one of us faces, I live *bastante bien*, fairly well. I eat well, that is I am well nourished. When I want ice cream, I can buy it. As we say vulgarly, *lucho mi dinerito*, I struggle to earn my bit of money. I go out. Sometimes I go to a *discoteca* in Havana with my young girlfriend. All in all, my life is quite satisfactory. For a poor person my life is very adequate.'

Juan's relaxed smile and self-confident pose convinced me that at that moment he was speaking candidly. He was satisfied with his life. While he would have wanted to have more, at least he had adequate food, music equipment, ice cream now and again, an occasional night out with his *young* girlfriend, freedom to roam the countryside, tranquillity, and respect. Juan had mellowed. In 2005 he was a frustrated thirty-six-year-old who dreamed of owning a car. Some ten years later, he claimed – and I believed him – that he didn't pine for anything, not even a mobile phone. The change was partly a question of age, partly of values. Juan was of the generation that grew up before the rise of consumerism, and he was critical of the new acquisitive culture. Juan derived pleasure from the things money can't buy.

The first time we interviewed Juan he lamented that in Santa Ana he wasn't regarded as someone of substance, he wasn't a somebody. Almost ten years later he told us with palpable pride that having taken the lead in uniting townspeople across the political spectrum he is considered an important person.

'My life has changed a lot, in fact. In this town people think of me as popular, as someone important. I managed to do something no one else has done since the Revolution triumphed fifty-some years ago. Every year on the 2nd of February I bring together everyone in town to celebrate the fiesta of Santa Ana. I came up with the idea and I am the principal organiser. The fiestas have been marvellous. Everyone says I have Santa Ana in my heart. What's more, I have brought the town together, though I never thought I would be able to. I have reunited people who would not be seen together for ten to fifteen years; people who wouldn't talk to one another.

'Teachers I had in school come up to me and say, "This is the most beautiful fiesta." People who left the pueblo *por el otro lado* tell me, "I didn't know you were doing this, what a beautiful idea." This is what I have accomplished, and it has made me stronger. People come to my house to tell me, "Don't let it fail, don't let it end, you are very strong, and while you have the strength do not let this go." I am going to organise the fiesta every year. I am very proud that my town, my people, hold me in such high esteem, treat me with such respect. Every place, every country, every city, every town, every tribe has its idol. Here in Santa Ana I am sort of an idol. People call out, "Juan, Juan." Someone answers, "He's not here right now." I feel this is my stamp of approval. I am the salad to the meal. People kid me, "What would happen if you left, we would miss you terribly." That's what they say. That's how they feel. That's how they regard me. It's not that I want it to be like this, it is the way I am. Wherever I go it's the same. If I go somewhere else, there it will be the same. That is how my life is.'

In his first interview Juan said, 'If my mother hadn't died when I was fourteen, I would have been a somebody.' Juan made himself a somebody. Organising a local fiesta where everyone in town mingles was no mean achievement. It was transformative in a particularly Cuban way. After the revolutionary government came to power, people who wanted to hold a meeting or an informal get-together of neighbours, artists, film buffs, baseball fans, whatever, needed official permission. Social life was inseparable from political life, and politics was controlled from the top.

Juan and his fiesta committee resuscitated a significant event in the town's social calendar, and its purpose wasn't either to support or to oppose the government. It didn't have a political purpose. Its purpose was to eat, drink, dance, party. Interestingly, when I asked Rosa if she had gone to the fiesta, she didn't know what fiesta I was talking about. My colleague Marisol reasoned that since the fiesta hadn't been endorsed by the local Party apparatus it wasn't on her radar; also Rosa was seventy-six. As a signal of a certain flexibility – or a survival instinct – town officials allowed it to take place. If Juan and his associates had tried to revive the traditional fiesta a decade earlier, it probably would have been banned.

'I would be a caged bird.'

Will you ever leave Santa Ana?

Hearing Juan describe his life, his reputation, his fiesta, I knew the answer. 'Perhaps tomorrow I will change my mind, but leaving would be very, very difficult. I have no intention of abandoning my country, ever... If someone invites me to visit, but to live, no. I don't like the United States. Why? I'm not afraid to tell you. You have to live inside the monster to know it.'[6] I felt that Juan was staring at me. 'When I watch TV I see a lot of mistreatment. People say to me, no that's just *bretes*, light disagreements. But how can it all be *bretes* when there's news twenty-four hours a day about it, and it's always about Blacks. In less than a year how many African-Americans have been injured? How many attacked? How many murdered? It seems to me that the US is not the place for me. I like living here. It's a detail, but here I get along with everyone. They accept me just the way I am, the way I live. My friends tell me, "You live in the countryside, in Miami you can't live the way you like to." Here we have the freedom to go out whenever we want to, to lounge on a mat on the floor and converse with friends. Someone calls out to you. My young girlfriend embraces me, calls me, "*Mi negrito*." No, there I would be a caged bird.'

Perhaps Juan used the word freedom deliberately. The freedoms that were of foremost importance to him – freedom from police brutality and brutal racism, freedom to wander the countryside, to relax with friends, freedom from the Miami rat race, were not the same freedoms that stirred up US policymakers.

Juan had made his peace with life in Cuba. In 2005, he began the interview saying, 'My story is about what it's like to live like a poor person in Cuba.' Ten years later he brought his life story to a close saying, 'For a poor person my life is very adequate.'

I ended the interview as I always did, asking Juan if he would grant me permission to tell his life story, and use his words, in books, on the web, in radio and TV programmes. 'I feel tremendous satisfaction that you have interviewed me, and I am proud that you came to find me again. I feel like a very important person. I feel like I am an ambassador. As Raúl Roa [Garcia – Cuba's first Foreign Minister] said to our Comandante [Fidel], "I feel like a missionary sending a message to the world." I am tremendously satisfied with everything I have said, and everything that I am doing for my people and for my country. I give you my total permission.'

Juan knew how to bring his story to a beautiful end.

*

Postscript

Marisol and I interviewed Juan twice more in 2016 and 2018. While he continued to organise the town fiesta, and the CDR president sign still hung beside his door, he complained that life was becoming much more difficult. When his friends in Miami managed to send him a box of this or that he sold them outside the market, but he said that his sales were way down because more people from Santa Ana had left, and those who remained had less money to spend. He repaired the leaks in the walls of his house, but he had not installed the shiny bathroom and the kitchen fixtures he had purchased. 'I couldn't complete the job because my economic situation is dire.' Juan tried to appear upbeat but he seemed to have lost much of his exuberance.

22

RAÚL CASTRO: THE GENERAL

Fidel was an idealist, a dreamer. Raúl Castro was a pragmatist, prepared to do the business. Fidel was one of the great charismatic leaders of the twentieth century. Raúl avoided the limelight and preferred to operate in the background. The differences in their politics and personalities played out in the oral history interviews. Almost every Cuban we interviewed spoke of Fidel with passionate admiration or vitriolic condemnation, or both. Few talked about Raúl by name, even when he was head of state.

Raúl Castro's greatest contributions stemmed from his practicality and his eye for business. His rendezvous with the commercial world began long before Cuba's post-Soviet crisis. In 1980, as Minister of Defence, he developed a strategy that, in effect, carried out warfare by other means. To evade the US blockade, he created military corporations that engaged in clandestine trade. The first, the Cuban Import-Export Corporation, CIMEX, owned by MININT, the security apparatus, and the armed forces, was notoriously corrupt in its early days. Although every general that headed the company in its first decade was convicted of embezzlement, CIMEX survived and prospered. The CIMEX story inspired Leonardo Padura's thriller, *Pasado perfecto*, published in English as *Havana Blue*.[1]

In the next forty years CIMEX grew into a global enterprise that operated in Cuba and overseas. The CIMEX empire included everything from hotels, resorts, supermarkets, tour agencies, warehouses, airports, down to neighbourhood shops. Its website described the company as, '*Un grupo empresarial privado de capital estatal cubano*,' a private business group formed of Cuban state capital.[2]

Three of the narrators in this book were employed by CIMEX at one time or another – indicative of the corporation's reach. Mario worked his way through university as a nightwatchman at CIMEX warehouses. One of Juan's few legal jobs was at a CIMEX warehouse in Santa Ana. Alejandro fulfilled his post-university, social service – an alternative to the military draft – working as an intern at a CIIMEX subsidiary that manages Cuba's airports.

Raúl Castro expected that the military would play a leading role in the new public-private economy, and as head of state he expanded the army-MININT empire. He founded GAESA, Grupo de Administración Empresarial, S.A., a megacorporation and holding company that dwarfed CIMEX, to build and administer the new harbour and free enterprise zone at the Port of Mariel, and to take over some of the tourist facilities formerly under the CIMEX umbrella.

Raúl Castro's pragmatism was evident in the state's response to the crisis of the Special Period. When the population was going hungry he coined the phrase, 'Beans are more important than cannons', and famously deployed the army to grow food on state farms. With the end of Soviet provision of military hardware, he created a number of profit-making enterprises to supply the army. And in a move greeted with scepticism by the Party leadership, he sent military officers to Western Europe and Latin America to study capitalist business methods.

A legendary anecdote bolstered Raúl's business credentials. According to the story, at the meeting where Cuba's leaders decided that tourism would become the driving force of the new economy, Fidel said to Raúl, 'I am putting you in charge of the tourist sector because the army is the only institution we have that combines business experience and a reputation for honesty.' The story was a gift. It papered over the scandals rocking CIMEX; it legitimated the army's future role, its takeover of the tourist sector, and it sealed Raúl Castro's reputation as a fixer. When Raúl succeeded Fidel, and began to lift restrictions on the private sector, foreign commentators expressed surprise. If they had been more familiar with Cuban history, they would have predicted it.

Under more favourable geopolitical circumstances, Raúl's programme to introduce limited market reforms might have generated economic growth. But it failed, and not because of opposition by Fidelistas within the Party; they had already been sidelined. The economic transformation that Raúl's government hoped to deliver was thwarted by the weight of outside forces.

23

ESTEBAN CABRERA MONTES

Fontanar, Havana, 2006

'Year after year I try to emigrate... That is the story of my life.'

In his pessimism and his desperation to leave, Esteban claimed to speak for a generation. To demonstrate that he is not an extremist, he invited friends, most of them university dropouts in their twenties, to join him for what turned out to be his last interview before he left Cuba. Yannis, his sidekick, who Esteban said was a mathematical genius, and Haydée, who was studying business administration at the University of Havana, joined the conversation. Several other friends wandered in and out, but seemed more interested in the music and food than the interview being recorded in the front room.[1]

'Capitalist society is monstrous. I know it is very crude.'

'Everything here is the same as always, nothing has happened since you left,' Esteban began. Julia had just returned to Cuba after six months in Britain. 'The monotony is tiring. I'm fed up and I need a change. You almost get to the point you will risk your life and you will do anything to leave. You look for something that will change your life forever, like going to the developed world. I say developed in quotation marks. I know that capitalist societies are monstrous; I know they are very crude. Don't think we're so backward that we don't know. We're well informed. Here almost everyone sees capitalism that way, but we haven't lived it, not yet anyway, and young people want to give it a go.' Esteban was laying the foundation for what he was planning to ask of Julia.

'You should say, *almost* all young people want to take their chances with capitalism,' Haydée said. 'Youth don't all think alike, and not everyone sees things the way we do, or talks like we talk.' At eighteen years old, Haydée was the youngest of the group yet she exuded the most self-confidence. 'In other countries young people can enjoy the fruits of their labour. They are paid decently and they have enough money to buy lots of things. Here the problem is that salaries are ridiculous and everything is very expensive.'

Esteban broke in to say that Haydée's parents were part of the revolutionary aristocracy. Her mother was an army colonel; her father was a university professor. Haydée interrupted to add that despite her parents' rank, they struggled economically. 'My father can't support himself, much less me, on his salary. He needs to *inventar para resolver las cosas*. That's the problem; the Cuban problem is a money problem.' Haydée's slang, the national slang, *inventar para resolver*, is deliberately evasive. She meant that her father had to have an illegal side-line to provide what they needed.

'We are not *chicos malos*.'

'The Cuban problem is bigger than that,' Esteban said. 'The government protects its own interests... *Este hombre* [this man, i.e. Fidel] tricked us all. Nothing is changing and everyone is feeling very negative. We haven't been given any opportunities, even when we go looking for them. That's why this country is in the state it is. It is not like we want to act like this. We are not *chicos malos*, bad little boys, but they won't give us opportunities. None. Not to anyone.'

'Some people don't see it that way, or they see it but don't want to admit it,' Haydée said. 'Or they are resigned to whatever happens and they claim it's good. As far as I'm concerned everything here is one great big lie,' Esteban said definitively.

What changes would you like to see? asked Julia.

After a long pause Esteban said, 'To have a little bit more liberty, be allowed to work.' He meant work in private business. Several years later Raúl Castro's government changed course and encouraged people to open small private enterprises. 'We want to be allowed to live independently from our family and pay our own rent, be allowed to work at two jobs, even three. It would be hard, it would be a sacrifice, but at least you would know if you could do it. If you couldn't, well that would be your problem. But here they don't give you the chance to try to make it on your own.'

'Many people here are talented,' said Haydée. 'They could accomplish many things. But they think why should I sacrifice myself, why should I give it everything I've got if in the end I'll be nothing but a martyr.'

Esteban and Haydée wanted the opportunity to earn a living from their own business. They believed that if you worked hard you could become rich.

'When I finish my degree I want to work in a hotel,' Haydée said. 'I could work as an accountant in a state company but why would I want to? Once a month they would pay me two hundred and some pesos cubanos and that would cover one shop at the farmers' market. No, not even. With what they would pay me I could buy a little rice on the ration, one pair of cheap trainers and that's all. And what if I had a child? Lots of girls my age are mothers. With a child they can't make it. People my age don't have the option of having a child, they simply cannot afford to.'

Cuba has one of the lowest birth rates in the world, and *Granma* frequently runs articles about how the government is trying to raise it. Haydée listed off the top of her head a number of practical pro-natal policies that she said the government would never consider.

'Cubans are constantly plotting ways to leave. It drives them crazy.'

Esteban turned the conversation to his favourite theme. 'Cubans are constantly plotting ways to leave. It drives them crazy. It gets so extreme that they can't function, and they forget that they need to figure out a way to survive. To make a living [he meant an illegal living] you need to keep your feet firmly planted on the ground and not be constantly obsessed with leaving, leaving, leaving. Your obsession can become so extreme that you lose your will to live; you become totally disillusioned and lose all hope. But me, I'm a realist. I don't go around Havana hunting for a tourist who would fall in love with me.' (I suspect that's exactly what he did with his girlfriend, the British anthropologist.) 'I get on with my life. I do what needs doing. I am a sociable person and I like to meet new people, but not because I have a fixation about leaving. Leaving becomes an obsession that perpetually eats away at your insides. As for me, I just live my life.'

Esteban wanted to sound level-headed in the presence of Julia and his friends. Evidently, he had forgotten that six months earlier, when he, Julia and the recorder were alone, he said the opposite. 'I need to leave by whatever means. I don't care if I risk my life, or, or if I need to, get myself a foreign girlfriend. I'll keep playing the [US visa] lottery. I'll keep doing whatever it takes to get out of here. I must leave, otherwise I will go crazy. I prefer to risk my life, knowing I might drown, to staying here. I must try, I must try, and I'll try again this year. Forgive me, Julia, forgive me. I lost control. As you can see, I have to get out of here.'

Narrators frequently forget what they said months, even minutes, before, but recording machines don't forget. An advantage, and a complication, of recording a life story over a span of months and years is that narrators tell you conflicting stories. They remember events differently, depending on their immediate circumstances, current social and political conditions, and their feelings at the time of the interview.

'Escape is our only hope.'

Minutes later, when Esteban and his friends were describing how it felt to be trapped in Cuba, Esteban muttered in a semi-hysterical whisper, 'It is madness, Julia, all madness. If you want to, you could shoot us a letter of invitation.' There, it was out. He said what he had been wanting to say. But the room was noisy, and Julia misheard or she misunderstood.

Did you say something about social workers? asked Julia.

His friends laughed nervously. Esteban seized the moment. To be sure that Julia understood him, he repeated slowly and clearly, 'If you give me a letter of invitation I could get away from all this. You could free me from my suffering.' The room went quiet; his friends were curious. 'I am very independent. I would never visit you, or only when you invited me, and then I would arrive with a bottle of wine, the very cheapest, of course. No, I should say, the most economical.' The room exploded with laughter, but the moment had passed. To preserve his dignity Esteban half pretended it was all a joke.

Next it was Yannis's turn to talk. Yannis was Esteban's best friend. To put Julia in the picture Esteban explained that Yannis had been a maths whiz at La Lenin Preparatory School, the hothouse for brilliant adolescents. When his mother died he dropped out of university because he had no one to pay for his food, books and clothing. This was the new Cuba.

Yannis said the American Dream was all hooey and he tried to disabuse his friends of their illusions. 'The other day I saw an old friend who now lives in Spain. I asked him, "With no work in Spain now how are you getting on?" He replied, "There is work, but the truth is you can't get rich by working."'

'Who wants to be rich?' Esteban said. I suspect he said it to garner favour with Julia. 'Not me,' Yannis replied. 'I just want a job that would allow me to buy clothes, go out, the normal stuff. I'm not thinking big... But it's amazing, absolutely amazing, incredible, super incredible how poor we've become. You think to yourself, it's really something that Cubans have adapted to being so poor... But you have to keep your mouth shut about these things.'

To Yannis's way of thinking the reason to leave was not to get rich, but to preserve your self-esteem. 'There's a huge difference between Cubans who live here and Cubans who live abroad. Living abroad changes you completely. How can I explain it? You become a different person, you change completely. On the outside you are the same person, but on the inside you change completely. Your self-esteem changes completely and you hold your head up higher.'

Esteban chimed in, 'You hold your head up higher because it's clear of all this garbage. You think more clearly; you are more organised and you can get on with your life. Here you can't take a step forward, every move is backwards... Sometimes we talk about getting a job, going to work, because we fear the vagrancy laws I was telling you about last time. But if you get a job, you have to deal with the daily monotony, and you get paid a salary that isn't enough to live on, and then you lose interest.' Esteban and Yannis – neither one had ever travelled overseas – believed that when you leave Cuba your problems go away. It's the myth of leaving.

'Last year I tried to emigrate, this year I will try again, because as I told you, I would rather that than... well, you know.' Yannis finished Esteban's sentence, 'Yes, before I do something bad, and I'm not talking about robbing a bank, because that wouldn't work here. Before I get myself into x number of difficulties, I would prefer to take a risk, and see if there's someone out there calling my name, if you know what I mean.'

Esteban said bluntly, 'What I mean is that I would prefer to risk drowning than staying here.' This sounded like another plea to Julia.

I know that salaries are a huge problem, but aren't there any jobs that would give you some satisfaction because you would be doing something that really interests you?

Haydée jumped in. 'Money is what makes the world go round and it is the money that really interests me. If I am not earning good money, I would lose interest.' She was too honest for Esteban's liking, especially as he was trying to elicit Julia's pity, and he launched into a story about applying for a job at a hospital. But he quickly realised it sounded phony. 'No, it is a disaster here, a total disaster. Julia, I wish you would stop saying things like that. I have told you about my experiences. I wish you could go to work with someone for a week. Then you would see what he does, how he lives... and then you would agree, *no es facil*, it's not easy. You would understand that there is nothing here that could motivate you, nothing.' Esteban burst into sing-song, 'What has youth come to. What has youth come to la, la, la.' He hoped singing and joking would dissipate the tension. '*No es facil, no es facil*. But soon we'll get ourselves a raft. Yannis, did you hear me, very soon we will get a raft.'

'No, an airplane; better yet a magic carpet,' Yannis shouted.
'A what?' Julia was bewildered.
'ALADDIN,' Esteban and Yannis chanted in unison.

OK, so what motivates people who do go to work?

Julia was trying to get the interview back on track.

'I worked last year, not for very long. What an experience,' Esteban burst out laughing. 'You watch people go to work every day. It's madness. You're right there; you see everything; you get inside their heads. You watch them arrive early and punch in. You watch them sacrifice themselves in order to collect a salary. Where I worked people didn't eat their lunch. They sold it; they sold their *merienda*.'

Yannis picked up the thread. 'They sell their *merienda* for twenty pesos. Twenty pesos is less than a dollar. [Twenty pesos was more or less what most state workers were paid for a day's work.] They bring food, pastries, other things to sell at work. In the *novela*, the soap opera, on TV right now, *la muchacha*, the girl, is always cross with her husband because she wants him to sell coffee and buns at work. The other workers tell him, "No, we're not interested, they're too expensive." She's doing all this to pay for her daughter's *quince* [fifteenth birthday party].'

'It's amazing,' Esteban said. I think he meant that it is amazing how much Cubans spend on fifteen-year-old's birthday parties. The *quince* extravaganzas never ceased to amaze me either. The revival of this costly, and sexist, tradition from before the Revolution at a time when most Cubans' salaries didn't cover the cost of food demonstrates just how difficult it is to change people's consciousness. And perhaps that was the message of the *telenovela*.

'Look around any workplace and you'd think they're all robots. They act like robots,' Esteban said. 'They do it as a conscious thing. Very few complain because the majority are older.' Esteban and Yannis took turns explaining what motivated Cubans to go to work. Yannis went first because Esteban was talking on his mobile phone.

'Yeh, the majority, what would they do at home all day? They go work because at least it gives them something to do. You wouldn't want to see them when they get home. They're in a foul mood, they get into fights. And the stress.'

Esteban finished his call and returned to the conversation. 'What really gets me is that for a lot of people work is a place to relax, a place to gossip, to laugh about other people's miseries. When they're at home they need to face up to their own problems, the crude reality of what they are going to *inventar* for dinner. What they have, what they lack, like soap to wash themselves, and other things, things no one should have to do without. When they get home it's like a nuclear bomb goes off, BOOM! At home a bomb explodes every single day. That's why, day in and day out, they wake up early and head off to work. It's their way of relaxing, getting rid of stress. They don't see going to work as an economic thing. Most people know – no, everyone knows – the salary doesn't cover what you need, so at work you try to *inventar*.'

Yannis continued, 'Ninety-five per cent of people manage more or less to *resolver*, to sort out their basic necessities, but not by working, by *inventando* when they're at work. Julia, do you understand what I'm saying? I prefer not to have to spell it out, but if you don't understand I will. At work they hustle on the sly, clandestinely, illegally. Now do you understand?'

Esteban picked up the thread. 'How they do it depends on where they work, and on...' He gave a long whistle, 'That's what it takes, and I won't let anyone tell me otherwise, because I have seen it with my own two eyes.'

'So, you see Julia, we are normal people,' Yannis said, meaning that in Cuba normal people steal from the state, and stealing from the state is normal behaviour.

278

'Everyone in this country does it. They go to work just to…'
Esteban whistled again. 'Someone who has an alright job, maybe
a job a little bit better than alright, they don't go to work because
they like whatever it is they do at work. They go to work because
that's where they can *inventar*.'

'It's nothing new. Ever since I was a child this has been going
on,' said Yannis. He was in his mid-twenties, and he was talking
about the period after the collapse of the USSR. 'People don't look
for a job they're interested in. They look for a job that allows
them to make money on the side. Take me, I am an architect, but
I would never, ever work again in that field. For years I've been
looking for a job that brings in some money.' Yannis did not mean
a state pay cheque at the end of the month. He meant a job that
pays partly in hard currency, or a job where you can *inventar*.

Esteban and Yannis's description of people's motives for going
to work chimed with the stories different narrators told. Cubans
regarded stealing at work as part of normal everyday life. I think
it is a sign of social disintegration.

'They label us anti-social.'

'They label us anti-social. It shouldn't be that way. It shouldn't
be that a person who is…' Esteban hesitated, 'is law-abiding
is labelled a delinquent.' The pause may have been caused by
embarrassment. Esteban was embarrassed to claim he was law-
abiding when by any measure he was a crook. He didn't pilfer
from the state in order to put food on the table. He stole from
the state, directly and indirectly, to buy himself a mobile phone,
parmesan cheese and steak. Esteban was an associate, albeit a
very junior one, in a criminal network.

'Let me explain, we are anti-social in the sense that we don't
work. But we are of a different period, and we have a different
outlook on things. How can I put it? We want to live our lives.

We want to live the way all young people want to live. We want to go to parties and all those kinds of things. In this country, with what they pay, you can't do any of that.'

'In addition, you wouldn't have the time,' Haydée said. 'You would need to get up at six in the morning, go to work, return at five in the afternoon and start cooking.' Haydée looked at everyday life from a female perspective. She thought about the ways babies and cooking and domestic chores ate into women's time. Esteban and Yannis showed no interest in her concerns.

'The way we see it, it doesn't make much sense. Work, work and more work. Not that I've anything against work, not at all,' said Esteban. 'If they paid us decently, we would do any kind of work. As for you, *chico*,' he said, turning to Yannis, 'Tell Julia what kind of work you do to support yourself.' 'Go on, don't be ashamed. Describe your life,' Haydée coaxed.

'Youth here are different than in other countries... They don't get together to demonstrate.'

'I'm not ashamed,' Yannis shouted, almost drowned out by Nirvana. 'We wake up, then maybe *inventamos*, we come up with something. Like we might go out for a little walk to enjoy ourselves, maybe take in a concert if the tickets are cheap, ten pesos or so, or go somewhere else. That's it. Then we go home in the wee hours of the morning.' 'That's about it. It's our daily routine,' Haydée and Esteban said in unison. Everyone in the room laughed.

'He likes to go to Vedado, to G and 23rd, to hang out with the freaks. Young people get together there at night. Some are students, but the great majority don't do anything,' Haydée said. 'They don't do anything because this is Cuba,' Esteban said. 'It is a socialist system, so youth here are different in many respects from youth elsewhere... They don't get together to demonstrate.'

What do young people do when they get together?

'What do they do? Well, they don't protest... Youth have turned to drugs. Some young people have become drug addicts. I know several but I don't want to talk about them in this *trabajo* [academic work].' Esteban enjoyed showing off his command of anthropologists' jargon. 'Now young people take drugs more than before. But we don't allow heavy drug users into our group.'

'If your idea is to conduct interviews about people's lives, you might have come to the wrong country.'

Suddenly Yannis seemed alarmed and muttered to himself (probably thinking the recorder wouldn't pick up his voice), 'Don't worry. Nothing will happen to us. It's not a problem. We're not really saying anything. Nothing will happen, but if it does we could be in a real mess.' Esteban ignored his friend. He knew our project had official links and perhaps the danger thrilled him.

'People who are *integrado*, who participate in state organisations, who carry a Party card in their pocket, you should find out what they think about living here,' Esteban said. 'What they might tell you confidentially is the opposite of what they would say at a political meeting or a march. Everything here is a lie, it's all a lie, I tell you. If your idea is to find out about the lives of ordinary people you might have come to the wrong country. It's not that life here isn't intriguing. The lives of people in this country are very interesting because of this country's history. North American imperialism, the Revolution, the blockade, and everything else that has happened to us makes interviewing here very interesting. But the people who live here have very limited experiences... It's pretty much the same year after year, nothing changes, nothing new happens. Living here you get mentally blocked. You ask about my life, the things I want, the things I need. To you it's all very interesting, but has anything transcendental happened to me? No, year after year I try to emigrate. Year after year I am unsuccessful. That's the story of my life.'

Esteban was saying that he felt exploited. What to him were matters of life and death, to Julia was an interesting research topic.

Racial problems

Are there racial problems?

Music, chatter, the clinking of glasses hummed in the background. 'When we go to Central Havana to walk around, I watch to see if there are police standing on the corner, hoping they won't ask me for my identity card. They frequently stop people for no reason,' Esteban said. 'For nothing,' Yannis agreed, giving a long whistle. 'Sometimes when they stop me, if I am in a rush, I ask… [Esteban switched to an ultra-deferential tone] "Please officer, is this going to take long? I know it is normal, and it's your job, but please officer, I have an appointment and I really don't have much time, and if this takes a while…" I speak like that, like I am a human being, a normal person, not like there is a file in some computer somewhere on me, or a poster with my photo under the heading Most Wanted. Nothing like that. I don't say, "Why are you stopping me for no reason at all?" They can stop you two or three times in one night, easily.'

'That's true, but don't take it like that,' Yannis said. 'I think it's OK. It's good and it's bad. It's good in that it keeps the streets safe. At the same time, sometimes it is… The truth is that it is normal for us, normal. You are walking along, you see a police officer, and inside you say to yourself, *coño*, they're going to stop me. If they let you walk by you think, aha, how divine. Julia, I bet you don't think of Cuba as a very violent country, do you?

So, doesn't it make you wonder why the police stop so many people on the street?'

'Julia, let me tell you what it's like living here,' Esteban said, picking up the story. 'There's lots of pressure and other stuff. Some of it is your own shit, personal shit. Then you go out for a walk and you have this too. It's the last straw. It's a bomb. Once one thing after another made me explode at a police officer, but only once. I always speak correctly, in the best possible way, so they won't take reprisals. But once I said, "*POR FAVOR*, ENOUGH." Do you understand what I'm saying? The worst that can happen is they ask for my identity card. If they phone headquarters on their walkie-talkie they'll find out there's nothing on my record. We've never had a warning, nothing. We are not delinquents. When it comes to the walkie-talkie we are completely clean. So why do they do it?'

Do they stop some people more than others?

'They stop everyone, even women, because they think they're *jineteras* and men because they think they're delinquents,' Yannis said.

They stop everyone?

'They do it because they feel like it, for no reason,' said Yannis.

'Yes, but there's also a racial problem,' Esteban said.

'It's their reputation, their reputation,' Yannis countered. Yannis probably meant the police stopped Afro-Cubans because of their reputation for delinquency.

'The problem is racial. The problem is racism,' Esteban repeated.

'No, no, it isn't racism,' said Yannis. 'It's their reputation, it's the *morenos*' reputation.[2] It's not racism because for years and years we haven't had racial problems here in Cuba. Do you see what I am saying? Not for years and years, not since...' Yannis seemed to be saying that stopping Afro-Cubans more than white Cubans on the street wasn't racist, it was crime-fighting.

'No, not true, not true,' interrupted Esteban. 'Here there's always been racism. Let me tell you something, it has always existed here.'

'Let *me* tell *you* something, what with education and other stuff, there isn't any. No, not at all,' said Yannis.

'Of course, of course,' said Esteban, his voice dripping with irony, 'There isn't racism here, there can't be any racism here, because this is socialism, this is socialism.'

Esteban and Yannis started shouting. After an indecipherable jumble of words Yannis allowed Esteban to speak.

'This is a revolution, so supposedly there cannot be any, supposedly there cannot be. As far as they [Cuba's political leaders] are concerned in Cuba there are no racial problems. But there are. Yes, there are racial problems now and there were in the past too. When you're looking for a job, a good job – I'm not talking about one of those crappy jobs they'll give to anyone. When you are looking for a good job you encounter racism. It exists. There are other problems, racial problems on the street. Like who gets labelled a *jinetero*, a male sex worker. Who? The *morenos*. They're viewed as thieves. The police do this, yes, the police. People say that at the top of the police force and in the Ministry of Interior most of the higher officials are white. That's how the system works. We have racial problems on the street; and then we have this. It's outrageous. I know there are problems like this all over the world, police harassment, and other stuff. But, please, it's not like we're living in Europe. We are in the Caribbean where everyone is a great mixture. We Cubans are a great mixture and there should be...' Esteban stopped. His speech about racism was getting drowned out by the music.

'To top all this off, the way our society is changing, there are people who have more money than I don't know who. The Black people you might have spotted hidden away somewhere, and the poor, they have less money. And now they are getting pushed aside by people who have a little more. Now you see people who have a little more money looking down their noses. I'm talking about people who have cars, people who live a little bit better than the rest of us. You can see and feel it happening. That's what Cuba is turning into, can you believe.' Suddenly, Esteban switched out of his serious mode. He snapped his fingers, and called out, 'Help me' in English. Perhaps he felt he had said enough. Talking about racism was difficult and even Yannis, his sidekick, didn't think there was racism in Cuba.

Afternoon was turning to evening. The talk session, interview, whatever you want to call it, had been going for almost three hours. Esteban complained that the conversation was making him feel depressed. 'The economy is getting worse, there is nothing to look forward to. Towards the end of the 90s things seemed to be getting better... Since then it's been going downhill. It feels now like it did in the early 90s, but without the long blackouts. Who knows how long this is going to last. We are in a very difficult stage, and people are psychologically exhausted. We face so many problems, we feel totally blocked. Everyone has their own personal problems and some problems are shared. What more can I say?'

On parting, Yannis whispered to Julia, 'Remember we didn't complain about a thing.' Someone shouted, 'Today is Saturday.' 'We had been thinking of buying a bottle,' Esteban said, 'But then you, Julia, fell from heaven.' It was his way of asking her to buy the drinks.

Esteban and his friends portrayed a world and a worldview familiar to many Cubans of his generation, and one that is entirely missing from the official narrative.

24

BARBARA VEGAS

Barbara believed in Santería but she wanted to deny it. 'Do you practise Santería?' Ada asked soon after they met. 'A little, but only when I have to.' Although the state granted religious freedom in 1991, fifteen years later Barbara was hesitant to say that she was religious. Religion carried a stigma, especially for Party members, and she probably calculated that it would be unwise to own up to observing Santería when she was applying for Party membership. Later, when she relaxed and came to regarded Ada as a confidant not an interrogator, she described the history of her family's religious practices.

Do you feel like an outsider at work because you are Black?

'Oh no. It's not that. Many of the staff are Black. It's true that I no longer get along with my colleagues at work. Perhaps it's because of my new position. Now that I am a *dirigente*, an official, I have to deal with the *compañeros* who are troublemakers. It's my job to enforce discipline and combat absenteeism. I think the *compañeros* resent me because I do what managers have to do, not because of my skin colour.' They criticise Barbara because she is part of the power structure, not because she is Black.

'Well, it's true there are always some neighbours who will blurt out right in my face, "Fancy that Black doing this and that," or "Wouldn't you know it takes a Black to say that." But no, I haven't had any serious problems… I live in my own little world… I never, ever drop in on neighbours. I don't go snooping around… Consequently, I don't know what people around here think about the race issue. For that matter, I don't know what they think about anything.'

Your husband, what is his skin colour?
'He's white.'

Describing his multiracial family, Barbara said, 'I don't feel they look down on me.'

Ada later told me that she suspected Barbara had married a white man to guarantee respectability. 'I think she has an inferiority complex. Unfortunately many Afro-Cubans do.'

Ten years after we first met, Ada phoned Barbara to arrange another interview. Barbara had moved and was living in a brand new house on the outskirts of town, close to the factory quarter and the cemetery. Barbara proudly showed off her new home, explaining that the municipal government had built two houses and given them to families who had contributed to town improvements and who were most in need of housing. Barbara didn't say whether Party members had priority, and we didn't ask.

25

PAVEL GARCÍA ROJAS

El Cerro, Havana

'I am a publicly declared opponent... I am what you see.'

Film school – the openness of political discussion – and having a daughter were, as Pavel tells it, formative events. They convinced him to stay in Cuba and campaign for democracy, the cause that took over his life.

After graduating with a master's degree from film school, Pavel taught at the Instituto Superior de Arte (ISA), Cuba's famed university of the arts.[1] 'My students were extraordinary. Though poorly educated, they were remarkably intelligent, hardworking, and had a passion for the arts.' I asked why in a country famous for schooling his students had received a poor education. Pavel explained that many teachers had left the country in the Special Period, or left the profession for better paying jobs as taxi drivers and chambermaids. 'But now my ex-students aren't worth a *centavo*. I know this sounds extreme, but most of them no longer care a hoot about art. What matters to them is how they're seen. They want to make a name for themselves and enjoy financial security. Now their work is dull; not all of them but most. They churn out banalities, and as far as I'm concerned they're lost.' Pavel doesn't mask his opinions and often it leads to difficulties.

'Liz, if you haven't seen ISA, you haven't lived. All human beings should visit Venice, London, Paris and ISA. You're probably thinking how outrageous is that; Pavel is exaggerating. But the buildings really are extraordinary. Some are open and extroverted. The ones that look like female and male genitalia are most people's favourites.' Pavel prefers those you enter via dark, narrow passageways. 'They feel claustrophobic, then suddenly the spaces open up.' Several days later I took the bus out to ISA, built on the grounds of what had been Havana's exclusive country club where Fidel and Che famously played a round of golf. The buildings are as exciting as Pavel said.

Pavel enjoyed working at ISA but resigned because the salary was too low to support his family. 'My wife and I together earned the equivalent of thirty-six dollars a month in national currency. Foreigners who applaud the government say Cubans can live on that. Please tell them we can't. Thirty-six dollars covers the rice and eggs you get on the ration, and not much else.' At that time Pavel's family lived with his wife's parents. Her father, an eminent jurist and loyal Fidelista, wrote textbooks to supplement his salary. After he died Pavel decided he needed to find a higher-paying job. 'It was humiliating, absolutely humiliating. There I was, thirty years old, working very hard, earning eighteen dollars a month. You could say that humiliation is part of the Cuban condition. Cubans do not live off the wealth they produce. The majority of Cubans have no wealth, but if you are one of the few who do your income is not the product of your labour; you live on the money your brother, sister or father sends you from abroad. It is unnatural and dehumanising.' Pavel was well acquainted with the syndrome; for years he lived off the money his father sent him.

Pavel was hired by the International Film School, his alma mater, as an administrator. He said the job was boring but he was thankful to have it. It paid well and he enjoyed mixing with illustrious filmmakers. 'These men are extremely humble, it's marvellous… They take the school bus along with the rest of us. Raúl Pérez Ureta doesn't go by car.[2] These days anyone of the slightest importance tries to get a car one way or another. They think, now that I'm a big shot I need a car – it's a sign of status. To my mind it is pathological. Nelson Rodríguez is happy to converse with anyone.[3] These are people who if they lived anywhere else in the world would be mega rich. Nelson Rodríguez's house is falling down. Raúl Pérez Ureta's is in a bit better shape because, despite his seventy-some years, he repairs it himself. These men are truly great. They exemplify dignity, commitment and humility: the ideals of the Cuban Revolution.' Pavel juxtaposed the celebrated filmmakers with the nobodies of his generation who if they have two hundred dollars in their pocket expect to be addressed as *usted* (the formal form of you). 'These people are preposterous,' Pavel said of Cuba's nouveau riche.

'Before the Revolution my parents belonged to the middle class. After the triumph Cubans immediately faced material deprivations. There were always acute shortages; it was a characteristic of the Fidelista system. But people had discipline and attitude, and despite the scarcities they knew how to conduct themselves. My parents always lived in poverty but they accepted it because they were revolutionaries. Living modestly was part of their identity. My generation is different; our discipline has broken down. If you examine the conduct of my generation you can't but notice that people are forever calculating: will I gain, will I lose, does this jeopardise my economic status? But to such an extent, it's very sad.' Pavel admired the proletarian morality of his parents and the generation that made the Revolution.

What are the major causes of inequality?

'The leading cause of social differentiation is whether or not someone sends you money from abroad.' Pavel explained the case of his neighbour, a leading surgeon, whose best friend from medical school lives in Miami. 'If not for the dollars his friend sends, the famous surgeon would be driving a taxi.' Pavel said that Cubans who received Spanish citizenship through their grandparents were also doing well, and he pointed out that most of them are white. He explained that with a Spanish passport they can travel back and forth between Havana and Miami smuggling goods. 'The FAR [Fuerzas Armadas Revolucionarias, Revolutionary Armed Forces] is another group that is prospering. If you are in the FAR or the Ministry of the Interior, you have privileges not enjoyed by the rest of the population. You have good housing, extra food, military hospitals, special stores, a nice car to drive. It's always been like this but with Raúl in charge it's become much more visible, particularly in the provinces where these privileges clearly separate military personnel from the rest of the population.'

'When Fidel Castro was about to give a speech on television it was like, "Whoa, Cuba hold on!"'

In 2016, Pavel told me with great excitement that he was developing a new interpretation of Castrismo.

'Since Fidel Castro stepped down the leadership feels under immense pressure and for the first time government policies are being written down. How did Fidel Castro govern? Simple, when someone accumulated enough money to buy a house the government allowed them to buy the house illegally. It was a way of releasing pressure. Under Fidel Castro everything was done outside the law. The advantage was that the government could crack down and confiscate the houses ten years later.

'Under Raúl Castro there have been minimal changes. People say to me, "Not true, there have been many changes." "No," I answer, "But there has been one very important change: instead of relying on ad hoc practices the government is enacting laws.

People can read the statutes and find out what are their rights. As a consequence, lawyers are much more willing to defend you in legal proceedings than before, and this is very important. It demonstrates that the Fidelista phase of Castrismo is being dismantled."'

Pavel's analysis was not unique. Many Cuban intellectuals were saying that with Raúl's succession the country's political structure was evolving from a system based on personalities, to a system based on laws. But Pavel added an interesting twist.

'From the 1980s until Fidel left office we had what I call politics made on TV. In the eyes of your average Cuban, Fidel Castro developed all, absolutely all, policies. Probably there were other people at various levels involved in decision-making, but it was Fidel who appeared on television. I think many of the policies the government implemented popped into Fidel Castro's head when he was on TV. You've taught classes, Liz; so have I. When you go into a class you have your lecture prepared, but during the class you feel liberated to say new things, develop new ideas. It must have been the same for Fidel Castro. He was planning to make certain announcements but while he was speaking other ideas occurred to him. The act of giving a lecture is very creative for teachers; the same goes for Fidel Castro. When Fidel Castro was going to give a speech it was like, "Whoa, Cuba hold on!" He might have been planning to say one thing, but out came something different... In speech-making Fidel Castro was a virtuoso, an absolute virtuoso. To my mind he was brilliant at nothing else, but in oratory yes, a total virtuoso... The charismatic leader is a feature of Fidelismo; it is characteristic of populism. Raúl Castro is totally different... He reads his speeches. He is incapable of speaking extemporaneously and it does not go down well.'

Pavel explained that Fidel's cult of personality allowed him to rule without the encumbrance of laws, giving him almost limitless power. With Raúl it was different; lacking a broad personal following he institutionalised his power through the legal system.

'Opening the border is a major change.'

How do the measures enacted by Raúl Castro's government affect you personally?

'Now there are private playgrounds. People import five bouncy castles and start a small business, but I've never taken my children to one of those. Opening the border, that is a major change. The freedom to come and go has made a big difference to me and to many Cubans. It allows me to go to international events and to visit my father. Even though I am a political opponent, I can leave and return. At this very moment I am waiting to see if they will renew my passport. A new law allows them to refuse a passport to anyone they consider a national security risk, and that happened recently to two important members of the opposition.' (Pavel's passport was renewed.)

'But let's be clear, we are talking about costs that are not within reach of most Cubans. A passport costs one hundred dollars; every two years you pay twenty dollars to renew it; every six years you have to pay another one hundred dollars for a new one. With an average salary of twenty dollars a month, few people can afford a passport. It is simply not doable. They would need to receive money from abroad.

'There is another important change: the liberalisation of the housing market. Now people are selling their homes – the one thing the Castros did not take away. I will never forget Yoani Sánchez's phrase: "*La casa como ida, cuando siempre ha sido ancla.* A house always tied you down; now it is the means to leave." What is happening is ironic.'[4]

Pavel talked about the incongruity of people selling their home to finance emigration – '*La casa como ida*' – when they were not permitted to move from one part of the island to another – *'cuando siempre ha sido ancla'*. The ban on internal migration was enforced by the police, but more effectively by a ration system that provided food to every household, but only at the address listed in their supply book. If a family moved without permission they forfeited access to food, healthcare and schooling.[5]

I asked why Yoani Sánchez is allowed to publish an anti-government blog that has something like a quarter of a million subscribers throughout the world.

'If this were the 1970s or 80s, Yoani Sánchez would be condemned to thirty years in prison. Antonio Rodiles [an opposition leader] probably would be shot. Me, I'd be thrown in jail for twenty years. It would have been very simple. But now Yoani Sánchez is internationally famous, and besides it's an entirely different epoch. The prestige of Castrismo is low, and there is less willingness on the part of the global intelligentsia to accept repression. The opposition is no longer invisible... I am a publicly declared opponent of the government. If I have anything to be proud of, it is that.'

Pavel described with evident satisfaction how the government tried to get him fired from his job at the film school, but the director refused. 'Fortunately, I work in an international school with many foreigners. The director told me the security apparatus paid him a visit and said they wanted me fired. His response – by the way, he is a foreigner – was that the school would not play the role of executioner.

'You need to understand; state security tries not to be seen. They wanted me fired, but wanted someone else to take the blame, and that would be the end of it. If the other person refuses it forces state security out into the open. This is very important because our society is built on fear. The state doesn't need to activate the repressive apparatus; Cubans police themselves. The police, the forces of repression, don't want to be seen bashing people in the street, like what happened recently to the Damas de Blanco [Women in White] when they [the government] called in their mobs.[6] But what happened? The behaviour of the mob was so pathological that it horrified people around the world [who watched it on TV.]. You only had to look into the eyes of the people on the government side, see them shouting, the postures they assumed, throwing stones, men dropping their pants and exposing their balls in front of the opposition demonstrators, it was grotesque. They [Cuba's leaders] finally realised that we live in a world of instant communication and a mob attacking the Damas de Blanco is not a good image. So long as Cubans police themselves the repressive apparatus is relaxed; that's true in every country. The problem comes when people begin to develop their consciousness and express themselves more freely.' Pavel said that since Raúl took over the leadership, Cubans feel they can speak a bit more openly than before.

However, two years later state security insisted that the school's director fire Pavel, and this time he bowed to the pressure. I interviewed Pavel soon afterwards and he was furious at what he felt was a betrayal.

He had gone to the Plaza de la Revolución on 30 December 2014 to participate in a speak-out organised by the celebrated Cuban artist Tania Bruguera, unaware the government had banned the event and that Bruguera was under house arrest. On his arrival, he and a handful of others were herded into a police van and taken to jail, where they celebrated the anniversary of the triumph of the Revolution – it coincides with New Year's Day – shouting anti-Castro slogans. Several days later Pavel was released without charges, and without having been allowed to contact his family or a lawyer while in detention.

The next week the director of the film school called Pavel into his office to tell him the Faculty Board had voted unanimously to sack him. 'It is a source of great satisfaction that in the future my children will be able to say, "My father said no, and for that he lost his job. And where are the men who raised their hands to fire him?" Getting expelled was a merit. I am lucky I was not among the eleven [on the Faculty Board] who raised their hands that day, the 5th of January. I have never voted to expel anyone. In Cuba, in 2015, that alone is transcendental, lucky and transcendental. It was a very sad experience. They were my *compañeros de trabajo*, work colleagues. I used to talk with them about the same things you and I are talking about.' Pavel's dismissal, with the complicity of the very colleagues he so highly prized, his role models, came as a terrible blow.

After losing his job his politics hardened, his language became more strident, he was more aggressive in confrontations with the police. The experience also made him more tender, more affectionate with his family, and with me.

'The state simply handed him to the dissidents on a silver platter.'

Pavel's exclusion from the film school was the making of his political career. If ninety-nine per cent of Cubans have never heard of Pavel, his sacking turned him into a minor celebrity among the opposition in Cuba and overseas. After he was fired, government officials promised him a menial job at ICAIC, Cuba's famous film institute, but the promise never materialised, and he has not been formally employed in Cuba ever since.

After losing his job he collaborated with an array of short-lived opposition groups. He was a spokesman for #Otro18, an organisation that petitioned the government to allow opposition candidates to run in the 2018 parliamentary selections – they were not elections in the usual sense. When representatives from #Otro18 went to the government offices to deliver the petition they were detained and jailed for several days without charges. Pavel said the handful of people who had put themselves forward as independent candidates, i.e., without Communist Party support, had been jailed or threatened. In the end, only government-backed candidates stood for office.

In 2018, after Raúl Castro delegated his administrative title and tasks to Miguel Díaz-Canel, the Communist Party announced it would revise Cuba's constitution. Pavel was a spokesman for a coalition of opposition groups that drew up recommendations for constitutional changes. In addition to his activism, he has made a name for himself as an independent journalist. In Cuba, independent is a euphemism for dissident. He is a columnist for *Diario de Cuba*, an online newspaper based in Spain that opposes the government, and occasionally for *14ymedio*, a daily online newspaper published by Yoaní Sanchez and Reinaldo Escobar in Cuba. Sporadically he publishes a blog whose banner reads, 'The dissidents of today will be the heroes of tomorrow', beside a picture of him laughing. Laughing is a side of Pavel I rarely saw during interviews; he approached them as part of his political work.

To advance his cause, and to make money, before Covid Pavel participated in academic meetings and political events in Europe, the US, and Latin America. Having made a name for himself in international opposition circles, he was invited to Mario Vargas Llosa's eightieth birthday party in Madrid, a gala that included right-wingers from across Europe and Latin America.

Who finances your activities?

Pavel's eyes clouded over and his gentle demeanour vanished. After a long silence he said, 'The problem is that is *the* question people always ask about anything to do with the opposition. I don't ask everyone who works for a state institution, who finances you? But when it comes to the opposition almost always it's the first question. People always want to find fault.

It's an ugly question, an unethical question. For example, if you are working for the Cuban government, and the US government gives you money, people regard that as clean money. But I oppose the Cuban government, and if the US government values what I do and gives me money people see it as dirty money. That attitude is disgusting. The word for that is *asqueroso*, nauseating. People come up to me and say, "It's all very well, but who is financing this?" I don't know who is financing these things. I have to live so I write for a foreign newspaper... I don't have an ideological problem with *Diario de Cuba* or with *14ymedio.*'

There was an uncomfortable silence.

How do your friends and neighbours react to your political involvement?

'In the first place my political activities are out there for all to see. When I tell people what I am doing they say, "But Pavel, just imagine if..." I say, "No, if I have something to be proud of it is that I am what you see." I move in artistic circles where my political conduct is accepted, maybe an exaggerated acceptance. People who don't dare open their mouths in public say to me, "*¡Coño!* You've got courage." Folks like me who openly declare themselves government opponents encounter two kinds of responses. There are those people who frankly admire me and sincerely appreciate what I am doing, and there are those who don't want to see me. Over the years they have been conditioned to be afraid. They don't want to acknowledge our stance because if all Cubans behaved as we do our behaviour would be validated.

'Cubans whisper. Inside the house we speak in one way, in the street another. When we say something against the government, we don't say Fidel. We make a gesture everyone recognises like pretending to stroke a beard, or we simply say "He". To my mind, not saying the name Fidel is an example of social schizophrenia. If we all behaved differently that alone would validate the behaviour. If suddenly someone were to stand up and say that they blamed Fidel Castro for the state of Cuban society, a situation that is truly criminal, I think it would genuinely upset people. Not because they are socialists, or Fidelistas, or leftists, but because it would reveal the cowardliness implicit in people's everyday behaviour. In short, some people show me genuine affection and appreciation, even if most of them don't yet dare to express themselves publicly, and then there those who clearly reject me, and who demonstrate their rejection with silence.

'In this day and age no one would come up to me and say outright, "I support Fidel Castro," and engage in a discussion. No, people do not speak their mind. They do not speak. A few say, "If you're so opposed, why don't you leave," but nowadays people say this less. I reply, "No, they are the ones who should leave. This is my country." Government opponents are still stigmatised, viewed as *gusanos*, the enemy. Over the course of many years we have erected a whole series of exclusions. We have excluded many things.'

Pavel's belief that no Cuban would say outright, 'I support Fidel,' may have reflected, in part, Raúl's success in changing people's attitudes to Fidel and egalitarianism. However, most older Cubans I interviewed expressed support and affection for Fidel. When I asked Ofelia, the one-time *jinetera* from Old Havana, who she hoped would succeed Raúl, she said, 'It doesn't matter who is president. The big people will get richer, the people at the bottom, people like me, will remain poor. We no longer have Fidel on our side.'

What would you like to see happen in Cuba over the next five to ten years?

'We in the opposition have no blueprint. Our primary political demand is democracy... But I don't accept a so-called gradual opening, step-by-step change. Gradual liberty? I don't even know what that means. No, they must give me my liberty immediately. I need my freedom now.' He listed the changes the opposition is demanding: free elections, freedom of assembly, a free press, and freedom to browse the internet. 'Who is to say what a Cuban democracy will look like. Whatever it is, it won't be ideal. But Yoani Sánchez should be on TV telling her truths and making mistakes just like everybody else. I might not like it when two million Cuban-Americans invest in businesses here, but their investments should not be prohibited. If we are going to have a democracy, a government that upholds freedom, investments should not be blocked.'

Beyond a vague call for democracy, Pavel said the internal opposition hadn't figured out what they hope Cuban politics and economics would look like in the future. 'It's very difficult to say what we are going to achieve. I can't envisage the result, so I have to see a virtue in the process itself by putting into practice everyday forms of democracy.' Pavel said everyday forms of democracy included helping those living in extreme poverty, assisting the elderly, acting courteously on crowded buses. His vagueness reflected the difficulties Cuba's internal opposition faces and their inability to unite and develop a programme.

Do you consider yourself a socialist?

'Personally, I repudiate the concept of socialism. Although many of my ideas are consistent with socialism I don't use the word because it's the word used to describe the Cuban experience.' He said that he might feel differently in the future, when Cuba is a democracy, but for now, to him socialism conjures up firing squads, prisons, violation of the rule of law, and arrogant officials. 'I might sound like a member of the Tea Party [a far-right movement in the United States], but I've always been absolutely clear about my social principles. I've always defended state provision of healthcare and education. I believe it is very important that a child's chances in life are not determined by their parents' class background... I want equality of opportunity. This is simply social justice.' I was struck that Mario, a Party member, and Pavel, a dissident, both espoused the Communist Party's new policy of equality of opportunities.

Who are your role models?

'People who have been engaged in non-violent forms of struggle: Nelson Mandela, Martin Luther King, Gandhi. People who have tried to change society from within, without causing harm. Very simply, I was not born to cause harm. I remember I once interviewed a man who had participated in the 1959 Revolution. They offered him a post in the police after the triumph. He answered, "No, your justice is not mine." Anyone familiar with the 26th of July movement and the crimes of Castrismo in 1960, the executions, knows what he meant. No, I was not born to commit violence against anyone. If I did, I know that I would turn into a different person. I never want to fall into the kind of frenzy that would lead me to commit violence. Nor was I born to exact revenge; whatever system we create, it will not seek revenge. Everything must conform to the rule of law. That's why I am so interested in creating a system of laws in Cuba. Everything must be done within the law.'

I last interviewed Pavel in 2018, shortly before Raúl Castro passed the presidency to his successor. Castro had promised to open wholesale markets, expand the private sector, strengthen the legal standing of small proprietors, create a single currency, and most importantly raise the standard of living. They were all on hold. 'Raúl Castro's government has been a failure,' Pavel said. 'All his promises remain unfulfilled, and the people who believed he would sort out the economy are completely disenchanted... The atmosphere reeks of political instability.'

Pavel felt a source of instability was fear among the nomenklatura that Raúl's successor would sweep away their power and prerogatives. 'High officials no longer have a strong sense of loyalty.' Pavel believed that Fidel's patronage system ensured his subordinates remained devoted to him. However, growth in the private sector altered the political dynamics. With money and business increasingly important, officials acquired a certain independence and the unity of the political class was breaking down. While Pavel's analysis is certainly interesting, the question is whether it is correct.

Has inequality increased during Raúl's term of office?

Pavel was certain it had but said that without official data it is impossible to measure, and he fell back on anecdotal evidence. 'But the issue of equality in post-Soviet Cuba is not what most people imagine. As Omar Everleny, one of our leading economists said, "Rather than attacking wealth, this government should attack poverty." For the last twenty-five years equality has meant that no Cuban can [legally] eat steak. The minimum state salary is nine dollars per month, and on that money no Cuban can afford to travel very far from where they live. These are characteristics of extreme poverty. From my point of view, in preserving this kind of equality we perpetuate extreme misery. A couple of days ago every child received ground beef on the ration. Everyone said "*Que bueno*. We're getting beef." Let me explain the reality. I had to remove the skin, and it was mostly skin and gristle. Once I threw that away there was hardly anything left, and the smell made me sick to my stomach. This is the quality of ground beef our state gives the children of this country. This is what people all over the world call Cuban equality.'

My interpretation of Pavel's story is that instead of an indictment of equality, the anecdote demonstrates his deep if unconscious attachment to egalitarianism and a residual belief that the state has an obligation to provide Class A beef to every child.

Pavel's happiest memories from the Raúl years are the times he spent with his family. 'My close family is a source of great riches. The government forced some members of the opposition into exile. They put them on a plane and said, "You have to go." If that were to happen to me I would protest in the Plaza de la Revolución until they allowed me to stay or they killed me. They can't take away my rights as a Cuban.'

I met with Pavel the final time on the eve of the presidential succession, and again asked how he envisaged the future.

'I am the littlest bit optimistic because I think the current system simply cannot last. Not because people are going to take to the streets, I only wish. We are not going to have the kind of protests they had in Berlin and Eastern Europe. I think the situation cannot continue because the kind of regime we have completely impoverishes the country. When you think about the leaders who will emerge in the future, wherein lies the valour of leading a population that lives in misery and has no rights, where human beings are treated practically like beasts? I think the totalitarian regimes of the so-called socialism of the past came to an end simply because the leaders found it tiresome to head countries that were like zoos. To my mind, there comes a time when statesmen, other than the totalitarian-minded like Fidel Castro, will not want to be the head of a nation living in misery. They will not find much to be proud of when they go home and look at themselves in the mirror.'

I'm sorry Pavel, but to me this sounds trite and far-fetched.

'The big question is, if there is a democratic opening, what will we do? In a society with no political culture, where misery has become the basis of human relations, where individualism is extreme because each person is responsible for their own welfare and the survival of their family, how are we going to construct a society based on consensus, a society that promotes the common good? How are we going to stop individual wellbeing taking precedence over the wellbeing of society? That is the big question, and on that I am not optimistic.'

Despite Pavel's journey from Fidelista to dissident, from socialist to anti-communist, he believes – no, more than that, he takes for granted – that governments should promote the common good. This is a legacy from his childhood, from the egalitarian milieu of his early years. To me it suggests that Pavel, and perhaps Cuba's internal opposition more widely, might not easily line up with the Cuban-American politicians trying to plot Cuba's future.

As Pavel drew his story to a close he mourned the lives he did not live. He imagined the filmmaker, the intellectual, the university professor he might have been had he not decided to campaign for democracy. He disparaged the Cubans who left to make a career for themselves abroad. 'It's incredible how many intellectuals and artists, rather than joining a collective endeavour, opt for personal gain.' He was sad that virtually none of his friends decided to stay and take a stand. 'I want to make films, write, study for a PhD, but I know that if I dedicate my life to social action I must sublimate my desires. In Cuba, you must choose.'

As we kiss goodbye, Pavel reminds me to tell readers he did not choose to remain anonymous. 'I am not bothered whether you use my real name or a pseudonym. What I don't want is that tomorrow someone comes up to me saying I had asked to be anonymous. I don't want anyone to think that. What I say is public, and as far as I'm concerned you can use my true name in your book. You are free to use my voice in your radio programmes, my face on your websites. I have no problem at all with this. But I respect your decision to use fictitious names for the narrators, so long as you tell readers it was not my idea to hide.'

*

Postscript

On 10 October 2019, the *Asemblea Nacional*, Cuba's parliament, announced they had elected Miguel Diaz-Canel president of the Republic. Hyped in the official press as a watershed moment in Cuba's democratic process, *Cubanos y Cubanas de a pie*, ordinary Cubans, were completely uninterested. They knew the announcement was of no substance. The 10th of October was business as usual for the population at large, but not for Pavel and several opposition activists who spent the night in jail. Detained without charges a few days before the inconsequential occasion, they were released soon afterwards.

Their detention highlighted something important. Cuba's leaders feared the mounting miseries – economic decline, food scarcities, petrol rationing, widening inequalities and Obama's decision to roll back Cubans' special privileges vis-à-vis US immigration – might dispel apathy and motivate people to take to the streets – which they did in July 2021.

26

ALEJANDRO ESPADA BETANCOURT

Havana, March 2015

'Today is the most important day of my life,' Alejandro pronounced as I opened my front door. He had come directly from his interview at the US Consulate, the final hurdle in a long wait to join his mother in Miami. He was agitated and sweating profusely; he said he had barely slept. When I turned on the recorder he talked compulsively, weighing up whether to leave his high prestige job that paid miserably, the lucrative side-line he built from scratch and Xiomara, the woman he lived with, sitting beside him, or stay in Cuba. I felt I was eavesdropping on the argument he was having with himself.

Alejandro was a product of his times. Just turned thirty, he had an enviable position at Cuba Ron, the state company that bottles Havana Club. With bonuses and perks he earned far more than most state workers, and to supplement his income he sold pirated digital entertainment on the sly. Alejandro was a small player in Cuba's emerging private economy.

'I could sell ice to a penguin.'

Alejandro attributed the success of his business to what he called 'my capitalist spirit'. 'I want to be successful, and I imitate the methods capitalists use. I try to get people hooked on my products. First I copy the TV series they ask for. Then I give them the first episode of another series for free, and tell them, "Maybe you'll like this one too, and then you will be buying two." That's how I do it. Slowly but surely my clients discover they are buying episodes from many different series... I built my business little by little and learned a new skill in the process: the art of selling, making people believe they need something. I tell Xiomara, "I could sell ice to a penguin." I enjoy it. It doesn't have much to do with my job at Cuba Ron where I am a middleman between the factories and the clients. Come to think of in both in my job and my business I need to know how to sell. I enjoy persuading people. It gives me great satisfaction.' Alejandro personified Cuba's twenty-first century New Man – the antithesis of the New Man Che envisaged in the 1960s.[1]

Alejandro was in Cuba's digital vanguard. In 2011 he began selling pirated episodes of *Game of Thrones*. He delivered the episodes to his subscribers on memory sticks the day after they premiered in the US. In a country that was largely offline, his business was state of the art. Then *El Paquete Semanal* came along. El Paquete Semanal delivered not only foreign TV series, newspapers and films, but Revolico (Cuba's equivalent to eBay), and antivirus software on external drives. Alejandro ran a one-man operation. He copied shows and delivered them himself throughout Havana by bus, taxi, and literally by running around. El Paquete employed who knows how many IT specialists and a fleet of couriers on motorbikes who delivered the devices to homes throughout the island. A subscription to El Paquete cost from one to three CUC a week. In a country where the internet was very expensive, very slow, and often down, a country virtually cut off from the world wide web until 2015, El Paquete was a sensation. According to Jon Lee Anderson, 'It had a large, almost insatiable, market, and was rumoured to be Cuba's most profitable illicit enterprise.'[2]

Alejandro complained he was losing clients to his mighty competitor because he didn't have the vast digital resources and the mountain of employees available to whoever owned El Paquete. He didn't even have a motorbike. He had only Xiomara, who helped out occasionally, but with an important job at Havana Club, Cuba Ron's partner company, and finishing an MA in business management, she had little time.

Alejandro said El Paquete was one of Cuba's great mysteries. It had millions of subscribers, yet nobody knew who owned it. It provided Cubans with news that wasn't available in the official media, yet it had managed to circumvent the censors. Alejandro believed that El Paquete's allure was that it gave Cubans something akin to the web, even though it was offline and non-interactive. 'It is curious that El Paquete carries no anti-government news.'

Assuming that Alejandro knew the business inside and out, I asked the question on everybody's lips.

How do you acquire the episodes so quickly?

'They are downloaded from the internet. Don't ask me who does it or how, because I don't know. It must be done by people at the highest levels who have access to fast broadband, and I am certain they don't pay for it. All I know is that I buy the episodes from someone who buys them from someone else. I am one link in a long chain and I don't know who is at the top. That's the big unknown.'

Many Cubans believe El Paquete is owned by the armed forces; they said the FAR is the only institution in Cuba with the business knowhow, the internet capability, the resources, and the political clout to deliver one terabyte of digital content per week. According to a study cited by Jon Lee Anderson, in 2015 El Paquete employed 45,000 couriers, reached 5 million people – almost half the population – and had gross profits of US$1.5

million a week.[3] These figures may be wildly exaggerated, but one thing for sure is that El Paquete Semanal is big business.

'I don't think they will ever close down El Paquete. It is a form of social control. It keeps people at home happily watching things that in the end don't cause any trouble to anyone. El Paquete is definitely regulated. There is nothing political, nothing pornographic, nothing opposed to the principles enshrined in the constitution. They don't include any vulgar shows from Miami. So long as the regulation works, El Paquete isn't a danger to anyone. Besides, by keeping people at home and entertained it reduces crime on the street. Things are not like they used to be; now even the poorest Cuban has a TV where they can plug in a memory stick. And even if they don't, they'll have a friend with an old computer they can use to watch films and other things.'

In addition to keeping people apathetic, entertained, and off the street, Alejandro said digital entertainment was educational because it inspired Cubans to take English classes.

'The FAR and MININT are normal businesses.'

Alejandro admired the FAR's efficiency but swore he would never work in one of its enterprises. He was remarkably outspoken, perhaps because he was leaving.

'At the end of the day the FAR and MININT, the Ministry of the Interior, will own everything in Cuba. They [Raúl Castro's government] are putting military men in charge of every organisation. I don't know whether in the long run it's good or bad, but it's a way of centralising things. The FAR has done good things. It invented a system called *gestión empresarial*, business management, to improve entrepreneurship.' (Mario's course for talented Party cadre taught *gestión empresarial*.) 'Businesses owned by the FAR pay higher salaries, about 100 pesos *nacionales* [US$4] more per month than the average wage.

That's not much, two pounds of steak, but it's something. Other enterprises imitate their methods. The FAR and MININT are businesses, normal businesses. The FAR still runs the military, but the business side is more important. Every day more organisations are absorbed into the FAR. The dollar stores are part of the FAR. I think it's a political strategy, but what do I know. I was asked to work for an outfit belonging to the FAR but I said no. I don't want to have anything to do with the military. Like I said, I think the FAR is mainly a strategic way of maintaining tight control.'

'The economic changes are too slow for us.'

Alejandro wanted to see an expansion of the private sector and complained that Raúl Castro was moving too slowly. Xiomara interrupted to say that they decided to leave because they didn't feel the changes would come fast enough to help people at their level.

'Normal people like us, people who live on their salaries plus a bit more, we have not benefitted from the new measures… The measures will have a positive impact on the lives of people who have more money. They will be allowed to own more than one house and buy one or two cars. For people who have greater economic possibilities this is a positive step. They will be able to go into business selling houses and cars, and they won't face much competition because the market for investment is practically virgin. They will be able to launch start-ups with small amounts of capital and grow their businesses.' Xiomara had just completed an MA in business management and spoke its jargon.

Alejandro agreed. 'I think the changes are super positive and I think they should continue. Now that they [the state] have given us the possibility of opening a business, it is up to each and every one of us to decide if we want to take it. You need to have money, of course. If I weren't leaving, I'd grab the opportunity to build a big company.'

'Cubans went into the Special Period together but came out one by one.'

Alejandro's words reminded me of an entry on Fernando Ravsberg's former blog *Cartas Desde Cuba*. 'Cubans went into the Special Period together but came out one by one.'[4]

'I believe that all human beings want to improve their standard of living. No one wants to stagnate,' said Alejandro. 'I am not saying this for myself, I am saying it for the mountains of Cubans above sixty or seventy years of age who say, "I have nothing. I have lived here my entire life, I worked at such and such, and where did it get me? I am no better off than I was before." Mind you, they don't live horribly. As I've always said, no one in this country dies of starvation. No one is homeless. Well, I take that back, now there is some homelessness. The problem here is that you cannot better yourself unless you do things that are illegal, and you must do them if you want to live decently and improve your situation year on year. I tell you, five years ago I lived about the same as I live now. My income is about the same, and I see no prospects of improvement.'

Alejandro presumed that Cubans of sixty or seventy years of age shared his aspirations. Many did, some did not. Older Cubans had a different history, and many had a different consciousness. In 1959, Cuba had a cultural revolution that engendered collectivist values. The country had another sort of cultural revolution at the turn of the twenty-first century, one that rewarded individualism.

Alejandro's philosophy of life turned the socialist ethos of the 1959 Revolution upside down. 'I feel really and truly fulfilled because when I wanted to do something I did it with my own resources. No one, absolutely no one helped me. The money I needed I earned myself. It gives me tremendous satisfaction to be able to say that.

Never ever in my life could I have imagined I would own a cellular phone. Now I have an iPhone 6 Plus, the latest model.'

Alejandro prided himself on being a self-made man. In some ways he was, in many ways he wasn't. He grew up with the freedoms all Cubans enjoyed: free education and healthcare. The food, clothing, transport, housing, resorts and movies he took for granted were heavily subsidised by the state. He and Xiomara lived in a comfortable house the state had given his mother before he was born. And now he hoped that thanks to the new property law he would able to sell the house for fifty thousand dollars which would finance his move to Miami. It's a classic example of Yoani Sánchez's saying, *La casa como ida…* The house is the means to leave.

Inequality

Is inequality growing?

'Look, there has always been inequality. Raúl said not long ago that there's a difference between equality of opportunities and egalitarianism. Egalitarianism is when everyone has the same things. We are never going to have egalitarianism here. There will always be some people who have more than others. Equal opportunities is having the same rights to acquire things, which doesn't mean you will have the money to buy them. Let's take the example of hotels. Now we all have the right to stay in a hotel, but most Cubans can't because they don't have the money. Take me, for example, I cannot afford to go to a hotel.' Alejandro was in favour of all Cubans having the same rights, rather than the same living standard.

Undercover

Towards the end of a long, emotional interview, Alejandro revealed that he had worked as an undercover agent in the

Juventud Comunista. I wondered why he was telling me this out of the blue. Perhaps his sleepless night brought to mind unsettling memories and he felt driven to confess before he left. Telling your life story can be cathartic.

In Cuba, university graduates have to complete a one-year internship, called *trabajo social*, social work, before embarking on a career as a way of repaying the state for their education. Alejandro landed a prestigious post at the Instituto de Aeronáutica Civil (Civil Aviation Institute), where his job was to develop more efficient systems for boarding and de-boarding planes. He said the work was dull, and his recommendations were ignored, but he enjoyed the year because he stayed at hotels for the first time in his life.

'There were only three of us at the Institute in the Juventud, so we didn't bother to holding meetings. Every month we submitted detailed minutes of non-existent meetings, along with mountains of other things. To tell the truth I think there was some criticism of our behaviour. And there's another thing I haven't told you, when I was at the Institute I was released from my regular duties for two months to be… err, to become a kind of inspector inside the Board of Directors of the Juventud. I was supposed to inform on what they were doing and all that. It was a condition of my promotion within the Juventud. I used those two months to paint my house because at the end of the day I wouldn't do anything like that.

'During that time I made friends with a lot of the people on the board. I still see them; we go to Tun Tun [a live music venue]. They were the first to take me there, the guys I was supposed to be informing on. We went drinking together, and to rap concerts. They used to invite me when they finished work at 6 p.m. I really enjoyed that whole experience, and I got time to paint my house. I went to one of their meetings but I never went back.'

I did not ask Alejandro to say more about his role as informant. I did not want him to say things he might later regret.

I thought rappers are critical of the government. Were there tensions between the leaders of the Young Communists and the rappers?

'Yes and no. Rap tries not so much to criticise as to change the concept of revolution. Change what needs changing. That's not my phrase, it's Fidel's. People in the Juventud go the same places as millions of others, the places where intellectuals go. I am sure that eighty per cent of those who go to Tun Tun are in the Juventud. They like to hear songs about the realities they face day in and day out. I am sure they go to hear Los Aldeanos too.[5] One of the guys in Los Aldeanos is Silvio Rodríguez's son.'[6]

Can you explain, please, what 'change what needs changing' means?

'Fidel said, "To change what needs changing is the essence of revolution." He said lots more too. I can't remember what book I read it in, but I'll look it up if you like. That's what a lot of rappers' songs are about. The truth is there have been important political changes in the last few years. Some of the changes I don't agree with, but I don't have anyone I can talk with. Another reason I don't talk is that nothing will come of it. What's the point? Nothing. People who go to hear rap like the music and the words, which are full of double meanings. I don't think going to hear rap has anything to do with being in the Juventud or not. Maybe some people in the Party think so, but they have retrograde ideas. The way I see it, the Juventud is a very passive organisation. In truth, most of its members are apathetic.'

Do some people face problems because of their politics?

'No one has problems because of their politics. Really and truly no one. Why would anyone get involved in politics when it isn't necessary? The Damas de Blanco, or any of that dissident nonsense, at the end of the day none of it matters. For those people it is a way of getting paid and all that stuff. Maybe you'll find some people are involved in one group or another, but if you delve you'll always find they do it to get some personal benefit. The truth is no one joins an organisation out of conviction, nobody, not one person. Not on the left, not on the right. Economic self-interest is at the root of every political affiliation. Either they are getting paid, or they do it to secure a job, or to get some other advantage. What matters is putting food on the table each and every day. What matters is defending your very survival, not defending an ideal which in the end won't help you. I truly believe that politics has nothing, nothing to do with our problems. Our problems are purely economic. If someone gets involved in politics, it is to solve their individual economic problems. No one gets involved in politics because of their ideals. Not one person, not now.'

Alejandro was cynical or realistic or both. It is true that almost everyone we interviewed griped about material difficulties – prices, houses, food shortages, salaries – and few complained about censorship, repression and undemocratic elections, and they were from the post-Soviet generation. Cubans may have been afraid to talk about political problems, or they simply did not care. As Alejandro said, what they cared about was putting food on the table.

Political apathy was not new; it began at the beginning of the revolutionary process. Fidel and the leadership circle discouraged political debate; they made it clear that raising problems was divisive, maybe even counterrevolutionary. Cubans were encouraged to be grateful for the food, healthcare, and education they received, and never to question.

'No one in Cuba is interested in politics. I may be wrong, but that's the way I see it,' Alejandro repeated. 'No one watches *Mesa Redonda*. It is usually about foreign affairs, but if it is about Cuba it never touches on water shortages, blackouts, or the high price of food. Why should we worry about the Middle East, or some place where people are killing each other, when I have millions of my own problems. In my neighbourhood we get water once every eight days, and I have to be home the day the water comes on, so I can fill my tanks.' Alejandro had two huge water tanks and he gave water to his neighbours. 'Tell me, why should I be worrying about some place I don't know, where they are killing each other, some place where there isn't enough water, when right fucking here I don't have water either. In my barrio we used to have water every other day. Not now. Now when I get home, if I wasn't there when the water came on, I have to ask a neighbour for a couple of bottles.'

'The problem is corruption,' Xiomara said. 'The state employees who drive the water trucks don't come to our house because other people pay higher bribes, and the drivers have to take the bribes because they can't live on their salaries.'

'The same goes on everywhere,' Alejandro said. 'The number one problem with our economy is corruption… But it is all very complicated… Everyone says, "The only issue that really matters is that I am paid decently for my work." The way I see it this will be very difficult to achieve in the next five years. The economy is devastated, our entire society is devastated… Society is falling apart because people think, why should I work at a job in the state sector if I can live better *inventando*.

'To tell the truth, this goes for me too. I earn more in one-week *inventando* than in one month at my job. People think, why should I put up with the responsibilities and the stress of going to work? Why should I wake up early every morning? It's just not worth it. All Cubans think this way. So how is our economy going to recover? Well, if they paid salaries that we could live on people would wake up in the morning and say, *coño*, I think I will go to work today. But they [the state] can't pay a living wage because productivity is low, and productivity is low because people are not motivated to work. How are we going to overcome this vicious cycle? I don't know and that's the truth.'

'Cubans are not the same people we were before.'

'It wasn't always this way. Cuban society has not always been the same. At certain historical moments there were major changes. Cubans are not the same people we were before. Cubans living right now are not the same Cubans who lived in the 1960s, 70s and 80s. We have turned into different people, and we will never ever go back to being like the Cubans we were before. Now we know what is going on in the world. Now there is the internet, and Cubans see how people in other countries live and we see that we are thirty to forty years behind. Take me, I watch lots of TV and I see new things. I watch foreign news. I have access to the internet at work, and [dropping his voice to a whisper] I have an internet connection at home. I can sit back on my sofa and see what's going on in the world.'

Why are you leaving?

Xiomara, who was planning to remain in Cuba until Alejandro got settled in Miami, answered for him. 'You have decided to emigrate because you want to be world class. With your dedication to work and your intellectual capacity, you want to be paid what industrial engineers earn in the rest of the world.'

Alejandro nodded, 'Yes, I want to be able to earn enough to pay for the basics and still have some money left over. Here with what they pay, you die... I want to live without the stress of whether there will be water in the house, whether I can pay someone to deliver it. I want to live without having to *inventar* to buy what I need. If that dream came true, I would not have to leave. Neither I, nor anyone else.

'It is very sad. Here I am, thirty years old, and I have not achieved anything of importance. True, I have done some good things, but I would have liked to have achieved much more... I know that professionally I can accomplish many things, and my boss agrees. It gives me great satisfaction to know I do things well; things I enjoy doing. I get pleasure from my work at Cuba Ron.'

Alejandro was leaving because he wanted to be recognised for his professional contributions. He wanted to live in a house that had running water when you turned on the tap. He dreamed of owning a car (most Cuban men dreamed about cars), of playing in the park after work with an imaginary son, instead of running around delivering memory sticks. He wanted to be able to live comfortably on his salary, to eat at restaurants, without having to resort to shenanigans. He wanted to dream.

*

Postscript

I interviewed Alejandro in Miami a year later, in 2016. He was trying to be upbeat. His first job was in a bookstore at the airport but after a few weeks the manager told him they didn't need him anymore. He thinks he was fired because if he had stayed longer he would have had some legal protection against arbitrary dismissal. After several months looking for work, a Cuban friend hired him to load trucks in the warehouse of his family's business. It wasn't Alejandro's dream job, but he was grateful to have it.

With his passion for efficiency – Alejandro admired Taylorism and time-motion studies to speed up production – he developed computer programmes to make the warehouse run more smoothly. He wasn't asked to, he did it because he enjoyed the challenge. Several years later he wrote saying he was still working in the warehouse but he was in charge of managing inventories and the work was linked to his professional training.

In 2016, Alejandro confessed that despite drawing on his mother's network of family and friends, his first year in Miami had been much more difficult than he ever imagined. Some months after arriving he was rushed to the hospital with an infection. The doctors refused to treat him until he proved he had arrived recently and was in the US legally. At the time, under the terms of the Cuban Adjustment Act that regulated Cuban migration to the US, Cubans received free health insurance for six months. Alejandro said it was lucky he got the infection within the grace period.

He complained that housing was very expensive. He shared with his girlfriend – not Xiomara, with whom he had lost touch – a tiny apartment in what he called a decent neighbourhood. The walls were flimsy, the space too small for two, but it had air conditioning, running water and electricity. Alejandro said he missed the spacious house and garden in Havana that he was still trying to sell. Despite all the difficulties, he was not sorry he had left Cuba.

While showing me around Miami, by car of course, he explained that he was applying for a loan to upgrade to a newer, fancier car, and was looking into a mortgage so he could buy a small house, which he would sell at a profit, and buy a bigger one. He had it all worked out. He would move up the property ladder until he could afford a better home. Alejandro was describing the American Dream.

His greatest pleasure came from going to concerts. He said he was thrilled to see his music idols live in Miami and Spain, where he had gone for a holiday. He and his girlfriend took a five-day cruise around the Caribbean, and he posted pictures of them in formal attire on Facebook. Although eating was one of the great pleasures of his life, he grumbled that with long working hours and commuting he rarely had time to relax over meals.

Alejandro was still in a hurry.

Conclusion

The magic that kept the Cuban system going evaporated. Some older Cubans remember a Revolution that gave their life meaning: Fidel, the Literacy Campaign, the Bay of Pigs, the struggle for national dignity. Younger Cubans see this as ancient history. They remember blackouts, shortages, low pay, friends who left, rising inequality.

The pandemic, Trump, and the Venezuelan crisis destroyed the economy and most of the population lost what little confidence remained in their political leaders. Instead of adopting a soft line to placate the opposition, the leadership became more repressive, targeting young Afro-Cuban artists from a poor barrio. Queuing for hours for food, many Cubans were unaware of the brutality. It took a song to galvanise them, 'Patria y Vida', a song that travelled the world. 'Patria y Vida' turned Fidel's signature slogan, 'Patria o Muerte', Motherland or Death, into a song about life.

In July 2021, thousands of Cubans marched demanding bread and freedom. Many called for individual rights, not social rights. They felt that social rights were part of the system they opposed, not major achievements of the early years of Revolution. Cuba had lost the promise of equality and Cubans lost their desire for it. The government cracked down, sentencing hundreds of first-time protesters to long prison terms. The leadership aimed to instil fear in the population and show it was prepared to use brutal methods to maintain control.

Socialism in Cuba is over, at least for the time being. At this point in its history a measure of social democracy would be good for the country, but it is hard to imagine how the government and its people would get there. The memories of the post-Soviet generation might serve as a beginning.

My Thanks

All books have a life story, and many colleagues, friends and family have helped me along the way. I thank my late husband, John Weeks, and my family Matthew and Rachel Dore-Weeks, Michael Schaadt, and Lukas and Hana Dore-Weeks. I appreciate the commitment and enthusiasm of the narrators, and the collaboration of the research team, the Cubans, Lilia Campos Zamora, and my long-time friend and colleague Carrie Hamilton. William Hobson's keen eye and editorial expertise improved – and shortened – the book, for which I am grateful. I thank the many Cubans who helped and encouraged me over the years: Olga Saavedra Montes de Oca, Ailynn Torres Santana, Diosnara Ortega, Norma Guillard, and others who asked that I not identify them by name. I appreciate Paul Thompson's and Elizabeth Jelin's guidance, and especially the workshops they led for the research team in Cuba. Brooke Larson, my graduate school soulmate, picked up my spirits when they flagged. I thank Sue Himmelweit, Therese Heemels and Kathy Chamberlain for their material and literary support, and hepatologist Professor Rajiv Jalan, who asked about my book at every appointment. I thank Head of Zeus, especially Neil Belton and Matilda Singer.

I am grateful to the Ford Foundation and the Swedish International Development Agency (SIDA), and their staff, for generously funding the Cuban Voices oral history project, the University of Southampton, and Mariela Castro, director of Cuba's Centro Nacional de Educación Sexual, Cuban National Centre for Sex Education, who secured permission to carry out the project.

Endnotes

Chapter 2

1. Lewis, Ruth M. 'Foreword', in Oscar Lewis, Ruth M. Lewis, and Susan M. Rigdon (eds), *Four Men, Living the Revolution: An Oral History of Contemporary Cuba,* Urbana and Chicago Illinois, University of Illinois Press, 1977, pp. viii–xi.
2. Ruth Lewis, the project co-director, wrote, 'Was it possible to record an honest, believable life history in socialist Cuba? ... We believe the life histories ... are as honest and revealing as those we have collected elsewhere... The advantages of a long autobiography [is it] allows the basic personality and outlook of the informant to emerge.' Lewis, 'Foreword', in Lewis, Lewis and Rigdon, *Four Men,* 1977, p. xxviii.
3. Gerald Martin, Lecture at the University of Southampton, 26 April 2010. See his book *Gabriel García Márquez: A Life,* London and NY: Bloomsbury and Alfred A. Knopf, 2009; Jon Lee Anderson, 'The Power of Gabriel García Márquez', *The New Yorker,* 27 September 1999, pp. 56–71.
4. Mariela Castro, Paul Thompson, dubbed the father of oral history, and Miguel Barnet, author of *Biography of a Runaway Slave,* gave the keynote speeches. See them on the Cuban Voices project website. www.southampton.ac.uk/cuban-oral-history

Chapter 3

1. Discurso pronunciado por Fidel Castro Ruz, Presidente de la República de Cuba, en el acto por el aniversario 60 de su ingreso a la universidad, efectuado en el Aula Magna de la Universidad de La Habana, el 17 de noviembre de 2005. www.cuba.cu/gobierno/discursos/2005/esp/f171105e.html

Part 1: The 1980s

1. In 2018, the wage ratio in the United Kingdom was 201:1 and 265:1 in the US www.statista.com/statistics/424159/pay-

gap-between-ceos-and-average-workers-in-world-by-country/
Retrieved 5 January 2020.

Chapter 4

1. This chapter is based on interviews Lilia Campos and the author conducted in 2006 and 2010.
2. José Marti, an essayist, poet and journalist, is Cuba's national hero. He was killed in Cuba's Second War of Independence in 1895.

Chapter 5

1. This chapter is based on the author's interviews with Alina Rodríguez in 2010.

Chapter 6

1. This chapter draws on many interviews Marisol, Victoria and the author conducted with Juan from 2005 to 2018 in Santa Ana de la Laguna.
2. Interview conducted by Lilia Campos, Marianao, Havana.
3. On 26 July 1953, a small group of revolutionaries led by Fidel Castro attacked the Moncada barracks in Santiago de Cuba. The armed attack is widely accepted as the beginning of the Cuban Revolution. The date on which the attack took place, 26 July, was adopted by Castro as the name for his revolutionary movement, Movimiento 26 Julio, which toppled the dictatorship of Fulgencio Batista, on 1 January 1959.
4. Holt, Thomas C., 'Marking: Race, Race-Making, and the Writing of History', *American Historical Review* 100 (1995) no. 1:7; in de la Fuente, A., *A Nation for All: Race, Inequality, and Politics in Twentieth Century Cuba* (Chapel Hill: University of North Carolina Press), 2001, p. 19.
5. Interview conducted by Julio César González Pajes and Juan Paz in Old Havana, 2005.
6. Interview conducted by Marisol and Victoria in Santa Ana de la Laguna, 2005.
7. Interview conducted by Julia in Holguin, 2006.

Chapter 7

1. www.cuba.cu/gobierno/discursos/1959/esp/f220359e.html Discurso Pronunciado por El Comandante Fidel Castro Ruz, 22 March, 1959. Retrieved 13 December 2018.

2. Quoted in Eugene Robinson, 'Cuba Begins to Answer its Race Question', www.washingtonpost.com, 20 November 2000. Retrieved 12 December 2019.
3. de la Fuente, A., *A Nation for All,* pp. 263–6.
4. Daisy Rubiera Castillo and Inés M. Martiatu, eds, Afrocubanas: historia, pensamiento y prácticas culturales, La Habana: Editorial de Ciencias Sociales, 2011.
5. www.afrocubaweb.com/club-espendru.html. Retrieved 16 December 2019.

Chapter 8

1. This chapter draws on two interviews conducted by Julia in 2005 and 2006.
2. Radical in Cuba means extremist. Although it usually implies that a person is implacably anti-government, it can also mean a person is fanatically pro.
3. Raúl Castro's programme of economic liberalisation reunited some, more affluent, Cuban families. Laws stipulating that only residents could open businesses encouraged Cubans abroad to connect with their relatives on the island to invest in real estate, restaurants, and B&Bs.
4. Perez, L., *On Becoming Cuban: Identity, Nationality, and Culture* (Chapel Hill, N.C.: University of North Carolina Press, 1999), p. 5.

Chapter 9

1. Two Cuban teammates, Ada and Georgina, interviewed Barbara in 2005 and 2006. Ada and the author interviewed her in 2015, 2016 and 2018.

Chapter 10

1. Alma Guillermoprieto writes that Cubans' relationship with Fidel was characterised by 'intimacy and awe'. 'Fidel in the Evening', *New York Review of Books*, 22 October 1998, vol. 45, no. 16.
2. Cubans received toasted chickpeas, instead of coffee, on the ration.
3. On the ration, *La Libreta*, only children were entitled to milk.
4. Olga Betancourt, b. 1948. Interview Marisol and the author conducted in Boyeros, 2005.
5. Salomón (b. 1962). Interview Elena Santos and the author conducted in Central Havana, April 2006.

6. Carrie Hamilton analyses Cubans' love of Fidel and the Revolución in *Sexual Revolutions in Cuba: Passion, Politics, and Memory* (Chapel Hill, University of North Carolina Press, 2012) pp. 65–74.
7. Yeyé (b. 1931). Interview conducted by Ada and Georgina, Regla, April 2005.
8. Petra (b. 1942). Interview conducted by Marisol and Victoria, Santa Ana, June 2005.
9. Jorge (b. 1942). Interview conducted by Julio César González Pajes and Juan Paz, Central Havana, February 2005.
10. Carlos (b. 1954). Interview conducted by Marisol and Victoria, Santa Ana, March, 2005.
11. Socrates (b. 1942). Interviewed conducted by Marisol and the author, Santa Ana, March 2006.
12. Lorenzo (b. 1932). Interviewed conducted by Elena and Maria, Central Havana, January 2006.
13. Interviewed conducted by Elena and the author, Old Havana, December 2010. Mario refers to Varela's song, 'Guillermo Tell' ('William Tell').

Chapter 11

1. This chapter is based on interviews the author conducted with Pavel from 2012 to 2016 in his apartment in El Cerro, Havana.
2. An estimated 10,000 Cubans occupied the Peruvian Embassy in Havana in April 1980, seeking permission to leave. The occupation set off a chain of events that culminated in the Mariel Boatlift in which approximately 125,000 Cubans emigrated to the US.
3. www.ecured.cu/Marcha_del_pueblo_combatiente Retrieved 15 December 2015.
4. Pavel subsequently sent the author an email saying he had been mistaken about the provenance of his uncle's car. His family told him that the state gave Uncle Joaquín a car in recognition of outstanding work.
5. Eckstein, S., *Back From the Future, Cuba Under Fidel* (Princeton, Princeton University Press, 1994) pp. 60–66; Habel, J., *Cuba, The Revolution in Peril* (London & NY, Verso Books, 1991), pp. 149–76.
6. Emails to author, 19 September 2013.
7. *Cuba Annual Report 1989*, prepared by Voice of America, Office of Research and Policy, Radio Martí Program. New Brunswick, NJ:

Transaction Books, 1992, Military Affairs, Chapter One: 'Cuba's Armed Forces', pp. 147–91. books.google.co.uk/books/about/Cuba_Annual_Report_1989.html?id=SveBSrKBnoEC&redir_esc=y Retrieved 19 September 2013.

Part 2: Fidel and the Collapse, 1990–2006

1. For US laws designed to encourage Cubans to defect see LeoGrande, W. M. and Kornbluh, P. *Back Channel to Cuba: The Hidden History of Negotiations Between Washington and Havana* (Chapel Hill: University of North Carolina Press, 2014), and www.govtrack.us/congress/bills/89/hr15183 Retrieved 15 August 2018.
2. Miguel (b. 1977). Interview conducted in Old Havana by Lilia Campos, 2008.
3. www.ipsnews.net/2014/08/cubas-balsero-crisis-still-an-open-wound-20-years-on/ Retrieved 15 August 2018.
4. Discurso pronunciado por Fidel Castro Ruz, Presidente de la República de Cuba, en el acto por el aniversario 60 de su ingreso a la universidad, efectuado en el Aula Magna de la Universidad de La Habana, el 17 de noviembre de 2005. www.cuba.cu/gobierno/discursos/2005/esp/f171105e.html Retrieved 25 February 2020.

Chapter 12

1. This chapter is based on interviews conducted by Lilia Campos and the author in 2006, 2010, 2012, 2014 and 2016.
2. Yanelis (b. 1976). Lilia Campos and the author interviewed her in Old Havana, 2012.
3. Raydel was an illegal *cuentapropista*. Interview conducted by Lilia Campos and the author in Old Havana, 2006.
4. In November 2018 Mario sent the author a Facebook message saying he found his brother on Facebook. He was out of prison and working at two jobs in Jacksonville, Florida.
5. america.aljazeera.com/articles/2015/8/13/amid-sweeping-changes-in-us-relations-cubas-race-problem-persists.html Retrieved 19 August 2018. Domínguez, E. M., *Desafíos de la problemática racial en Cuba* (La Habana, Fundación Fernando Ortiz, 2007).
6. Statistics on the racial composition of the Cuban population vary. worldpopulationreview.com/countries/cuba-population Retrieved 19 August 2018.
7. The prime example is Morales Domínguez, *Desafíos de la problemática racial en Cuba*. Books on racial themes include

Rubiera Castillo, and Martiatu (eds), *Afrocubanas: historia, pensamiento y prácticas culturales* (La Habana, Editorial Ciencias Sociales, 2011, published in English by Rowman & Littlefield, 2020); Rubiera Castillo and Martiatu (eds), *Mujeres negras en la historia de Cuba* (La Habana, Editorial Ciencias Sociales, 2016).

8. de la Fuente, Alejandro, 'How Did Seeking "Strong Men of Color" Ever Become Acceptable in Cuba?' *The New York Times*, 28 May 2019, www.nytimes.com/2019/05/28/opinion/cuban-revolution-racism.html Retrieved 28 May 2019.

9. Letter to María Mantilla, 9 April 1895. cubalmater.wordpress.com/2009/05/16/jose-marti-carta-a-maria-mantilla Retrieved 3 June 2019.

Chapter 13

1. *Lucha tu yuca Taíno*, words and music by Raymundo Fernández Moya.

2. *Memories of Overdevelopment* (2010) directed by Miguel Coyula.

Chapter 14

1. Interviews conducted by Marisol, Victoria and the author from 2005 to 2010.

2. Alejandro de la Fuente, conversation with author.

3. A blatantly racist and sexist Cuban saying.

4. Dore, E. 'Hearing Voices: Cuban Oral History,' *Hispanic American Historical Review*, 96:2 (2016) 96:2, p. 239–47. hahr-online.com/sound-forum Retrieved 19 September 2018. Audio clips, transcriptions and translations at dx.doi.org/10.1215/00182168-3484114. Retrieved 19 September 2018.

Chapter 15

1. Julia conducted interviews with Esteban in 2005 and 2006.

2. The US government runs a programme in many countries, including Cuba, where people apply for resident visas supposedly allocated randomly. On the US State Department website it is called 'the visa lottery'.

3. Oswaldo Payá founded the Varela Project in 1998 to collect signatures on a petition calling for constitutional protection of freedom of speech, assembly, press, religion and private enterprise. In 2003, twenty-five leaders of the Varela Project were sentenced

to prison. In 2012, Payá died in a mysterious automobile accident in Cuba.

4. Before the US and Cuban governments re-established diplomatic relations in 2015, the office representing the US government in Cuba was called the Interest Section. The Cuban government had a reciprocal Interest Section in Washington, DC.

5. Probably Esteban had in mind the legendary occupation of the Peruvian Embassy in Havana in 1980. At the start of the occupation security agents announced that the government would not allow the people inside to emigrate. A week later Fidel said the government had decided to allow them to leave. The events at the Peruvian Embassy set in motion the Mariel boatlift.

6. Stephen Sondheim (1957).

7. Cascarilla is used by Santería/Yoruba believers to ward off evil.

Chapter 17

1. This chapter is based on interviews the author conducted from 2012 to 2018.

2. Oswaldo Payá founded the Christian Liberation Movement in 1987. In the late 1990s he and other opposition activists founded the Varela Project. He died under suspicious circumstances in an automobile crash in 2012. Esteban hinted that he was connected with the Varela Project.

3. Hamilton, C., *Sexual Revolutions in Cuba* (UNC Press, 2012) pp. 214–31.

Chapter 18

1. This chapter is based on interviews the author conducted with Alejandro in 2012, 2014 and 2015 in Havana, and interviews Marisol and the author conducted with Olga in 2005 and 2007 in Havana.

2. Cuba's internment of gay people was in line with international practices of the time. In the United Kingdom, same sex sex between consenting adults carried a prison sentence, and homosexuality was not decriminalised until 1967.

Part 3: Inequality, 2006–20

1. I interviewed Alina Rodríguez (b. 1983) in November–December 2010.

2. Dayma Echeverria León and Mirlena Rojas Piedrahita, 'Mercado y nuevas desigualdades: ¿Que está pasando en Cuba?', *Nueva Sociedad*, November 2019. nuso.org/autor/dayma-echevarria-leon/ Retrieved 12 May 2020; Mayra Espina Prieto and Dayma Echevarría León, 'Reforma y equidad social en Cuba: apuntes sobre la política social y el cuadro socioestructural de la "actualización"', *International Journal of Cuban Studies*, 12:1 (Cuban Scholars on the Cuban Economy and Society, Summer 2020), pp. 29–52. www.jstor.org/stable/10.13169/ intejcubastud.12.1.0029. Retrieved October 2020.
3. LeoGrande, W. M. and Kornbluh, P. *Back Channel to Cuba: The Hidden History of Negotiations Between Washington and Havana.* (University of North Carolina Press, 2014)
4. 'Lineamientos de la política económica y social del partido y la revolución para el período 2016–2021,' www.granma.cu/file/pdf/ gaceta/Lineamientos%202016-2021%20Versi%C3%B3n%20 Final.pdf Retrieved 22 June 2020.

Chapter 19

1. Chapter based on interviews Lilia Campos and the author conducted in 2006, 2010, 2012, 2014. The author conducted the interviews in 2016 and 2018, after Lilia Campos moved to Miami.
2. CUC = Cuban universal currency, i.e., hard currency, divisas. 1 CUC was roughly equivalent to 1 US dollar.
3. Raúl Castro, Speech to the National Assembly, December 2010. www.cuba.cu/gobierno/rauldiscursos/2010/ing/r181210i.html Retrieved 27 August 2018.
4. 'En la política económica que se propone, está presente que el socialismo es igualdad de derechos e igualdad de oportunidades para todos los ciudadanos, no igualitarismo.' ['In the economic policy that is hereby proposed, socialism is equality of rights and opportunities for all citizens, not egalitarianism.'] *Lineamientos de la Política Económica y Social del Partido y la Revolución. Aprobado en el VI Congreso del Partido Comunista de Cuba, 18 de abril de 2011.* www.prensa-latina.cu
5. Subsequently, cell phone use, though expensive, expanded rapidly.

Chapter 21

1. Marisol and the author conducted the interviews for this chapter in 2010, 2014, 2016, 2018.

2. Only Cubans living on the island were allowed to purchase land and houses.

3. Fidel Castro, *Discursos de Fidel en los aniversarios de los CDR 1960–1967* (Havana: Instituto del Libro, 1968); Discursos del Comandante Fidel Castroen la constitución de los C.D.R. www. youtube.com/watch?v=aCvBm8jiALI Retrieved 17 March 2021.

4. From interviews the author conducted with Ofelia in 2006, 2010, 2012, 2014, 2016, 2018.

5. Gramsci, A., *Selections from the Prison Notebooks of Antonio Gramsci* (London: Lawrence & Wishart, 2005).

6. José Martí, Letter to Manuel Mercado, 'I have lived inside the monster and I know its entrails.' 18 May 1895. José Martí, poet, essayist, and soldier, is Cuba's foremost national hero, revered by Cubans regardless of their politics.

Chapter 22

1. Padura, L. *Pasado perfecto* (first published in Spanish in Mexico, 1991); *Havana Blue* (London: Bitter Lemon Press, 2006.)

2. www.ecured.cu/corporación_CIMEX Retrieved 8 December 2019.

Chapter 23

1. Chapter based on the interview Julia conducted with Esteban and his friends in 2006.

2. Cubans tend to use moreno/a interchangeably with mulato/mulata. The names imply a person of African descent who has light brown skin.

Chapter 25

1. Chapter based on four interviews the author conducted with Pavel in 2014, 2016 and 2018.

2. Raúl Pérez Ureta is a cinematographer, a cameraman and director.

3. Nelson Rodríguez is a film editor and director.

4. Yoani Sánchez's internationally celebrated blog, Generation Y, is about the difficulties of everyday life in Cuba.

5. Alina Rodríguez's award-winning documentary, *Buscándote Havana* (2007) records the experiences of Cubans who moved from *Oriente*, the eastern provinces, to squatter settlements surrounding Havana.

6. Damas de Blanco, founded in 2003 by the mothers and wives of Cuban dissidents jailed in what is called Cuba's black spring, hold a weekly protest calling for the release of political prisoners.

Chapter 26

1. Che Guevara, *El socialism y el hombre en Cuba*, 1965. Marxists.org/espanol/guevara/65-socyh.htm Retrieved 24 March 2021.
2. Jon Lee Anderson, 'Letter from Havana: Opening for Business', *The New Yorker,* 20 July 2015.
3. Jon Lee Anderson, 'Letter from Havana, Opening for Business', *The New Yorker,* 20 July 2015.
4. Fernando Ravsberg, '¿Una Cuba con todos y para el bien de todos?' *Cartas Desde Cuba*, 24 Septiembre, 2015. When the government rescinded Ravsberg's credentials as a foreign journalist in 2017 he had to stop blogging.
5. Los Aldeanos is a rap band famous for its anti-government lyrics. Their song 'Viva Cuba Libre' calls for a more open, democratic, society.
6. Silvio Rodríguez, frequently criticised for his unwillingness to call out repression, is Cuba's most famous singer-songwriter.

Index

Notes are indicated by 'n.' after the page number.

About the Author

ELIZABETH DORE was a professor of Latin American Studies, specializing in class, race, gender and ethnicity, with a focus on modern history. She was Professor Emeritus at the University of Southampton, Associate Fellow of the Institute of the Americas, University College London, and had a PhD from Columbia University. Elizabeth was Project Director of the oral history project 'Memories of the Cuban Revolution' and wrote extensively on Cuban history and politics. She died in 2022, while this book was being sent to press.